THE CHALLENGE OF CHANGE FOR THE LEGAL AND POLITICAL SYSTEMS OF EURASIA

THE IMPACT OF THE NEW SILK ROAD

Cultures juridiques et politiques
Vol. 15

Cultures juridiques et politiques Vol. 15

Les conceptions du pouvoir, du droit et de l'ordre se réfèrent inévitablement à l'ensemble du système de représentations qu'est la culture de chaque société. Toute forme de culture ayant donc nécessairement une dimension politique et juridique, la collection « Cultures juridiques et politiques » publie des travaux, tels que des thèses, synthèses de recherches, ouvrages collectifs et actes de colloques, se proposant de faire connaître les systèmes politiques et juridiques des pays européens, d'évaluer les grandes tendances des processus d'intégration politique et d'harmonisation juridique en cours dans l'Union européenne et d'éclairer les interférences entre le politique, le juridique et les autres aspects « culturels » dans le contexte de ces processus.

AMANDINE CAYOL
ZHULDYZ SAIRAMBAEVA
PIERRE CHABAL

THE CHALLENGE OF CHANGE FOR THE LEGAL AND POLITICAL SYSTEMS OF EURASIA

THE IMPACT OF THE NEW SILK ROAD

PETER LANG
Bruxelles · Bern · Berlin · New York · Oxford · Wien

Cover picture from iStockphoto.com © by jgroup.

The book was subject to a double blind refereeing process.

Éditions scientifiques internationales
Brussels 2020
1 avenue Maurice, B-1050 Brussels, Belgium brussels@peterlang.com; www.peterlang.com

Printed in Germany

ISSN 2235-1078
ISBN 978-2-8076-1382-9
ISBN 978-2-8076-1383-6 eBook
ISBN 978-2-8076-1384-3 ePub
ISBN 978-2-8076-1385-0 Mobi
DOI 10.3726/b16535
D/2020/5678/01

Bibliographic information published by "Die Deutsche Nationalbibliothek". "Die Deutsche Nationalbibliothek" lists this publication in the "Deutsche National-bibliografie"; detailed bibliographic data is available on the Internet at <http://dnb.d-nb.de>.

CIP available at the British Library and the Library of Congress.

Table of contents

PART II
THE BELT AND ROAD INITIATIVE: CHANGES FROM ASIA TO EUROPE

PART III
REGIONAL AND NATIONAL CHANGES: SECTORAL CASES

Part IV
The Challenges of Change in Civil Law and Human Aspects

Acknowledgements

Amandine Cayol

Caen Normandie University, Demolombe Institute, Caen, France

Zhuldyz Sairambaeva

al-Farabi Kazakh National University, Almaty, Kazakhstan

Pierre Chabal

Le Havre Normandie University, LexFEIM, France
& Europe-Asia Campus of Sciences Po

This book stems from the fourth Kazakh-Franco-Korean Law seminar, held in Almaty, Kazakhstan, on 25 and 26 April 2019, made possible by the support of several institutions. Its editors wish to express their sincere appreciation to the Department of International Law of al-Farabi Kazakh National University in Almaty; to the Eurasia Business Association in Korea; to the research Centre LexFEIM (Le Havre) and the Demolombe Institute (Caen) in France; to the InHa University Graduate Law School, Incheon, in Korea; to the Russian Foreign Trade Academy, in Moscow; to the Faculty of Law, Nankai University, Tianjin, in China; and to the Institute for the History of Law (IHD), University of Poitiers, in France.

The growing importance of Asia in academic cooperation and in particular the need for restructuring and renovating the Central Asian systems has led, in recent years, Kazakh and Korean law-colleagues from *al-Farabi* University (Almaty, Kazakhstan) and InHa University (Incheon, Korea) to reflect with French colleagues on how to conduct joint research. This has led to the holding of international conferences, the proceedings of which were published in Belgium (Peter Lang) in French or English (and in Russian in Kazakhstan) on the following three general themes: i/ *Regionalism and its limits: Franco-Kazakh cross-views* (2016a in French in Belgium; 2016b in Russian in Kazakhstan, 182 p.), ii/ *Mutations of society and legal responses: Franco-Asian perspectives compared* (2017a in French in Belgium; 2017b in Russian in Kazakhstan, 280 p.) and iii/ *On the*

Asian and European origins of legal and political systems (2018 in English in Belgium, 298 p.).

The will of Eurasian partners was expressed to hold the fourth conference in 2019 at *al-Farabi* Kazakh National University, Almaty, Kazakhstan, thereby starting a new cycle of three conferences in order to confirm the long-standing synergy between the Kazakh, Korean and French partner-universities and, most appropriately, to open up joint research to Chinese and Russian colleagues as contacts were established in 2017–2018 with Nankai University (China) and the Russian Foreign Trade Academy, in Moscow. The enthusiasm of our Chinese and Russian participants in Almaty in April 2019 suggested an even greater involvement on their part for the 2021 and 2023 editions of these conferences.

As always, we wish to say to the innumerable colleagues, staff members and students who helped with the organisation in Almaty that without their constant care and loyalty nothing would have proven possible.

To Peter Lang publishers, we say again our long-standing, professional and human gratefulness!

Foreword: The importance of the Chinese mega-project 'One Belt, One Road' for the destiny of Eurasia and the world

Sagyngaliy Aidarbayev
Dean, Department of International Law, al-Farabi Kazakh National University, Almaty, Kazakhstan

Yong-Ho Yang
Eurasia Business Association, Korea

The American political scientist Z. Brzezinski in his book *The Great Chess Board* determined the importance of the Eurasian continent for the destinies of the world in the early 1990s. According to his conclusion, the question of world domination is decided precisely in Eurasia: without domination over Eurasia, there is no world domination. It is possible to argue with certain provisions of the doctrine of Z. Brzezinski, but the most important thing in his reasoning is noted correctly – the Eurasian continent plays a crucial role in the future of all humanity. Therefore, those processes that occur in the depths of this complex and diverse continent, attract the attention of researchers.

One of such significant processes that promise to have a significant impact on the political and economic map of Eurasia, and therefore the whole world, is the Chinese megaproject 'One Belt, One Road' that is rapidly developing before our eyes, which China itself recently renamed to the project the 'Belt and Road Initiative'. The initiative to revive the historic Great Silk Road can have a great influence on the direction of movement of large commodity-money masses and technologies between East and West of Eurasia. Already more than sixty States are involved in this process, which is actively promoted by its initiator – China.

With the aggravation of trade and economic relations between China and the USA, the sanctioned opposition between Russia and the West, the 'Belt and Road Initiative' is able to restructure the system of international trade, economic, political and legal relations throughout Eurasia. The volumes of allocated investments and implemented infrastructure projects are impressive in their scale. Already today practically all countries of the former Soviet Union, States of Asia, Africa and a number of EU Member-States have joined the orbit of this project. The efforts of the SCO (Shanghai Cooperation Organisation) are directed to the implementation of the 'One Belt, One Road' project; other organisations, such as the Eurasian Economic Union (EAEU), are making adjustments to their activities; third organisations are considering the possibility of pairing with this megaproject.

The Chinese initiative is being actively studied by the research structures of the USA, the EU and many other countries in terms of the possible influence on their interests and policies in Eurasia. Many Eurasian States adopt strategic plans for their development, taking into account the project 'One Belt, One Way'. Thus, a vivid example of such a State is Kazakhstan, which from the very beginning supported the Chinese initiative and adopted its strategic programme 'Nurly Zhol' (Shining Path).

Particular importance for the successful implementation of the 'One Belt, One Road' initiative are the countries of Central Asia and Russia, which are located in the centre of the Eurasian continent and connect the East of Eurasia with its West. In addition, it is very important to connect to this project of States located in the extreme east (South Korea) and the extreme west of Eurasia (France). In this aspect, it is very important to hear what opinions exist among the expert community of these States regarding the participation of their countries in the 'One Belt, One Way' project.

Using the unique platform of the conference, which brought together representatives of the scientific community of Kazakhstan, China, South Korea, Russia and France, an exchange of views was held around the political, legal, trade and economic aspects of the implementation of the 'The Belt and Road Initiative'. I believe that the results of the international conference, held on 25–26th of April in 2019 in Almaty (Kazakhstan) within the walls of the *al-Farabi* Kazakh National University, will be of interest to researchers dealing with the problems of the development of the Eurasian continent. It is very important that the conference revealed a number of issues that require separate study and may be the subject of discussion in other scientific forums. The conference participants agreed to continue joint activities in areas of mutual interest.

Preface

Bing CHEN
Nankai University, the People's Republic of China

Politics and laws are mostly moved by society and economy development. Meanwhile, the evolution of society and economy also receive significant influence from politics and the legal system. A closing interactive relationship exists among them. The Forth Asian and European Conference of Law and Politics: "The Challenges of Change for the Political-legal Systems of Eurasia" has successfully ended. Nevertheless, the more profound cooperation among China, France, Kazakhstan, Korea and Russia has just begun and will step onto a higher stage of a comprehensive development under the 'Belt and Road Initiative'.

This year's conference reveals the fruits that we have obtained through communication and cooperation among Asian and European countries. At the same time, these collaborating countries aim to lighten a path for the future. Tremendous possibilities of all-round cooperation have achieved since the 'Belt and Road Initiative' has been brought up five years ago. Currently, more than 150 countries have signed the Belt and Road cooperation contracts with China. Kazakhstan, who generously held this conference, is the first country that the 'Belt and Road Initiative' been raised, and also the first station of western construction. For the five years, China and Kazakhstan have realised remarkable accomplishments at trades, infrastructure constructions, investments and so on.[1] Great foundation has been solidly laid on. The cheerful collaboration among China, France, Kazakhstan, Korea and Russia presents possibility and practicality for the wider scope of cooperation with other Asian and European countries. It is not difficult to visualise, in the future, China and other collaborating countries will continuing deepen interaction to promote the further development of the 'Belt and Road Initiative'.

---

1 Xiao ZHANG, Chinese Ambassador of Kazakhstan, https://www.yidaiyilu.gov.cn/xwzx/hwxw/92151.htm, last accessed on 13 June 2019.

Meanwhile, China has experienced forty years of reform and opening up. To profoundly govern the country by rule of law is also stressed many times. The 'Belt and Road Initiative' is thriving on an open ground and escorted by rule of law. The forty years of reform and opening up enable China to provide both material support and strategic guidance for collaborating countries. Moreover, the implement of rule of law shoulders the responsibility to ensure safe and professional trades and investments.

It is of vital importance that the scholars and specialists from collaborating countries to gather here at Kazakhstan, sharing thoughts and changing opinions, also to witness the achievements of cooperation under the 'Belt and Road Initiative'. We believe the enlightening thoughts and opinions from this meeting will provide the most direct reflection of the 'Belt and Road Initiative'. Also, by summary of past experience, it is a great opportunity to look forward to the brightening future that the collaboration will constantly upgrade and expand among Asian and European countries.

Introduction

Yesbol Omirzhanov
Al-Farabi Kazakh National University, Almaty, Kazakhstan

More than two thousand years ago, a road appeared in Eurasia, connecting European and Asian civilizations that were completely different from each other. The Great Silk Road allowed many nations to get to know their neighbours better, to establish trade, to get acquainted with the latest religious and philosophical teachings and to establish diplomatic relations with the most distant countries. Many years later, the Great Silk Road returns to life and again becomes one of the important connecting threads of many states. If once the Great Silk Road was laid as a result of various military campaigns, then in the modern world this was possible through diplomacy. This time the idea of reunification of the East and the West was reflected in official documents and proposed by the official authorities of one state. The initiator of the idea was China proposed to the world the megaproject 'One Belt, One Road'. The concept of 'One Belt, One Road' is an international initiative of China to improve the existing and create new trade and transport corridors, which connects more than 60 countries of Central Asia, Europe and Africa.

On September 7, 2013, during his first state visit to Kazakhstan, Chinese President Xi Jinping delivered a speech at Nazarbayev University and officially launched an ambitious initiative to jointly build the Silk Road Economic Belt, which immediately received support from the President of Kazakhstan and an active response from various circles societies in Kazakhstan. Subsequently, Kazakhstan became one of the earliest states that took part in international cooperation within the framework of the initiative "One Belt, One Road".[1]

1 'One Belt, One Road' – the path of mutually beneficial development and joint prosperity of China and Kazakhstan //site inform.kz, 7 September 2018.

Every year the project is gaining popularity and, till this time, China has signed cooperation agreements under the 'One Belt, One Road' initiative with more than one hundred countries. The implementation of this project stimulated a change in the national policies and legislation of the participating countries, and this in turn led to changes in various sectors of public life. At the moment, there are a lot of different opinions and views regarding this project. Some support the initiatives of China and some are sceptical of this project. As well as politicians, businessmen, scientists from various countries also united for making scientific discussion on the project 'One Belt, One Road'. As a result, scientists from France, Russia, China, Kazakhstan and Korea shared their research at the fourth Kazakh-Franco-Korean Law seminar, held in Almaty, on 25 and 26 April 2019.

The participants of this seminar considered the specifics of the implementation of the 'Belt and Road Initiative' and the challenge of change in the legal and political systems of Eurasia. Each of the participants of the seminar considered certain aspects of this topic and made his own conclusions. This book is the result of the painstaking work of individual researchers on the study of modern changes in the legal and political system of Eurasian states.

The first part of this book is devoted to "Historical and conceptual approaches to change". The authors have devoted this part to the historical development of the state and law in the territory of Eurasia on the example of individual countries. This part provides a historical overview of the development of the constitutional system, the judicial system, the political course, the relationship between religion and the state, and the reform of the legal system of individual states of the Eurasian continent. First section of this part begins with a historical excursion to France, where the history of the development of the French Parliament is analysed. Then the reader will become familiar with the new challenges of change in the legal system of Arab countries and how they were influenced by European values.

The next author focuses on the secularism of the Central Asian countries and concluded that it is possible to create a specific local organization, including all these secular Muslim countries, as a confederation. Having analysed the influence of other powerful countries in this region, the author expresses his concern about the growing Chinese expansion in the Central Asian countries. Next section devoted to the legal system of modern China. This section provides a full overview of current

Chinese legislation and analyses existing laws in the field of private law. The following section is dedicated to the Eurasian Economic Union (EAEU) where the focus is on the activities of the Eurasian Economic Union (EAEU) court. The authors did not ignore the European Union, they considered the main dangers for the entire European Community and analysed the institutional reforms carried out. Also, in this section you can read about the history of the development of constitutionalism in North Korea and get acquainted with new proposals for the conduct of constitutional reforms in North Korea. In this section, the author conducts a comparative analysis of the political system of North Korea, Vietnam and China. But, about the effects of China on neighbouring countries is written in detail in the second part of this book.

The second part of the book is called "The 'Belt and Road Initiative': changes from Asia to Europe". In this part, special attention is paid to the implementation of the project 'The Belt and Road Initiative'. The second part begins with an analysis of the political aspects of the interaction between Belt and Road and Nurly Zhol. Analysing the activities of Kazakhstan in cooperation with other countries in the framework of the Eurasian Economic Union (EAEU) and the Silk Road Economic Belt (SREB), the author concluded that Kazakhstan patiently sought, first, mutual conjugation of the EAEU and SREB projects and signed the documents for conjugation of its national 'Nurly Zhol' Programme with the SREB Project. The following section is also devoted to the prospects for the implementation of the SREB Project. In the opinion of the authors, Kazakhstan, initiates cooperation with China not only in the field of transit transport, but also in the processing industry, the creation of industrial and industrial parks, in the sphere of finance, agriculture.

The authors did not overlook the Shanghai Cooperation Organization (SCO) and considered its impact on the internal affairs of its Members. Further you can familiarize yourself with the opportunities and risks of Kazakhstan's participation in 'Belt and Road Initiative' (BRI). Also, in this section, the features of migration between Kazakhstan and China within the 'Belt and Road Initiative' (BRI) are considered. You can also get acquainted with the analysis of the current situation in Kazakhstan related to labour migration from China. The authors of the above section adhere to different opinions regarding the implementation of the 'Belt and Road Initiative' (BRI) and each made an individual reasoning on this issue. But, one thing is obvious: in time, all states will meet with the problem of reforming their legislation in favour of new interstate associations. More about this in the next third part of the book.

The third part of the monograph is called "Regional and national changes: sectoral cases". This part begins with an article about US influence on the Eurasian market. The author of this section, after analysing the trade policy of the United States, made his predictions about trade policy of USA. The following section focuses on recent investment arbitration cases in some Eurasian countries. The author, considering the Recent Investment Disputes in the Region, made his conclusions on the development of investment arbitration in the region. Also, the reader is offered a section on legal aspects of trade cooperation in the framework of the 'Belt and Road Initiative'. The authors did not ignore China's economic cooperation with African countries. On the example of economic cooperation between China and Mali, you can see the features of economic cooperation between China and other African countries. Then you can read notes about how China implements the Maritime Economic Cooperation (MEC) in East Asia as part of the 'Belt and Road Initiative' (BRI). This section analyses China's cooperation with South Korea in the framework of the 'Belt and Road Initiative' (BRI).

As is known, the implementation of the 'Belt and Road Initiative' (BRI) covers not only the economies of the countries cooperating with China, it will primarily concern the legislation and human aspects.

That is why the fourth part of the monograph is called "The challenges of change in civil law and human aspects". This part begins with a note on international humanitarian law. You can also get acquainted with a section about new problems of personal data protection in European countries. The issues of dematerialisation in law were not left without attention and an '*apostille*' was taken as the example. As you know, when everything around is subject to changes, this will also affect the human body, therefore a separate section was devoted to this problem. At the end of the book you can get an information about problems of quality of palliative care for old people in South Korea.

In general, this monograph serves as a very good assistant in studying contemporary issues of improving the political and legal systems of Eurasian countries in the light of the implementation of megaproject 'One Belt, One Road'.

Part I

Historical and conceptual approaches to change

Introduction

Tai-Uk Chung
Law School, Inha University, South Korea

Part 1 of this book outlines changes in Eurasian law and politics. Starting from France at the western end, it covers major regions of Eurasia, from Arabic countries, Central Asia, Russia, China, and to the eastern end of Korea. After the Cold War, Eurasia is once again moving into a period of transformation. China's 'One Belt One Road Initiative' poses one of those challenges. Understanding the current state of Eurasian law and politics will serve as a preparation for the changes.

The first chapter is about the French Parliament. É. Frêlon introduces the historical changes of the French Parliament, evaluates its current situation, and looks into its future. Frêlon criticizes the French Parliament as failing to truly represent the people. Her model is the Republic of Ancient Rome. Readers can feel her democratic and republican aspirations for the French and European parliaments.

The second chapter is about the Arab-European relationship. N. El Hage deals with legal convergence and divergence in terms of acculturation and legal pluralism. El Hage asserts that their convergence in economic transactions is noteworthy, but both systems don't share the same standards on human rights, criminal procedures, women's legal status, and religious matters. Readers may have hopes in legal assimilation between Europe and Arabs, but they may still feel frustrated by the mutual heterogeneity.

The third chapter is about secularism in Central Asian countries, Kazakhstan, Kyrgyzstan, Tajikistan, Turkmenistan and Uzbekistan, as former Soviet territories and traditionally characterized by moderate Islamism. Ph. Gast anticipates that China's expansion and its 'Belt and Road Initiative' should bring about new challenges. He names the Russian Orthodox Church, Chinese Confucianism, Islamic fundamentalism (like in Turkey, Iran, Saudi Arabia), and American Protestantism as the four competing forces. This chapter offers a creative and interesting imagination on the future of Central Asia for the readers.

The next chapter is about change within the Chinese legal system. As we all know, in the vortex of the cultural revolution, the Chinese legal system was almost dismantled. However, with the introduction of Deng Xiaoping's leadership in 1978, Chinese legal system began to be newly constructed. B. Chen refers to this as "forty years of reform and opening to the Chinese Rule of Law". Readers can obtain an organized and concise information about the history and current status of Chinese rule of law.

The next chapter is about the legal issue of Central Asia in the former Soviet Union. While globalization is being promoted, the block economy of regions is newly under way. It resulted in the Eurasian Economic Union (EAEU). I. Lifshits asserts that the EAEU has sought to base its model on the European Union. He focuses on the Court of the EAEU. Readers will be able to obtain focused and detailed information about the jurisdiction of the Court.

The next chapter is about the future of the European Union. M. Bruno says the European Union is no longer sustainable. He thinks of the prospects of reconstructing the Union. He regards the five members of the Schengen Convention of 1990 as the core countries of the EU. He claims that it should be necessary to exclude the populist governments and perhaps the Eastern European Members-States from the euro-zone. His radical and sincere proposal may be an inspiring stimulus for further discussion.

Finally, a chapter looks at the possible constitutional transition of North Korea. T.-U. Chung claims that, first, North Korea needs to move from totalitarian monolithic rule to a normal communist Party – State system such as China or Vietnam. For that transition, it is necessary to separate the leadership of the supreme leader from the party-state system. As reference for that, Chung presents the distinction between the 'dignity part' and the 'efficiency part' in the constitutional monarchy of England, which was elaborated by W. Bagehot.

In all, Part I of the book set the scene for further analyses of the economic, strategic and individual dimensions of the challenge of change.

Parliament: the challenges of legal and political change in historical perspective[1]

Élise Frêlon
University of Poitiers, France

"Europe is a State composed of several provinces".[2] This statement is by a French parliamentarian of the 18th century, Montesquieu, in whose time – to stick to the French example – a parliament was an institution of justice and a royal institution. In our times, it is an institution of law and a republican institution. Changes have occurred. Taking stock of these past changes enables us to question the challenges of future changes. This chapter proposes an analysis of a historical-legal[3] nature about a particular object: the parliament.

Etymologically, parliament belongs to the lexical field of – in French – *parole*, *parler*, which refers to speaking, speech. Thus, parliament is the institution of the speech. For there to be an institution, there needs to be one or more persons, an established time and a stable location. So, parliament is both an assembly of people who speak (the parliamentarians),

1 May the craftsmen of this 4th Kazakh-Franco-Korean Law seminar – especially our colleague Pierre Chabal – be here once again thanked by the author for having associated her to their magnificent work.

2 G. de MONTESQUIEU, *Pensées et fragments inédits de Montesquieu*, Bordeaux, 1901, p. 333.

3 In the Latin language, the terms *ius* (juridical issue) and *lex* (legal issue) are clearly distinct, by a double common error of translation: *ius* = law and *lex* = act (but literally, *lex* = law). So the Latin term *ius* is confused with that of *lex*, where confusion between the juridical and the legal. On the causes and consequences of the translation errors, see É. FRÊLON, "Les erreurs de traduction des *Institutes* de Justinien. Exercice de philologie juridique", in J.-L. PIOTRAUT et S. ÉVRARD (dir.), *Le droit et l'édition. Regards français et étrangers sur les mutations engagées*, Paris, L'Harmattan, 2016, p. 67–86.

a speaking moment (the parliamentary session) and a location for that speech (the parliament building – originally a chamber of a palace).

A first historical question arises: which is the origin of parliament? When does it appear? It is a properly medieval institution (thirteenth century). But, in the time dimension, it is not a perpetual institution. Indeed, the eras that precede the Middle Ages have no parliament. So, a parliament is not indispensable as great civilisations – Greek, Roman, to name but a few – have lived without a parliament for centuries.

If the institution of a parliament has not been indispensable in the past to a political system (that of the ancient Greek *polis*), nor to a legal system (that of the ancient Roman *ius*), it may not be indispensable in the future in a political system or in a legal system. Lawyers and current politicians can give up on parliament. Nothing prevents them. And certainly not the 'weight' of history, the political or 'legal' tradition. There is no human institution that cannot be abolished. In essence, no human institution has an eternal vocation. The French parliament, subordinate to the European parliament, is less and less necessary. In term (short, medium or long), when it will no longer be recognised as a utility, it will disappear.

The evolution for an institution can take several forms: appearance or disappearance, abolition or restoration, conservation or alteration… In this perspective – historical: from yesterday to today and from today to tomorrow – what juridical (including legal) and political changes are conceivable for the parliamentary institution? And, if so, what challenges do these pose? What lessons for tomorrow can we remember from yesterday? To answer these questions, let us remember the legal changes (I) and the political changes (II) affecting parliaments from the past.

I. Legal changes in the parliamentary institution

Legal science – better said, juridical science[4] – is of ancient Roman origin. Jurisdiction – which means 'to say the *ius*' (from the Latin *iuris dicere*) – is ambivalent: the jurisdiction means both to apply the

---

4 The basics of the traditional juridical science are set out in a manual of learning named *Institutes*. Their author is the Roman Emperor Justinian († 565), who compiled all of the classic 'legal' science. The book was translated into English with an introduction by P. BIRKS and G. MCLEOD, with the latin text of P. Krueger, London, 1987, 3rd ed., 1998.

existing law (to give justice, to do right) and to produce a new law (to make law, if not make the law).

In France, before 1789, parliaments were *a priori* judicial assemblies (A). Since 1789, these are *a priori* legislative assemblies (B). For there is another ambivalence: in a civil legal order, not everything is law: there are other juridical and civil sources (written[5] or unwritten[6]).

A. The parliament: a Judicial Assembly

Originally, a parliament was an assembly held to help and advise the prince to deliver justice. The parliamentarians were judges, whose function was to render sovereign justice in the name of the king. This sovereignty referred to their ability to judge in the last resort, after a hierarchical appeal-mechanism. So, their judgment was called '*un arrêt*' (because this act '*arrête*' in French – 'stops', brings an end to the litigation). Apart from cases of dispute, parliamentarians could issue a 'settlement' judgment. It was for judges to put order in the province. More than legal, this regulatory activity was administrative. It was none the less 'legal' in the sense of producing of a legal writing (one would say today 'normative').

In France, after the Revolution, parliaments lost this main attribute of rendering justice. Nevertheless, this remains – even today – an accessory attribution. This is called 'political jurisdiction' because politicians (heads of State or ministers) are judged by parliamentarians. On the other hand, what was an ancillary task to them – producing legal writing, even law – becomes a primary one. This inversion, a consequence of the revolution, is above all an acculturation.[7]

In fact, in 1791, French parliaments were abolished. As such, in their French structure, mainly judicial, they have not been restored since. But – under the guise of the same term – another parliamentary model has been introduced since, of an English type. This English model (bi-cameral: House of Lords and House of Commons) was even established while the kingship (also abolished to the revolution) was restored (in France in 1815). Today, the chambers assembled have the function of

---

5 Juridical civil written sources are: *lex, plebi scita, senatus consulta, principum placita, magistratuum edicta, response prudentium* (J. Inst. 1.2.3).

6 Juridical civil unwritten sources are *mores* (morals).

7 See the text by Nassreddine El Hage in this book.

promulgating legal acts. Such acts are nominally laws. However, are these acts voted by parliamentarians really laws?

B. The parliament: a Legislative Assembly

In France, before the Revolution, parliamentarians never voted a single law.[8] Their actions were nevertheless sometimes referred to as an 'edict' or 'ordinance', two terms also used for royal acts at the same time (Middle Ages and Modern Times). The edict,[9] since antiquity, is the written juridical act of the magistrate. The king is the highest magistrate in the kingdom. The parliamentarians are high magistrates in the provinces of the kingdom. Also, it is not surprising that the king or the parliamentarians enact, respectively in the kingdom or in the province, like the Roman magistrates. The ordinance,[10] since the Middle Ages, is the act which consists, for a superior, in giving an order to a subordinate. In the inegalitarian (hierarchical) society of the *Ancien Régime*, it is not surprising that the king orders the subjects of the kingdom, nor that the parliamentarians order to the litigants of the province (of their judicial competence).

Moreover, in the old imperial model, the modern king of France had arrogated to himself the privilege of making the law. In all exactitude, in Rome in antiquity, the prince promulgated acts according to his pleasure which had the force of the law, but which were not exactly laws.[11] Because, in the pure and hard civil law tradition, a law[12] (lat. *lex*) is a

---

8 Except misnomer, parliamentarians of the old French regime are judges, not lawmakers. For a study of a provincial parliament on this topic, see É. FRÊLON thesis in law: *Le Parlement de Bordeaux et la "loi" (1451-1547)*, Paris, 2011.

9 "The edict of the praetors is also an important source of law. They form what we call honorarian law. The term derives from the fact that the offices of the magistrates who developed this law were called honours", Just., Inst., 1.2.7, translated by P. BIRKS and G. MCLEOD, *op. cit.*

10 A detailed definition is in Cl.-J. DE FERRIÈRE, *Dictionnaire de droit et de pratique*, Paris, 1771, t. II, p. 310 et s.

11 "A pronouncement of the emperor also has legislative force because, by the Regal Act relating to his sovereign power, the people conferred on him its whole sovereinty and authority", Just., Inst., 1.2.6, translated by P. BIRKS and G. MCLEOD, *op. cit.*

12 "An act is the type of law which the Roman people used to make on the motion of a senatorial magistrate, for instance a consul. [...] The people is the citizen-body including the patricians and senators", Just., Inst., 1.2.4, translated by P. BIRKS and G. MCLEOD, *ibidem*.

constitution of the people[13] (that is to say of all assembled citizens), not of the prince. Nor is it the act of an assembly of only a part of the people (whether this assembly be named Senate in Ancient Rome, or parliament in Medieval Europe).

If one attributes (in equity, in justice) to each person their written juridical act, according to the classical model, to the people: the law, to the senators: the senatus-consulte and to the prince: the pleasure. According to these dogmatic categories, parliamentarians' resolutions, just like their memoirs written on the occasion of the verification of royal acts (which were called *remonstrances*) are, so to speak, *senatus-consultes.*[14] Still according to these dogmatic categories, the ancient law of the Romans disappeared in the *Ancien Régime* of the Franks and others from *Germains* times. Moreover, citizenship has disappeared with the republic. Subjection to the king (and then to the State) gradually replaced it.

The modern king having confiscated the law (and this, to the detriment of the people, even if it is in the interest of the same people), the modern parliamentarians have acquired – from the king himself – a right to oversee the law. It was for them to check the royal deeds. An audit, of form and substance, which made it possible, if necessary, to rectify the errors, substantive or formal. In this audit, the parliamentarians remained in their role of aide and advice to the king. If they had pretensions of participation in the elaboration of the royal acts, it was only under British political influence[15]: the English lords were a model for the French parliamentarians. At the end of the French revolution, the parliaments – which were at the origin 'consultative royal' assemblies – became 'deliberative republican' assemblies. But power is about political change rather than legal change.

---

13 The people (comprising all the citizens) is a dogmatic category of Roman law. See L. HECKETSWEILER, "*Populus*. Éléments romains d'une restitution doctrinale de la catégorie juridique", *Diritto e storia. Rivista internazionale di Scienze Giuridiche e Tradizione Romana*, 2013, 11, 27 p.

14 "A resolution of the senate is a law decided and enacted by the senate", Just., Inst., 1.2.5, translated by P. BIRKS and G. MCLEOD, *ibidem*.

15 The French parliamentarian (from Bordeaux) the most under influence of English parliamentarianism is Montesquieu. This influence (acculturation) runs through all of his main work: *De l'Esprit des Lois* (1748).

II. Political changes in the parliamentary institution

Political science is of ancient Greek origin. Classical authors[16] classify modes of government according to two rational criteria:[17] i/ the number of leaders (one person, or a few, or all); ii/ the finality of the government (virtuous, good: in the public interest of all, governors and governed, or vicious, bad: in the private interest of the sole governor(s)). A virtuous institution can be described as royal or republican depending on whether it is in the hands[18] of a king (of a single virtuous citizen) or of the people (of all virtuous citizens). On these classic bases, the parliament in France is an institution *a priori* royal until 1789 (A) and *a priori* republican since 1789 (B).

A. The parliament: a Royal Institution before 1789

At their medieval origin, parliaments were created by the Capetian kings. In the following modern era, they were perpetuated by the Valois and Bourbon kings. In all sovereignty, the king could appoint such or such person to the parliamentary offices (offices which he created as and when the needs of justice appeared). Conversely, he could dismiss such or such person from their office. For the theorists of the absolute monarchy, the power of appointment, and – the opposite – that of revocation, were royal prerogatives. In theory, therefore, the old parliaments of France were royal institutions. Nevertheless, in practice, the king has had more than one difficulty in preserving his sovereignty intact. Parliamentarians were willingly rebels, competing with the king in the exercise of public

---

16 Especially Plato (428–348 B.C.) and Aristotle (384–322) who wrote each a book titled Πολιτεία (Politics).

17 If we combine these two criteria, there are (in theory and in practice) six dogmatic categories of governments. 1. Monarchy (translated by 'royalty' in Latin): good government of a single citizen. 2. Tyranny: bad government of a single citizen. 3. The aristocracy: good governance of some citizens. 4. The oligarchy: bad governance of some citizens. 5. Politics (translated by 'republic' in latin): good governance of all citizens. 6. Democracy: bad government of all citizens (which is the worst regime in that it inevitably leads to tyranny).

18 The prerogative of *appointment* (and of dismissal) of parliamentarians is useful for this qualification: if this prerogative belongs to the king, the institution is royal (the parliamentarians are subordinate to the king, of whom they are subject in addition); if it is with the people, the institution is republican (the parliamentarians are subordinated to the people, of which they are mandatary in addition).

powers which they did not hesitate to confiscate: this is the *patrimonialisation*[19] of the offices.

If we go back to classic categories,[20] the question can be raised of an aristocratic or of an oligarchic regime. The parliamentary assembly indeed, if it obliges the king, is a limit to its absolutism and even, it disqualifies his monarchy. In his government, the king is free to appoint people to help and advise him (advisory function). It is even a medieval principle of good government. But if he is obliged by the acts of these auxiliaries and advisers (deliberative function), by their remonstrances for example, he is no longer monarch, no longer the sole holder of power. If the acts of the king must be authorised by his parliamentarians, there is no longer a question of pure and simple monarchy (or absolute). If the obligatory political force of the parliaments in the government of the kingdom is a reality, then this is no longer a question of royalty but of aristocracy or oligarchy.

In France, at the beginning of Modern Times, parliamentarians formed an intermediate body between the prince and the rest of the litigants. Was this body aristocratic? Alongside the medieval military nobility, known as 'of the sword' nobility (*noblesse d'épée*), parliamentarians formed a modern judicial nobility, known as 'of the feather' nobility (*noblesse de plume).* They practised judicial excellence. The finality of their function was public: they enabled the king to render sovereign justice to his people. Was this body oligarchic? By a progressive corruption by money (corruption more marked in a bourgeois and Protestant society), parliamentarians were able to confiscate (from the king) the most majestic public functions.

B. The parliament: a Republican Institution since 1789

In France, the revolutionaries guillotined not only the king, but also many parliamentarians (clergy and nobles stigmatised as privileged). The monarchical restoration did not stand up with time. The French Republic was first proclaimed in 1792, abolished and restored several times since, notably in 1875 and established in its current form in 1958.

---

19 The **public** functions are acquired in **private** property (called by Roman Lawyers '*patrimonium*') by their holders by means of heredity and venality.

20 See note n° 20.

As such, it now has a parliament, consisting of two chambers: a national assembly and a senate.

In ancient Roman history, in the absence of a parliament, the senate was an institution which, from royal, became republican.[21] The Senate belonged to the highest Roman antiquity: the patricians who composed it with King Romulus from the very foundation of Rome (753 B.C.). In 509 B.C., the last king of Rome was expelled on the grounds (resumed in modern revolutions) that he was a tyrant. The consular republic has been established. The senate was kept by the favour of this new regime but its members – the patricians – confiscated the said regime for their own benefit (which is another oligarchic experience) and to the detriment of the rest of the people – the plebeians. The latter then made several secessions.

These secessions caused as many civil wars between patricians and plebeians (we would say today between representatives and represented). Civil peace has been restored. The senate was maintained as a republican institution (it could have been abolished by the plebeians), on this double condition: i/ that this patrician assembly have a plebeian equivalent to temper it: the *concile*. ii/ that the assembly of the people, of all the citizens – the *comitia* – be superior in deliberation to the two assemblies of a part of the people (*senate*: assembly of the sole patricians, *concile*: assembly of the sole plebeians). On the strength of this sovereignty (lat. *maiestas*), the assembly of the people voted the law by itself. It is a historical example of a fair and republican structure: to each political force its assembly, and the sum of the two alone makes the republic (that the patricians and plebeians meet together, in *comitia*, or that they meet separately but their respective assemblies,[22] senate and *concile* are balanced).

The French model, since 1789, is based both on the old Roman model (the restored term '*senate*' attests this) and on the modern English model (with a national assembly as a House of Commons), but with a contemporary confiscation: that of representation.

*

In conclusion, what lessons can we draw from yesterday for tomorrow? In essence, both legal and political lessons.

---

21 As the French parliament: from organ of council for the king (before 1789) it became organ of deliberation for the people (after 1789).

22 Patricians and plebeians also have their respective magistrates which co-existence allows Republican balance. On the plebeian magistrate by excellence, the Tribune, see P. CATALANO, *Tribunato e resistenza*, Torino, Paravia, 1971.

i/ Legal lessons

Yesterday's parliamentarians applied the law more than they made the law. Today's parliamentarians make the law more than they apply it. In these two attributions, it is finally a single function: jurisdiction. The 'jurisdictional' genre has been perpetuated from yesterday to today, with its two species: judging according to the legal rule and producing legal rule. In both cases, parliament remains the institution of speech.

The citizens of antiquity voted laws. Yesterday's parliamentarians issued edicts, ordinances, settlement orders. Today's parliamentarians enact laws. This shows a great deal of terminological and semantic confusion. By definition[23] (which, literally, is definitive, insusceptible of alteration, unless there be a mistake), the law is the constitution of the people, which means of whole citizens. It is precisely for this reason that the law obliges the people: the citizens, in freedom and in will, legally bind themselves. The law cannot therefore be the written legal act of only a part of this people (king, president or parliamentarians, who have their own written legal acts available). Except for abuse of language or common mistake, yesterday's parliamentarians did not really produce law (but nominally yes). Except for abuse of language or common mistake, today's parliamentarians do not really produce law (but nominally yes).

ii/ Political lessons

To govern was, in the ancient Roman republic, the attribute of the whole people. In the medieval and modern Germanic royalties, the government was confiscated by the king. In contemporary republics, the government has been confiscated by the representatives of the people. And this, to the detriment of the people (the citizens have lost their majesty, their sovereignty or even their freedom).

A royalty can succeed a republic: medieval history and modern history attest this. If a single citizen, the first of them – be he elected by them –, lays his hand on all the public functions, then this is the end of the republic: it is a monarchy (royalty or tyranny according to the virtue or the vice of the prince). Today, in France, a president can not only govern, but also make law, judge, appoint and dismiss the main offices of the State. But he does not have the monopoly of these public functions: he

---

[23] Definition given on Justinian's Institutes, see note 14.

is in competition with other public persons. The royalty is not yet fully restored, but this is always a possibility.

Conversely, a republic can succeed to a kingship: ancient history and contemporary history attest this. But if some of the citizens, the best or the richest of them – be they elected by them –, lay their hands on all the public functions, then this is the end of the republic: it is an aristocracy or an oligarchy (depending on whether the representatives act for the public interest or for their private interests). Today, in France, representatives govern, but also act, judge, appoint and dismiss the main offices of the State. Representatives have no right of suffrage except for the election of the supreme (soviet?) magistrate (the president), of some parliamentarians (348 senators, 577 deputies for more than 67 million inhabitants) and by referendum.

A parliamentary republic (or representative democracy) has of a republic only the name if the representatives (of which the parliamentarians) confiscate the power from the people (sum of the representatives and of the represented). But, to this day (for want of secession of the plebs: the revolutions in France have been until now only bourgeois, not proletarian ones), only the representatives have the power, as did the Roman patricians. The represented, like the Roman plebeians, have acquired neither their own assembly (bringing them all together like the *concile*) to temper the parliamentary assembly, nor the recognition of the superiority of the assembly of all the people (representatives and represented like the *comice*) on any other assembly whatsoever. The republic is not yet fully restored, but this is always a possibility.

A judicial or legislative assembly, a royal or republican institution… it is not only at the State level that the history of parliaments questions us. Except if we consider Europe (and Eurasia) as a State composed of several provinces.[24]

---

[24] See note 3.

Acculturation, pluralism and legal change in Arab countries

Nasreddine El Hage
Le Havre Normandie University, LexFEIM, France

Throughout their existence, cultures evolve permanently in order to fulfil the needs of human societies. The latter produce these cultures; and develop them thanks to exchanges among civilisations, yet without losing their identity. This can be explained by the universal phenomenon called '*acculturation*'.

Acculturation is the result of an interaction between two cultures. Each one influences the other, to various degrees. The process relates to two cultures with nearly an equal influence on each other – otherwise, interaction is between i/ a dominant culture and ii/ a minority culture. As for cultures that interpenetrate each other, novel technologies have introduced a new mode of communication that no longer requires the previously indispensable condition of having direct physical contacts with one another.

When diverse populations are present that differ culturally and socially, their cultures and their social, economic and political conditions always results in a plurality of sources of law governing the different situations and activities within a society. It is precisely this multiplicity of simultaneous sources of rules of law differently applicable to similar situations within the same society that is called *legal pluralism*.

Regarding the interaction between *acculturation* and *legal pluralism* in the Arab countries (I), the predominance of Shari'a in almost all of these countries (II) explains the persistence of important differences between Arab and European legal systems despite their numerous convergences in various fields (III).

I. The interaction between acculturation and legal pluralism in Arab countries

Legal pluralism, the logical consequence of armed conflicts, migration and commercial and cultural exchanges between Arab countries and Europe – the latter hosting a very large number of nationals of these countries, is not unambiguous. Although European laws, particularly French ones, have greatly influenced Arab legal systems (A), the opposite in some matters, even if to a lesser extent, is also true (B).

A. The influence of European acculturation on Arab legal regimes

The influence of European legal systems on those of the Arab countries took a historic turning point at the end of World War I. The Ottoman Empire collapsed, revealing several new Nation-States such as Lebanon, Syria, Iraq or Palestine.[1] None of these countries or of the Maghreb countries has, during the 20th century, escaped the influence of European laws, notably that of France, even if the extent of this influence has varied from one country to another. This influence has engendered a legal pluralism marked by an intelligent cohabitation between the rules emanating from the Shari'a and the laws drawn from the French Civil Code, Penal Code or Commercial Code. Yet, in some areas, the freedom of Arab legislators to transpose rules from European laws was still limited by the presence in the Quran or Sunnah of mandatory and precise norms. For example, the right of inheritance, which the Quran regulates with extreme precision, has remained unalterably subjected to Shari'a law, while the law of contracts, of which the Shari'a only specifies the basic principles, was marked by a degree of flexibility dictated by the need to adapt it to the diversity and permanent evolution of contractual techniques. Nevertheless, Arab legislators regained their full freedom when they were to legislate in matters that are not regulated in the Quran or the Sunnah. This is the case with transport law or labour law.

The influence of European laws, especially French law, on the legal systems of the Arab countries mainly concerns constitutional law (marked

1 Palestine was divided into two parts in 1923: the Jewish National Home on the west bank of the Jordan (now Israel) and the Hashemite Emirate of Transjordan on the east bank of the Jordan (now Hashemite Kingdom of Jordan).

by separation between legislative power, executive power and the judicial authority), administrative law, the system of jurisdiction, criminal procedure, civil procedure, criminal law, contract law, civil liability law, the regime of obligations, labour law, commercial law, company law and insurance law. In the area of jurisdictional organisation, for example, the French system, comprising a Court of Cassation, a State Council, a Constitutional Council, a Court of Accounts and a Superior Council of the Judiciary, served as a model for creating structures more or less similar in all Arab countries.

Unlike legal pluralism which, in the Arab countries, results from European acculturation, there is another kind of legal pluralism in European countries, even in France, which is surprisingly the consequence of the application of rules derived from Shari'a law.

B. The application in France and other European countries of rules derived from Shari'a

Over many decades, many European countries have been hosting foreigners who decided to keep the nationality of their country. Among these foreigners, there are, especially in France, a very large number of citizens from Maghreb countries. In accordance with the principles governing private international law, Moroccan nationals are subject to family law legislation in their country, which is based on Shari'a law. For example, article 9 of the Franco-Moroccan Convention of 10 August 1981 provides that 'the dissolution of marriage shall be pronounced according to the law of the State of the two States whose spouses have both the nationality on the date of the presentation of the request'. It follows that the divorce of two spouses of Moroccan nationality residing in France is pronounced, according to the French procedure, by the judge in French family affairs, but the causes and consequences of this divorce are assessed in accordance with Moroccan law.

The only reservation formulated in this Convention is provided by article 4: 'the law of one of the two States designated by this Convention may be excluded by the courts of the other State only if it is manifestly incompatible with public order'. European Regulation Number 1259/2010 of 20 December 2010 on the law applicable to divorce and legal separation[2] goes further than the Franco-Moroccan Convention since it provides, in article 25, that the courts of the Member-States of

2 Article 14 of the European Regulation states that "to provide spouses with the freedom to designate an applicable law with which they have close ties or, in the absence

the EU should not be able to apply the public policy exception to remove a provision from the law of another State when it is contrary to the EU Charter of Fundamental Rights, in particular its article 21, which prohibits any form of discrimination.

Despite the European acculturation that has, to varying degrees, influenced different subjects within the legal systems of the Arab countries, Shari'a still remains the main source of law in these countries.

II. Shari'a as the main source of law in Arab countries

Shari'a is the set of dogmatic rules based on the Quran and Sunnah of the Prophet Muhammad[3] and governing i/ the situation and activities of the Muslims as well as their relations with others and ii/ the mode of life and the legal, social, political and economic organisation within the Islamic society.

Shari'a defined the *halal* (permitted), the *haram* (forbidden) and the *makrouh* (abhorred) that emanate neither from nature nor from reason and it is the *Fouqaha* or *Ulema*[4] who interpreted its rules, referring to *Fiqh*[5] and practicing *Ijtihad.*[6]

The influence of European rights, at the origin of legal pluralism in the Arab countries, progressively developed from the second half of the 19th century as backcloth of colonisation and protectorate imposed notably by France and Great Britain.

Today, the implementation of legal pluralism in the Arab world varies from country to country according to the place given to Shari'a within the legal system of each country. Explicit in some countries (A) and implicit

---

of choice, to apply that law to their divorce or separation, this one should apply even if it is not that of a participating Member State".

3 The Sunnah is made up of hadith which are the narratives of the words and deeds of the Prophet and his companions listed and validated in the 9th century AD in two collections entitled *Sahih Al Bukhari* and *Sahih Muslim*).

4 *Fouqaha* or *Ulema* are the scholars who know and interpret the rules of Islamic law.

5 *Fiqh* is the knowledge of the Qur'an and the Sunnah.

6 *Ijtihad* is the effort of understanding and interpreting the Quran and Sunnah to adapt Shari'a prescriptions to every era. Among Sunni Muslims, *Ijtihad* ended under the Abbasids.

in others (B), the predominance of Shari'a gives way to an equivalence of sources of law in only one country, Lebanon (C).

A. Legal pluralism marked by the explicit pre-eminence of Shari'a

Among Arab countries clearly confirm the supremacy of Shari'a within their legal system, for example Saudi Arabia (1) and Egypt (2).

1. The Saudi legal system

Saudi Arabia is the Arab country most attached to Shari'a, but thanks to a sometimes direct and often indirect acculturation, which has become necessary for essentially economic reasons, its legal system has not remained totally hermetic. Indeed, despite the affirmation, in article 23 of its Constitution, that "the State protects the belief of Islam", Shari'a, commands the good and prohibits evil and assures its mission of *daawa* (call for conversion to Islam), this country has adopted various codes borrowed from foreign rights, such as the Commercial Code, which transposed the Ottoman Code of Commerce inspired by the French Code of Commerce created in 1807 by Napoleon.

a. The explicit pre-eminence of Shari'a law on Saudi regulatory texts

Article 7 of the Saudi Constitution provides that the kingdom's political regime derives its authority from the prescriptions of the Qur'an and the Sunnah which constitute the two criteria of validity of the Constitution itself and of all the *anzima* (regulatory texts of the State).[7]

The Saudi legal system has two distinct but closely related branches: Shari'a from the Qur'an and Sunnah, which is the highest standard in the country, and the *anzima* established by the Shari'a-based public authorities. The *anzima* aims at governing, without contradicting Shari'a, different activities such as banking, commerce, transportation or work. It is often inspired by foreign laws. For example, the regulation governing the organisation and activities of commercial companies is based on the French Companies Code. According to article 48 of the Saudi Constitution, the courts apply *ahkam al sharia al islamya* (the

---

[7] In Saudi Arabia, no text emanating from the public authorities can be described as 'law' because this term is reserved for the 'word of Allah'.

prescriptions of Shari'a), as they emanate from the Quran and Sunnah, and the *anzima* (regulations) established by the public authorities which cannot contradict Sharia.

As it results from the Qur'an and the Sunna, the pre-eminence of Shari'a is also binding on international texts ratified by Saudi Arabia.

b. *The prominence of Shari'a law over international texts ratified by Saudi Arabia*

In Saudi Arabia, the adoption of standards from foreign sources is generally limited to professional activities linked to industry or trade. It remains excluded in certain areas, such as, for example, personal status, human rights in general, rights of women, religious freedom or the prohibition of discrimination. This explains the refusal of this country, a founding member of the UN, to vote for the Universal Declaration of Human Rights of 10 December 1948, on the grounds that the freedom to change religion, proclaimed by this declaration, is qualified by the Saudi legal system of apostasy, punishable by the death penalty by beheading with a saber.

Regarding the rights of women, the main obstacle to the adoption by the Saudi legal system of standards from foreign sources lies, mainly in the inequality between men and women in matters of succession, marriage, polygamy, repudiation, parental authority, legal capacity, etc.

Among the Arab legal systems which affirm, with fewer rigors, the pre-eminence of Shari'a, is the Egyptian one.

2. *The Egyptian legal system*

Egypt's legal system has always been marked by legal pluralism due to the very history of a country located at the crossroads of three continents. It used since 1875 a Civil Code reproducing the French Civil Code of 1804. In 1948, it adopted a major reform of its civil code inspired by various European legal systems, including the French Civil Code.[8] The two main architects of this reform, later transposed into several Arab civil codes, were the Egyptian Abdelrazzak Alsanhouri and the French Édouard Lambert.[9]

---

[8] S. JAHEL, *La place de la Chari'a dans les systèmes juridiques dans les pays arabes*, Paris, Éditions Panthéon Assas, 2012, p. 77.

[9] It should be noted that Abdelrazzak ALSANHOURI studied law in France and obtained a doctorate at the Faculty of Law of Lyon under the direction of Édouard LAMBERT.

However, in Egypt, where Coptic Christians make up about 10% of an overwhelmingly Muslim population, the Constitution provides that Islam is the religion of the State and Shari'a the main source of law. In some areas, the imperative of respecting these two principles leads to the adoption of laws or regulations which are at least questionable. For example, in the area of personal status litigation, Muslim law applies not only when the dispute is between a Muslim and a Christian, but also when it opposes two Christians since they belong to two different churches.[10]

The difficulty of implementing Egyptian legal pluralism also manifests itself through the decisions of the judiciary, which remains attached to the pre-eminence of Shari'a, even on the international texts ratified by Egypt. For example, despite the country's adopting the Universal Declaration of Human Rights of 10 December 1948, article 18 of which guarantees each person the freedom of religion and the right to change their religion, the Court of Justice Appeal of Cairo, by judgment of 14 June 2014, pronounced the divorce of a Muslim qualified 'apostate' for his writings deemed heretical, on the grounds that a man who abandons Islam no longer has the right to remain married to a Muslim woman.[11]

The pre-eminence of Shari'a, which applies in some countries through an express stipulation in the Constitution, only benefits in others from implicit recognition by the judge.

B. Legal pluralism marked by the implicit pre-eminence of Shari'a

Among the Arab countries recognising the implicit pre-eminence of Shari'a is Tunisia, as the country having had the audacity to move away from the Sharia's personal status requirements. Directly inspired by the French Civil Code, Tunisia, in its Family Code, promulgated on 13 August 1956 and entered into force on 1 January 1957, prohibited polygamy, suppressed repudiation, and authorised adoption.[12]

---

10 M. CHARFI, "L'influence de la religion sur le droit international privé des pays musulmans", Rec. Cours La Haye, 1987 – III, t. 203, p. 386.

11 M. CHARFI, *Islam et liberté : le malentendu historique*, Paris, Albin Michel, 1999, p. 86.

12 Islam prohibits adoption according to the prescriptions of verse 5 of Surah *Alahzab* (The Allies).

However, despite this historic advance, Tunisia has remained attached to an implicit pre-eminence of Shari'a manifested, for example, through the decisions of the courts which, under the privilege of Islam, prevail over the application of Islamic law, when a dispute arises between a Muslim and a non-Muslim.[13] The implicit pre-eminence of Shari'a in Tunisia is also evident in another example of family law. The Tunisian courts annulled the marriage between a Tunisian Muslim and a non-Muslim,[14] on the grounds that it is contrary to Shari'a, while the Tunisian Family Code does not prohibit such a marriage. Similarly, the Tunisian Court of Cassation, by a judgment of 31 January 1966, decided that a Tunisian woman, who had married a non-Muslim Frenchman, should become a renegade and, as a result, be deprived of the estate of his mother deceased in the Muslim religion, on the grounds that a non-Muslim cannot inherit a Muslim.[15]

Of all the Arab countries, Lebanon is the only one with a pluralistic legal system marked by the equivalence of its sources.

C. Legal pluralism marked by the equivalence of sources of Law

Lebanon offers a remarkable illustration of legal pluralism marked by the equivalence of the sources of its law. Indeed, Lebanese legal pluralism, based essentially on a confessionalism linked to the tumultuous history of the country,[16] is characterised by equality between all denominational legal orders, which is not the case in other Arab countries where there is still a dominant Muslim community that tolerates the practice, by members of other minority religious communities, of cults specific to their

13 M. CHARFI, "L'influence de la religion sur le droit international privé des pays musulmans", *op. cit.*, p. 412.

14 This prohibition is recalled by a circular dated 5 November 1973 (M. CHARFI, *op. cit.*, p. 448).

15 Tunisian Court of Cassation, judgment of 31 January 1966, *Rev. tun. de droit*, 1968, p. 114, note DELA-GRANGE – Quoted by S. JAHEL, *op. cit.*, p. 52.

16 Lebanese confessionalism finds its foundation in Ottoman, French and Lebanese texts, which we note the following: the Ottoman Firman of 18 February 1856, the French Decree No. 60 LR of 13 April 1936, the Lebanese law of 2 April 1951, the Lebanese law of 23 June 1959, the Lebanese legislative decree No. 18 of 13 January 1955, the Lebanese law of 19 December 1967 and the two Lebanese laws of 13 July 1962.

religion. The specificity of Lebanon lies indeed in the coexistence on its soil of many religious communities governed by rules of law some of which apply to all Lebanese, regardless of their religious affiliation, and others apply only to only members of each community. In Lebanon, the Constitution provides neither for a State religion nor the predominance of religion as a source of law. Article 9 of the Constitution provides that freedom of conscience is absolute and that the State respects all denominations and guarantees and protects their free exercise, provided that it does not undermine public order.

According to the Lebanese legal system, which is unique in the Muslim world, the citizen can exercise his rights and obligations only through his membership of a religious community legally recognised and which is, in principle, that of his birth. This system, whose scope extends to the family,[17] spiritual, professional and political life of each citizen, divides the presidencies of the Republic, the Government and the parliament between the three main religious communities, those of the Maronite Christians, Sunni Muslims and Shia Muslims.[18] The same is true of ministerial portfolios, parliamentary seats and public-service posts, even within the army and the national police, which must also be distributed among religious communities in proportion to their historical and numerical importance, being reminded that atheism and agnosticism have no place in Lebanese society.

In Lebanon, Shari'a rules of personal status, which apply only to Muslims, are part of the State legal system. Indeed, Muslim-religious jurisdictions are incorporated into the State judicial system and judges (*cadis*) have the status of State officials. Other Lebanese religious communities, whether Christian or Jewish, enjoy an autonomy which allowed each one of them to establish its own personal status, to organise its own religious jurisdictions and to appoint its own judges for resolving disputes relating to the personal status of individuals who are compulsorily attached to it, and it being specified that these judges do not have the status of civil servants of the State. In case of a positive or negative conflict between two confessional jurisdictions belonging to two religious

---

17 Every Lebanese citizen must be attached to a religious community to marry, divorce, exercise parental authority or to collect an inheritance.

18 Political confessionalism in Lebanon is recognised by the Constitution of 23 May 1926, the unwritten National Pact of 1943, Decree Law No. 112 of 12 June 1959, and the Taif Agreement of 22 October 1989.

communities or between a confessional and a civil court, this conflict will be submitted to the Court of Cassation convened in Plenary Assembly.[19]

Apart from the personal status[20] which is the main source of divergences between Arab and European legal systems, the secular exchanges between these systems today explain their many convergences in different subjects.

III. Convergences and divergences between the European legal systems and those of Arab countries

The interaction between the European legal systems and those of Arab countries, which is reflected today in many convergences in certain subjects (A), is in sharp divergences in others (B).

A. The convergences between the European legal systems and those of Arab countries

The close examination of the general principles of law in Europe, particularly in France, and the *kawaed kulliya* (global legal norms) which form the basis of different branches of law in the Arab countries[21] reveals many similarities. *Kawaed kullia* are the general rules that *cadis* (judges) apply to all the particular questions attached to them.[22] These rules, whose development began at the end of the 3rd century of the Hegira (early 10th century AD), were incorporated into the Ottoman *Majallat*[23] promulgated on 16 September 1876 and applied in the Arab countries forming part of the Ottoman Empire. The similarities between the general principles of law applied in Europe and the *kawaed kullia* on the territory constituting the current Arab countries can be explained by the trade and wars that have led to cultural interaction between the two sides of the Mediterranean.

---

19 S. JAHEL, *op. cit.*, p. 50.

20 In Arab legal systems, personal status includes family law, matrimonial property regimes and the right of inheritance.

21 With the exception of the personal status which is set exclusively by Shari'a law.

22 S. MAHMASSANI, *Falsafat al tachri' fi al islam* (Philosophy of Jurisprudence in Islam), Beirut, 1980, p. 297.

23 The *Majallat* means *Majallat Alahkam Aladlya* (Collection of Rules of Justice) promulgated on 16 September 1876.

Among these similarities, we cite, as examples, i/ the Arab principle that '*al tabe' tabe*' (which is attached must follow) and the European principle that 'the accessory follows the principal'; ii/ the Arab principle according to which '*al darar la yazoulou bi mislihi*' (one does not repair damage by a similar damage) and the European principle according to which 'no one can do justice to oneself'; iii/ the Arab principle that '*al darourat toubih al mahzourat*' (necessity authorises what is prohibited) and the European principle of 'state of necessity'; iv/ the principles of contractual freedom, the binding force of the contract, the relative effect of the contract, the prohibition of unjust enrichment, etc. These different principles apply on the condition of not contradicting Shari'a law in Arab countries, nor public order or good morals in European countries. Today, all transactions of a pecuniary nature (*mouamalat malya*) such as, for example, contract law, civil liability law, securities law or insurance law, are governed by rules containing contributions foreigners, especially French. The same is true of constitutional law, administrative law, civil service law, procedural law and jurisdictional organisation.

Among the European legal texts that have influenced the Arab legal systems, the French Civil Code occupies a special place since it is very largely transposed into almost all of the Arab civil codes, especially its parts devoted to contract, civil liability, obligations and special contracts. These codes are also based on other European civil codes. For example, they borrow the notion of 'abuse of rights' from the Swiss Civil Code of 10 December 1907.[24] They also borrow from the Italian Civil Code the notion of 'unforeseen circumstances' in contractual matters and the German Civil Code the concept of 'injury' which the judge retains when a contractor takes advantage of the weakness of the other contractor.[25]

The application of rules emanating from European rights has not been achieved without difficulty in Arab countries, whose legal systems have, for centuries, been deeply marked by Shari'a law. For example, many Arab countries have enacted legal or regulatory texts permitting the

---

[24] Article 2 of the Code provides that "Everyone is bound to exercise his rights and to perform his duties according to the rules of good faith. Obvious abuse of a right is not protected by law".

[25] S. JAHEL, *op. cit.*, p. 81 (Article 1467 of the Italian Civil Code and Article 132-2 of the German Civil Code).

perception of interest in lending money. While some of these countries, such as Lebanon, Syria, Iraq or Egypt, allow it, others, such as Bahrain, the United Arab Emirates or Kuwait, have it – under the prohibition of *riba* (usury) by Shari'a – prohibited in non-commercial financial transactions and in financial relations between individuals.[26] The interaction between European legal systems and those of Arab countries based to varying degrees on Shari'a has, so far, have been remarkably successful in many areas, including those of an economic nature. However, in some areas, such as human rights, it faces a crippling incompatibility between Shari'a law and several European and international texts.

B. The divergences between the European legal systems and those of Arab countries

Several Shari'a rules, whether from the text of the Quran or from the requirements of the Sunnah, are resolutely incompatible with the provisions of the texts of the Council of Europe, the EU and the UN, which deal with human rights. The incompatibility of Shari'a law with the Council of Europe and the EU human rights texts concerns many issues, including the death penalty for apostasy, the amputation of the two hands of the person accused of theft,[27] the whipping[28] and stoning[29] for adultery, the submission of the woman to the man and the right of the latter to strike her if she disobeys him,[30] the inheritance inequality between man and woman,[31] the legal incapacity of the woman in different

---

[26] These countries tolerate, on the other hand, the perception of interest in commercial and financial operations.

[27] Verse 38 of the Surah *Al Maaida* (the table) states: "The thief and the thief cut off both their hands in punishment for what they have acquired and as a punishment from Allah".

[28] Verse 2 of Surah *Al Nour* (The light) states: "The fornicator and the fornicator, inflict a hundred lashes on each one. And do not be pitied for them in the execution of the law of Allah".

[29] Stoning for adultery is not prescribed in any verse of the Quran.

[30] Verse 34 of Surah *Al Nisa* (Women) states: "Men have authority over women because of the benefits that Allah has bestowed upon them and because of the expenses they make for their upkeep. [...] The wives of whom you fear disobedience, exhort them, leave them in your marriage bed and strike them".

[31] Verse 11 of Surah *Al Niasa* (Women) states: "Concerning your children, Allah commands you to give the son a share equivalent to that of two girls".

fields, polygamy of the husband,[32] the repudiation of the woman by her husband.[33]

This incompatibility is expressly noted by the European Court of Human Rights in its judgment of 13 February 2003 in the case *Refah Partisi* (Prosperity Party) and others against Turkey. Indeed, sitting in the Grand Chamber, the European Court of Human Rights in this judgment clarified its position of Shari'a in the following terms: "It is difficult at the same time to declare oneself respectful of democracy and human rights and to support a Shari'a-based regime, which stands out clearly from the values of the Convention [European Convention on Human Rights], particularly with regard to its rules of criminal law and procedure, the place it places on women in the legal order and its intervention in all areas of private and public life in accordance with religious norms". It should be recalled that this incompatibility is not limited to the texts of the Council of Europe and the EU. It also concerns many texts adopted under the auspices of the UN in the field of human rights.

The accession of Arab countries to international organisations, in particular the UN, has led them to juxtapose to their internal legislation, marked by the Shari'a, certain legal norms emanating from international conventions and covenants. However, the articulation of and international standards within the legal systems of the Arab countries is not always easy, due to the prominence of Shari'a overall international, constitutional, legislative or regulatory texts. For example, the International Covenant of 16 December 1966 on Civil and Political Rights normally takes precedence over the national laws of the countries that have signed it. But the application of article 18 of the Covenant, which provides for freedom of belief and the right to change one's religion, and article 23, which provides for equality between men and women, runs up against in the majority of Arab countries, faces an absolute incompatibility with the prescriptions of Shari'a law.

*

In conclusion, the History of humanity and of its civilisations, in their convergences and divergences, shows that acculturation and legal pluralism were and will always be inseparable. Recent reforms adopted

---

32 Verse 3 of Surah *Al Nisa* (Women) states: "If you are afraid of being unfair to orphans, marry, as you wish, two, three, or four women, but, if you are afraid of being unjust, then only one woman or slaves you own".

33 The 12 verses of Surah *Al Talak* (Divorce) are devoted to this question.

in various Arab countries, including Egypt, Sudan, Mauritania, Jordan, Iraq, the United Arab Emirates and Oman, marked by an ostensible return to Shari'a, do not go in the direction of respect for human rights and principles of secularism, prohibition of all forms of discrimination and equality between men and women in all fields. With regard to secularism, the application of which automatically leads to the elimination of many forms of discrimination and injustice, it can only find its place in the Arab countries if freedom has previously found its own.

Secularism in Muslim Central Asian republics: challenges from religious nationalism as linked to the upheavals of New Silk Roads

Philippe Gast
Le Havre Normandie University, LexFEIM, France

'Secularism' – in French *laïcité* – comes from the Latin *laicus* meaning 'he who is not a member of the clergy'. This concept echoes the idea of separation between religious institutions and the State. The latter does not recognise nor subsidise any religious activity and the former cannot intervene in the normative process of the State.[1]

Thus defined, *laïcité* can be deemed i/ democratic[2] secularism (e.g. in France, Japan, South Korea, etc.), entailing separation between State and religion in such a way that freedom of religion is guaranteed, as is equality among all religions; but some systems can be ii/ secular without being democratic (the USSR, China during the cultural revolution, Vietnam, etc.); iii/ some can be democratic but not secular, recognising freedom of religion but having a State religion (the UK, Denmark, etc.) with privileges in regard to others, thereby maintaining inequality (use of religious monuments free of charge; salaries paid to clergymen, etc.).

This separation between State and religion draws a distinction between *legal* rules, that come from the State, and *moral* rules which are of religious essence. The word 'morality' comes from the Latin *mores*

---

1 As in the Japanese constitution of 3 November 1956, article 20.

2 With 'people in power', through a voting majority's will and interest (or referendum on people's initiative, a *votation* in Switzerland), associated with liberty and equality, as Pericles theorised it. Democracy needs to respect *a minima* the majority's interest and free will in elections, freedom of expression, equality of electors and candidacy in institutional and indirect aspects, necessary even for direct democracy...

meaning 'ways of life' (*mœurs* in French): we have the morality of our ways of life and the ways of life correspond to our morality. Moral rules are personal and facultative:[3] we can change morality as we can change religion. Sanctions – paradise, hell, reincarnation – have a metaphysical nature. Legal rules, by contrast, are collective/mandatory, sanctioned *hic et nunc*, positively/physically: fines, imprisonment, etc.).

This chapter aims at using these reflections in a field that has *prima faciae* little to do with religion (b) and more with State affairs (a).

a) The new Silk Roads, inspired by China's president Xi Jin-Ping, or 'One Belt, One Road' target Central Asia,[4] a formerly soviet zone[5] under Russian influence since the 17th century. The regional context is a competition between China and Russia. i/ Beijing strives to place CA nations under influence, purchasing/exporting hydrocarbon energy, as well as wishing to recreate its cultural influence as in the Middle Age when some Chinese cities (in Kirghizstan, etc.) were a prolongation of the Chinese province of Xinjiang (*the new border* in Chinese), going as far as wishing to 're-educate'/convert its Muslim Uyghur population.[6] ii/ Russia, the former colonial power, attempts to 'reconquer' these republics, which still count in their population 15% to 20% ethnic Russians.

China and Russia attempt to impose themselves in Central Asia by massive investments in the local markets, still little developed due to former soviet policies. These Muslim republics, mostly those with

3 It is essential to distinguish moral rules from juridical rules. Cf. Thomas of Aquino in his *Summa theologica* (question 90, article 2) and Kant in his *Metaphysic of mores*: "law has the ability to constrain" (I.D); "ethical law is the one that cannot be external" (I.III)

4 China has built a railway and a highway between Chongqing, a large industrial city in central China to Kazakhstan and Kirghizstan.

5 Kazakhstan, Kirghizstan, Uzbekistan, Turkmenistan Tajikistan and, less directly, Mongolia.

6 *Le Figaro*, 12 October 2018, http://www.lefigaro.fr/international/2018/10/11/01003-20181011ARTFIG00051-la-chine-legalise-les-camps-de-reeducation-pour-ouigours.php; *Le Monde*, 31/08/2018, one million Ouigours are said to be locked up: http://www.lefigaro.fr/international/2018/10/11/01003-20181011ARTFIG00051-la-chine-legalise-les-camps-de-reeducation-pour-ouigours.php; *Libération*, 10 October 2018, where China recognise 800,000 prisoners: https://www.liberation.fr/planete/2018/10/14/ouighours-la-chine-reconnait-des-camps-pour-eduquer_1685316.

a common border with China (Kazakhstan, Kirghizstan, Tajikistan), facing possible Russian intervention, as in Crimea, strive to alleviate that risk by allying with China. Yet, opening up excessively to China carries a risk, due to their low population: Chinese investments entail migrations from China, notably to sites where China buys oil- and gas-extraction sites, a tilt some call neo-colonialism. The Collective Security Treaty Organisation (CSTO), a defence organisation was established by several ex-Soviet Republics (but without China) to tackle these issues from the military point of view. The Shanghai Cooperation Organisation (SCO), set up to monitor economic plans, includes China, Russia, Central-Asian Republics and now India and Pakistan. Together, the CSTO and the SCO maintain a balance. A Eurasian Economic Community (2014) turned into a *Union* in 2015, with Russia, Belarus, Armenia, Kazakhstan and Kyrgyzstan, tries with difficulty to balance Chinese influence.

b) A religious dimension, however, clearly exists. These Muslim countries of Central Asia are secular (due to their history) but Islamic nationalisms are equally at work, particularly in 'West-Asian' Turkey under President Erdoğan, as they share the cultural linguistic link of Turkish languages (except for Tajik, of Persian origin) and a religious origin with Shiite Iran and with Taliban Afghanistan, and also with Wahabi Saudi Arabia and the latter's petrodollars.

Three main poles of influence exist: i/ Russian-Orthodox; ii/ Sino-Confucian; iii/ Islamist (Turkey, Iran, Saudi Arabia that finance many mosques); maybe iv/ a pole of American influence through the creation of universities, with a Protestant influence.

This chapter deciphers how these secular Muslim republics resist these various religious, cultural and economic pressures. The situation of the Muslim republics of Central Asia, that are secular and could be models for other Muslim countries (I) is a context in which the New Silk Roads challenges this secularism (II).

I. Secularism in the Muslim republics of Central Asia: an exception in the Muslim world

We will study first the position of the *Koran* in regard to secularism (A) and then how some Muslim republics became secular (B).

A. Secularism and the Koran

Many *suras* are used in the Muslim world as legal ones but, in reality, only few of them are juridical and positively sanctioned. An example of a positive, juridical rule is the death sentence for polytheists: After sacred months, kill the polytheists wherever you find them (…) (S.9: v.5 called saber, same meaning as S.4: v.89).[7] Thus, a literary and juridical interpretation of the Koran is incompatible with democracy both as to public-law fundaments (a) and to positive private-law rules (b).

a) The sharia as juridical rules, that one should better call fikh,[8] is an ideological inegalitarian system that rejects the sovereignty of the people to the benefit of that of God[9] (and of the Ulemas). Muhammad, after winning the battle against the Meccas, became a monarch and a cousin of the 3rd Othman caliph, Mu'âwiya, and instituted the Umayyad dynasty. The monarchic principal was imposed. Only Karijites kept the elective principle.[10]
b) In regard to private law rules, the Koran contains few rules with positive, juridical sanctions. Most are moral rules (with metaphysic sanction as 'hell' for the apostate, for example (S.4: v.115). However, some general positive sanctions appear for the Thief (so the thief must be hand-cut – S.5: v.38)[11]&[12] and for the unfaithful (After sacred months, kill the polytheists wherever you find them, *op. cit.*). Those who fight against Islam must be killed and crucified or their limbs will be cut (S.5: v.33).

Yet, some positive rules can be identified that are liberticidal (a) and other discriminating (b) in opposition to democracy, if there is a juridical interpretation.

---

7 *The holy Koran*, Masson's translation, Paris, Gallimard, La Pléiade, 1967.

8 The word *sharia*, meaning 'the way to the source' differs from *fikh*, meaning 'law'. This linguistic difference leads precisely to the fact that *sharia* means moral rules and *fikh* juridical rules. A confusion thus makes Islamists, as Muslim theologian Al Ajami says: "the Muslim law must be distinguished from the *sharia*". A.N. al-AJANI, *Que dit vraiment le Coran* (Molsheim, SRBS, 2008, p. 7, 9, note 4).

9 "The One to whom pertains royalty of skies and earth" (S.25: v.2).

10 M. ELIADE, *History of religious beliefs and ideas*, Paris, Payot, 1978, 3 t., p. 86, 90, 91 and 92.

11 "Cut the hand of the thief; that will be the retribution for what they have done, a God's punishment".

12 God forgives the one who repents (S.5: v.39)… more moral than juridical.

a) Some rules are liberticidal because they undermine sexual freedom. The adulterous woman must be enclosed until death (S.4: v.15) but this rule is difficult to apply as it is not precise enough: if a woman is violated, is she adultery? The woman suspected of infidelity must be beaten (S.4: v.34). Women do not have the choice of their husband (this affects private life) mostly if he is not Muslim – don't marry your daughters to polytheists (S.2: v.221). As there is no positive sanction, this is a moral rule, but in many Muslim countries it became a juridical rule. As to the headscarf – o prophet, tell your wives, daughters and believer's wives to be covered by their vale [djilbab= cloth] (S.33: v.159). Again, this is a moral rule, as there is no positive sanction; yet, in Iran or Afghanistan, women without headscarf (chador or burqa) are beaten.

b) The Koran also contains several discriminations which, if interpreted juridically, violate democratic principles. i/ Sexual discrimination, as we saw about women adultery (men are beaten not put to death – S.24: v.2), women's inheritance is half that of the men (S.4: v.11)[13] due to being sexually submitted to men.[14] Yet, these rules, carrying no positive sanctions, are moral ones. ii/ A religious discrimination tax appears in Koran as a juridical rule in regard to Christians and Jews qualified as dhimmi – fight them until they pay directly the tribute (S.9: v.29). iii/ A social discrimination through the recognition of slavery in several verses: the Law of Talion is prescribed in case of murder: free man for free man, slave for slave (S.2: v.178); a Muslim slave is better than a polytheist one (S.2: v.221); be good (…) toward your slaves (S.4: v.36). There are also many references to women slaves (S.4: v.3 – as takes of war –, 36; S.24: v.58, take women as slaves S.33: v.52); and also the marriage of salves (S.24: v.32).

The question is simple. Either one interprets the Koran juridically, which leads to an incompatibility with democratic public order (violating equality and liberties). Or one interprets the Koran morally or spiritually, and there is no problem of compatibility because morality is

---

13 This gender-discrimination comes from the idea that "Men have authority upon women by virtue of the preference that God cast upon them" (S.4: v.34).

14 Here, "Your wives are for you fields for ploughing; go to the field whenever you want" (S.2: v.223), "Men have […] pre-eminence upon them (S.2: v.228) and can repudiate them unilaterally" (S.2: v.230, 241).

of free application in private life as are the five pillars of Islam,[15] not in opposition to it.[16] Furthermore, the historical evolution shows that some Muslim countries can be secular.

B. Muslim countries formerly part of the USSR

The long-dating Muslim republics of the Russian empire that became the USSR[17] have been *de facto* secular due to an anti-religious communist ideology, for which religion is 'the opium of the people' (Marx) or made to 'contain slaves' revolt' (Nietzsche).

Traditionally, Central Asian republics practice a moderate Islam among nomads. Under Russian and Soviet influence, Islam still stood moderate. After independence, they became systems claiming democracy, with elections, equality and various private liberties, among which secularism.

The Constitution of Kazakhstan proclaims itself as democratic, secular (art. 1). It proclaims freedom of consciousness (art. 22-1), no discrimination in regard to personal attitude toward religion (art. 14) which can be secret (art. 19). It forbids religious 'enmity' and religious propaganda destined to undermine the constitution (art. 20) and control of foreign religious associations (art. 5-5).[18]

The Constitution of Kirghizstan proclaims also to be democratic and secular, to respect human rights and personal freedoms, to forbid any discrimination based on 'beliefs' (art. 16-2). Freedom of religion is guaranteed and no restriction can be put upon religious choice (art. 20). Freedom of expression is also guaranteed, but religious hatred is forbidden (art. 31). Religious associations do not have the right to engage in politics or express religious hatred (art. 4). Secularity is very precise: "religion and all cults shall be separated from the State […] the involvement of religious associations and ministers of religion in the activity of State authorities shall be prohibited' (art. 7). This is a remarkable definition, as

---

15 Profession of faith, five prayers a day, Ramadan, donation, pilgrimage to Mecca.

16 As explicitly written "Anyone who makes jihad, fights against his own soul [ego]" (S.29: v.6).

17 http://www.oxfordislamicstudies.com/article/opr/t125/e414.

18 T. ABDRAKHMANOV, "L'islam au Kazakhstan : les rapports États-religion (XVIIIe-XXe siècles)", 2012 : https://tel.archives-ouvertes.fr/file/index/docid/817205/filename/These_-_Abdrakhmanov.pdf.

in the Japanese Constitution, but no in the French one, where secularism is not defined.

The Constitution of Turkmenistan proclaims also to be democratic and secular (art. 1), with equality and no religious discrimination (art. 19); freedom of opinion and expression (art. 28), and of association (art. 30), but forbids religious hatred and politic parties based on religious principles (art. 29).

The Constitution of Tajikistan proclaims to be democratic and secular (art. 1), adding that no (religious) ideology can be recognised as 'State ideology'; religious organisations will be separated from the State, and will not be able to interfere into State affairs nor to develop religious hatred (art. 18). The State guarantees individual (religious) freedoms (art. 17): anyone is free to determine himself toward religion, individually, collectively or without practice (art. 26). Freedom of expression is also guaranteed, but not if there is religious hatred (art. 30).

The Constitution of Uzbekistan proclaims itself as democratic (art. 1); secularism does not appear explicitly, contrary to previous countries, but it forbids any (religious) State ideology (art. 12). It proclaims freedom and equality, no religious discrimination (art. 18), freedom of thought, of speech, of belief (art. 29) and consciousness (art. 30), and the right to practice or not a religion: imposing a religion is forbidden (art. 31); freedom of (religious) association is guaranteed (art. 34).

As can be seen, Central Asian republics are secular, contrary to most Muslim States (except Turkey, secular, maybe not for long). Freedom of religion is accepted more (Tunisia, Morocco) or less (Saudi Arabia, Iran). Central Asian republics are really a model for the other Muslim peoples that want modernity, with liberty and equality.

Yet, this secular model seems challenged by the changes that occur around the New Silk Roads.

II. Secularism challenged by religious nationalism linked to changes around the New Silk Roads

During the antiquity, the Silk Road was a pathway for communication, commerce but also for the exchange of ideas, among which religious ones. Buddhism thus reached Afghanistan (Buddhas of Bamiyan, destroyed by the Talibans) and spread to China as shown by the 7th century Chinese monk Xuanzang, who brought 600 Sanskrit manuscripts from India to China and translated them into Chinese. These were peaceful exchanges. In most cases, however, the Silk Roads proved a path of invasion for Muslims into India (Moghols) or Turks (Constantinople).

The New Silk Road presents itself as an economic project (A) but seems to conceal a politico-religious ambition that could threaten the secularity of Muslim Central Asian republics (B).

A. The new Silk Road or 'One Belt, One Road': Chinese neo-colonialism?

The official goal of the NSR is to facilitate international exchange, creating 'win-win'[19] infrastructures (roads, harbours, airports) that enable gas and oil to reach China and, reciprocally, Chinese products to spread West, mostly to Europe (China joined the WTO in 2001).[20] Chinese products represent 16% imports by Europe.[21] China's GDP has grown in the double-digits in the last twenty years, making the Chinese economy the second in the world with financial reserves of 3,118 billion $ (July 2018[22]) for investments.[23] These reserves enabled China to create the Asian Infrastructure Investment Bank (AIIB) in 2015,[24] in which Beijing holds over 30% of the capital.[25] In the AIIB statutes, China imposed

19 But outside democratic values, where the (majority's) general interest can manifest itself through free elections and free critics.

20 But still without respecting the rules of the WTO as its economy is planned and subsidised (ceramic, aluminium, etc) and not yet liberal (R. HIAULT, *Le Figaro*, 1 January 2018: https://www.lesechos.fr/01/01/2018/lesechos.fr/0301073040549_commerce---le-systeme-economique-chinois-dans-le-viseur-de-bruxelles.htm.

21 In 2017, $2300 bil. of exportations and 1800 of importations ($500 bil. of commercial benefit), of which $372 bil. of exportation to the EU (and $244 bil. of importations): https://www.tresor.economie.gouv.fr/Pays/CN/commerce-exterieur.

22 See in *Capital*, 7 August 2018: https://www.capital.fr/entreprises-marches/chine-hausse-inattendue-des-reserves-de-change-1301981.

23 But China violates in particular liberal rules for foreign investments that have to make joint-ventures with Chinese companies, and that cannot own more than 49 % of the capital. See part I.8 of the report of EU commission 20 December 2017: http://trade.ec.europa.eu/doclib/docs/2017/december/tradoc_156474.pdf.

24 G. GRÉSILLON, *Le Temps*, 27 October 2014 : https://www.letemps.ch/economie/chine-va-lancer-banque-asiatique-dinvestissement.

25 https://www.imf.org/external/np/sec/memdir/members.aspx, See *Le Monde*, 24 October 2014: http://www.lemonde.fr/asie-pacifique/article/2014/10/24/pekin-signe-avec-20-pays-pour-etablir-une-banque-regionale-en-asie_4511772_3216.html.

(art. 25)[26] that the governing Board be constituted of nine local members and three external members, that the president be local (art. 29) and that the AIIB headquarters be in Beijing (art. 32). Clearly, China created a financial instrument in which she dominates and that enables her industrial production to be exported widely. Central Asia thus appears to be the Chinese 'new border' – *xin jiang*… China's Constitution proclaims to be a "popular democratic dictatorship" (*sic*)[27] for the benefit of a minority in power, with no popular expression by referendum[28] nor by free elections as the system has but one single party and public liberties are monitored, namely freedom of association, political expression and the right to strike.

Private life is freer in China nowadays[29] but through social-monitoring by a *social card* that contains a number of points reduced with each offense.[30] Pervasive video surveillance is ensured with facial recognition. Hence, the 5G-system of Huawei is so sustained by the regime and at the international level and many western countries intend to counter this monitoring-oversight system. Such evolutions exist elsewhere: some GAFAs manipulate personal data, including in electoral times (2016 in the USA; in the Brexit referendum[31]). Chinese neo-colonialism manifests itself through the new Silk Road, by securing local oligarchies[32] in order to get access to public markets, thereby creating real liabilities to obtain concessions (the British did the same against China for Hong Kong). The recent example is the Sri-Lankan harbour of Hambantota: in 1997,

---

26 https://www.aiib.org/en/about-aiib/basic-documents/_download/articles-of-agreement/basic_document_french_bank_articles_of_agreement.pdf.

27 Preamble, paragraph 10, modified by 4th amendment alinea 18, 14 March 2004: notice the new word for 'dictatorship of the proletariat'.

28 The slogan 'win-win' proclaimed for the 'belt and road' project concerns really oligarchies in power in China and in the bribed countries. Referendum by citizens' initiative is the only instrument against corruptions of oligarchies, as Switzerland has shown for centuries.

29 In most authoritarian States today (Russia, China, Turkey, etc), a certain freedom in private life is tolerated by powers, as long as individuals do not contest the regime.

30 E. TRUJILLO, *Le Figaro*, 27 December 2017: http://www.lefigaro.fr/secteur/high-tech/2017/12/27/32001-20171227ARTFIG00197-la-chine-met-en-place-un-systeme-de-notation-de-ses-citoyens-pour-2020.php.

31 W. AUDUREAU, *Le Monde*, 22 March 2018: https://www.lemonde.fr/pixels/article/2018/03/22/ce-qu-il-faut-savoir-sur-cambridge-analytica-la-societe-au-c-ur-du-scandale-facebook_5274804_4408996.html.

32 https://www.courrierinternational.com/article/comment-la-chine-fait-main-basse-sur-le-sri-lanka.

the Sri-Lankan government gave China concession over this harbour for 99 years with a 15,000-ha zone (a large area for such a small island) as repayment of a loan by China of 1,4 billion $ necessary to build the harbour. Note that experts have from the onset denied the profitability of the harbour, suggesting that corruption touched the family heading Sri Lanka at the time of the signature of the contract.[33]

The New Silk Roads appears to be a Chinese expansion, indeed a neo-colonialist one, with large delocalisation of Chinese workers (5,000 Chinese in Kazakhstan, with a total flux of up to 100,000 in one year, for example in 2008).[34] But factors other than economic ones are active in Central Asia: religious factors (B).

B. Politico-religious ambitions threatening secularism in Central Asian Muslim republics

Four poles of religious influence are present in Central Asia: Russian-orthodox (a), Sino-Confucian (b), Islamist (c) and, less important, Americano-evangelist (d).

a) The Russian-orthodox pole has been present in this region since the Russian empire, from around the 17th century[35] and still existed after independence, at the collapse of the USSR. Between 15% and 20% of the population of these republics are Russian-orthodox. V. Putin is very close to the patriarch of Moscow, Kirill.[36] Both were trained under the soviet system and at the time of universalist (international) communism and

---

33 https://www.epochtimes.fr/sri-lankais-protestent-contre-concession-gouvernement-a-chine-dun-important-port-de-pays-492072.html. It is easy for an authoritarian government to give a bribe to a corrupted one in a fiscal heaven (Singapore for example) in exchange of a concession.

34 S. PEYROUSE, "La présence chinoise en Asie centrale : portée géopolitique, en jeux économiques et impact culturel", *Les Études du CERI* (Paris, Sciences Po), n° 148, septembre 2008: https://www.sciencespo.fr/ceri/sites/sciencespo.fr.ceri/files/etude148.pdf.

35 Kazakhstan and Kirghizstan since the 3rd c. have had Christian Nestorian communities. Apostles Thomas and Matthew are said to have reached these regions. These communities where almost erased by conversion to Islam of Turcoman, but some may have reappeared in the 17th c., with the expansion of Russian Empire.

36 C. COSTIL, *La Croix*, 19 March 2018: https://www.la-croix.com/Religion/Orthodoxie/Presidentielle-russe-Poutine-beneficie-soutien-Patriarcat-Moscou-2018-03-19-1200922064.

nationalist hegemony. Kirill ambitions to be the 'Pope' of orthodoxy[37] even against the main patriarch '*primus inter pares*' of Orthodoxy[38] who recognised the new patriarch of Ukraine.[39] Putin envisions to recreate the Russian Empire (annexing Georgia's northern Ossetia, then Crimea, probably the Ukrainian Donbas; refusing Chechenia's independence). Wherever lives a Russian minority, Putin wishes it to 'return' to Russia (as Germany in the 1930s did of German-speakers of Alsace, etc).

This suggests an objectively common view between Putin and Kirill, in contradiction with Russian constitutional secularism. And an indication that, should Kazakhstan one day contest Putin's politics, there might be a risk that the Russian minority in the north claim (or be said by the Russians to claim) re-attachment to Russia (as with the Donbas population).

b) As for the Sino-Confucian pole,[40] recently, China opened a 5th Confucius institute in Almaty, Kazakhstan, in the Ablai Khan University in relation with the 'One Belt, One Road' initiative.[41] The link is clear between the new Silk Road and the Chinese purpose to create in Central Asia an ideological instrument to extend Chinese culture and religion (Confucius was the founder of the traditional Chinese religion). These Confucius institutes monitor eight teaching centres and have already trained 8,500 students in this country.[42]

Confucius institutes also exist in Kirghizstan, with the same purpose: to spread the Chinese culture (and then Chinese religion). Most recently, such an Institute was created on 26 December 2016, in Jalal Abad, an ancient

---

37 https://www.la-croix.com/Culture/TV-Radio/Le-patriarche-Kirill-lautre-voix-Russie-2018-09-04-1200966059.

38 S. LIEVEN, *La Croix*, 3 December 2017: https://www.la-croix.com/Religion/Orthodoxie/Le-patriarche-Kirill-convoque-lorthodoxie-mondiale-Moscou-2017-12-03-1200896659.

39 C. COSTIL, *La Croix*, 19 March 2018: https://www.la-croix.com/Religion/Orthodoxie/Presidentielle-russe-Poutine-beneficie-soutien-Patriarcat-Moscou-2018-03-19-1200922064; *La Croix*, 10 November 2018, based on an AFP despatch: https://www.la-croix.com/Monde/Le-Patriarcat-Constantinople-reconnait-Eglise-orthodoxe-independante-Ukraine-2018-10-11-1300975366.

40 The creation by China of numerous Confucius' cultural centres relates to the cultural and religious nationalist purpose. China did not promote Buddhist culture and philosophy although it has been the dominant practiced religion in China…

41 http://french.hanban.org/article/2017-04/25/content_682471.htm.

42 http://french.hanban.org/article/2017-06/29/content_691810.htm.

city of the old Silk Road, not a random location.[43] There are in total four Confucius institutes in Kirghizstan.[44]

The situation in the rest of the region is the following. In Uzbekistan, there are also two Confucius institutes, one in Samarkand and another in Tashkent, totalling 4,000 students.[45] In Tajikistan, there has been a Confucius institute for ten years, with 4,000 students trained each year.[46] There is none, yet, in Turkmenistan,[47] but probably soon, through the development of the SCO.

This Chinese 'soft power' spreads along the Chinese language (for business) and Chinese culture (martial arts, acupuncture, Chinese medicine related to Taoism etc.), in itself a good thing as traditional Chinese culture is rich and of great quality. Yet, behind these Confucius institutes, there occurs also a capturing of information about these host-countries.[48]

Does this suggest a return Taoism, against communism?[49] Is Confucianism back, as President Hu Jintao suggested in 2005, after creating many Confucius institutes all over the world?[50] Possibly. If so, however, not *a priori* in the ancient sense of humanistic values (harmony, mastering passions[51] by study, education, a certain equality of access to education and administrative functions, according to competence – not to hereditary rules – etc.). Rather in the sense of respect toward the people, the weakest (the elderly, the poor) and, above all, respect of authorities (family, ancestors)[52] and mostly in the sense of obeying State authority,

---

43 http://french.hanban.org/article/2017-01/20/content_671450.htm.

44 http://fr.cctv.com/2016/11/03/ARTIWYF4CJz7hmslKh0JDNg3161103.shtml.

45 http://french.hanban.org/article/2016-12/09/content_667786.htm.

46 https://www.japanpolicyforum.jp/archives/diplomacy/pt20180729151525.html.

47 https://www.japanpolicyforum.jp/archives/diplomacy/pt20180729151525.html.

48 https://www.japanpolicyforum.jp/archives/diplomacy/pt20180729151525.html.

49 *Le Nouvel Économiste*, 8 December 2015: https://www.lenouveleconomiste.fr/le-retour-au-confucianisme-28330/.

50 E. PUIG, "The contemporary influence of Confucianism in Chinese politic", July 2012: http://www.centreasia.eu/sites/default/files/publications_pdf/note_linfluence_contemporaine_du_confucianisme_dans_la_politique_chinoise_1.pdf.

51 In this, Confucianism is close to Greek antique morality as taught by Aristotle in *The politics* (chap. 2) where he talks about those who have the political intelligence and can master their passions by using their reason, then to master others: those who, like animals, are driven by their bodily passions and obey them… This objective of mastering passions is almost universal: in Buddhism, Christianism, Islam…

52 Mencius (Meng Zeu), Book 1, chap. 1 of *The four books* tr. Couvreur isbn n° 957-546-075-8; Taipei, Taiwan, 1972, p. 308.

which are all also Confucianist values. The diversion of Confucianism is easily swept towards imperialism, as in the Chinese secular imperial tradition…

In reality, Taoism in a general way and Confucianism (or political Taoism) a particular way, with its aspiration to harmony (in the family, the society, the Sky-and-Earth where the Emperor balances out both with his good morality). The latter would be closer to modern ecological ideas, with a circular economy, recycling garbage, non-polluting energies, short distribution circuits, balanced social relations with participative democracy than to an imperialistic economic system where national or multinational companies impose their rules onto politics, only motivated by oligarchic interests, etc.[53]

c) The Islamist pole is partly Turkish,[54] Iranian and Saudi. It finances many mosques and madrasas. Since the independence of Central Asian Muslim republics, a large number of mosques have been (re)-built. Their architectural style shows frequently, and clearly so, the origin of the funding: either Turkish (the main Mosque of Bishkek, for example), or Saudi style,[55] etc.

The link with Turkey is obvious. These Republics are members of an international organisation created on 12 July 1993 by the Turkish government, called TURKSOY[56] and based in Ankara. It is named after *Turk* and *Soy* ('ancestor'), thereby grouping peoples with a Turkish origin – at least by the language. The TURKSOY has a cultural purpose and is related to UNESCO (Paris agreement, 4 April 1996).[57] Such an organisation cannot balance out Chinese economic power through the new Silk Road. Mostly so, as these Republics have understood, early on, the danger of opening their borders to Islamist religious organisations. Hence the numerous restrictions imposed onto these religious organisations.

---

53 See China's project of the world's largest farm with 100 000 cows! Joagri, 10 November 2017: http://www.agriavis.com/news-9678-la+chine+construit+la+plus+grande+ferme+du+monde%25E2%2580%25A6+91+millions+d%25E2%2580%2599hectares+.html.

54 https://www.trt.net.tr/francais/turquie/2018/08/21/deux-types-de-diplomatie-publique-en-asie-centrale-la-turquie-et-la-chine-1033851.

55 Talgat Abdrakhmanov's doctoral thesis, *op. cit.*, p. 284.

56 *Ibidem.*

57 https://unesdoc.unesco.org/ark:/48223/pf0000103511.

d) As for the American-evangelist pole, some protestant cults exist in the region in the form of evangelist groups. These proclaim a primary reading of the Jewish *Torah*, a juridical one – as there are many juridical rules in Torah –, as Islamists do. Attempts to penetrate this region are made through people who are in a weak situation. Recent independence, as in Central Asia, often entails poverty or low education (as in Brazil for President Bolsonaro, in Africa – Rwanda), who feel drawn to puritans. The USA have created American universities in these countries, for example the AUCA in Bishkek, that are open doors to these organisations. Yet, at the moment, this influence in Central Asian countries is low.[58]

*

In conclusion, the best that these Republics could play, in order to protect their democratic secularism, would be to impose reciprocity in exchanges. At present, China invests everywhere but does not accept that foreigners own more that 49% of the capital of a company in China. It is virtually impossible for a person to own a building or land in China. Yet, the most efficient would be to create a specific local organisation including all these Muslim secular countries, as a regional community, or better still a confederation. The question as Europe suggests is a tricky one.

58 As T. ABDRAKHMANOV puts it, *op. cit.*

Development and transformation of the Rule of Law (法治) since 'Reform and Opening' in the PR China

Bing CHEN
Nankai University, the People's Republic of China

In forty years of reform and opening-up, under the leadership of the Chinese Communist Party, socialism with Chinese characteristics has built great achievements. Along with the sustained and rapid development of Chinese economy and society, the socialistic rule of law with Chinese characteristics also reveals its advance and nationalism, heading gradually toward maturation. Historic steps took place during this period, which this chapter reviews as evolution of legislation and partial implementation. It summarises the accomplishments and experiences of the rule of law system construction and its significance for promoting the modernisation of the national governance system and thus the governance capacity.

I. Forty years of reform and opening to Chinese Rule of Law

Since the Third Plenary Session of the 11th CPC Central Committee in 1978, substantial achievements in socialism with Chinese characteristics have taken place, along with the development in the rule of law in China. China's rule of law construction experiences three historic stages, considered as milestones.[1]

---

1 W. ZHANG, "A Review on the Building of Rule of Law in China for 40 Years: Historical Track, Evolution & Experiences", *Jilin University Journal Social Sciences Edition*, 2018(5), p. 5.

These three stages can be summarised as i/ the reconstruction of society and massive legislation period, ii/ the preparation and inception of rule of law period, and iii/ the comprehensive promotion of law-based governance period.

Among these milestones, two are particularly meaningful for the purpose of this chapter: i/ the establishing of the rule of law as the fundamental strategy for governing in 1997; ii/ the 18th National Congress of the Communist Party of China in 2012, which opens a new era of comprehensive promotion of law-based governance.

A. Economy reconstruction and active legislation to fuel steady social development 1978–1997[2]

After the end of the Cultural Revolution, the Chinese society was in need of reconstruction in almost every all its aspect. Among these aspects, economy restoration seemed the most important mission at the time. Economy requires a steady and orderly social environment as the foundation.

Therefore, the rebuilding of the legal system is of vital significance. An important, related historical event is *the seven laws of the day*. The 2nd Session of the Fifth National People's Congress passed seven laws within one day on 1 July 1979. With *the seven laws of the day* as the forerunner, China then adopted number of important laws.[3] Another influential event is the revision of the 1978 Constitution.[4] The 1982 Constitution helped re-established China's polity, economy, culture and legal systems in the form of a fundamental law. It worked as a guidance for the development direction, and laid down basic principles for the reform of China's political and economic system. The 1982 Constitution also provided the foundation for the further implementation of reform and opening-up. The construction of progressive democracy and the rule of law have opened a new era of rapid development.

The legislative activities at that time mainly focused on economic and administrative aspects. The legal system operated as a tool to ensure the steady development of the State. The 1992 *South Tour Speeches* established the destination of building a Socialist Market Economy System.

---

2 *Ibidem.*

3 *Ibidem.*

4 *Ibidem*, p. 6.

Consequently, on the basis of continuing enhancement of legislation and law enforcement, a system of a law-based administration was stressed.[5]

During 1978–1997 period, the social and institutional foundations were laid down for governing the State based on the rule of law.

B. *The stage of establishing and ruling the State by Law: 1997–2012*[6]

In 1997, the 15th National Congress of the Communist Party of China adopted for the first time the rule of law for governing as the basic principle. Meanwhile, it was the first profound expansion of the essential features and significance of governing the State complying with law.[7] The establishing of ruling the State by law marks the transformation from building 'a legal system' to realising the 'ruling by law'.[8]

The principle of governing the State by law went forward steadily during this period. In 1999, ruling the State by law was written into the Constitution. In 2002, the 16th National Congress of the Communist Party of China further raised the principle of *ruling the State according to law and building a socialist State ruled by law* into the category of political civilisation.[9] In 2007, the 17th National Congress of the Communist Party of China deepened the principle as *fully implementing the basic strategy of governing the State according to law and accelerating the building of a socialist State ruled by law.*[10]

The prominent characteristics of legislative activities at this stage were: gradually delivering the principle of rule of law into the economic and administrative fields; turning the attention to the field of social legislation; promoting judicial reforms, and optimising the approaches of law-enforcement.[11]

---

5 D. YAN and G. LI, "The Traceback and Foreclose of Reform and Open 40 Years on China Rule of Law Construction. Based on 1978-2018 the Government Work Report of China State Council", *Study & Exploration*, 2018(12), p. 9.

6 *Ibidem*, p. 7.

7 *Ibidem*, p. 8.

8 Y. CHEN and B. LI, "Theory on Rule of Law of China in Forty Years: Development, Innovation and Prospects", *Political Science and Law*, 2018(12), p. 66.

9 *Ibidem*, p. 8.

10 *Ibidem*.

11 *Ibidem*, p. 9–10.

C. A new moment for ruling the State by law: 2012 to present[12]

Since the 18th National Congress of the Communist Party of China in 2012, socialism with Chinese characteristics has entered into a new era, and the rule of law in China also steps onto a higher stage.[13] Comprehensively promoting the 'ruling the State by law' principle was put forward at that moment. The socialist rule of law system with Chinese characteristics is one of the most original concepts brought forward by President Xi Jinping. It explicitly formulates the concept of the rule of law and proposes building a socialist system of rule of law with Chinese characteristics. It is a significant theoretical and institutional innovation.[14]

In this new era, ruling the State by law encloses new goals: i/ strengthening the authority of the Constitution, which requires every activity need to conduct within the boundary of the Constitution; ii/ to enhance human rights protection through perfecting the rule of law legal system; iii/ reinforcing the Party's concentrative leading of ruling the State by law with the measures of supervision system improvement and consummating inner-party laws and regulations.

In the new era of comprehensive promoting of law-based governing, it is essential to continually insist on the socialist rule of law path, together with the efforts of promoting economic growth, to lay down a solid foundation of new development.

II. Development of China's legislative system over forty years of reform and opening

A. The Constitution Law: 宪法

On 4 December 1982, the 5th Session of the Fifth National People's Congress passed a comprehensive revision of the Constitution of the People's Republic of China. Successive and substantial modifications in 1988, 1993, 1999 and 2004 were conducted of individual articles and parts thereof accordingly. A total of 31 amendments were passed through these four revisions.

---

12 *Ibidem*, p. 9.

13 *Ibidem*.

14 *Ibidem*, p. 11.

The 2018 amendment was adopted at the first meeting of the 13th National People's Congress. The core essence of the 2018 Constitutional Amendment mainly reflects in:[15]

i/ establishing the guiding position of Socialism with Chinese Characteristics of Xi Jinping's New Era in the State's political and social activities;

ii/ promoting measures to rule the State according to law and the implementation of the Constitution; revising the Constitution preamble from "improve 'legal system' in socialism" to "improve 'rule of law' in socialism", reflecting the new connotation of the concept of ruling the State by law at constitutional level;

iii/ enacting relevant provisions of the National Supervisory Commission.

The revision of the Constitution is for the purpose to better coordinate with the pace of social development. The integration of insistence of the Party's leadership, rule by the people and rule by law is the inner logic of the 2018 revision.[16]

B. Civil Law and Commercial law

1. Property Law of the PE China: 物权法

On 16 March 2007, the 5th Session of the Tenth National People's Congress passed the *Property Law of the People's Republic of China*, which came into effect on 1 October 2007.

This assured the State's basic economic system, the socialist market economy order, and laid a solid foundation for the establishment of a complete legal system for China socialist market economy.[17]

It established China's basic economic system in the form of basic principles, notably systematically stipulating State, collective and private ownership; strengthening and perfecting the specific content of China's basic economic system; and is conducive to the full play of their respective advantages and mutual promotion.

---

15 Constitution of the People's Republic of China (Amended in 2018).

16 Z. LIU, "Political Logic and Legal Basis of the 2018 China Constitution Revision", *Study and Exploration*, 2019(1), p. 58.

17 Property Law of the People's Republic of China [Effective].

2. Company Law of the People's Republic of China: 公司法

On 29 December 1993, the 5th meeting of the Standing Committee of the Eighth National People's Congress passed the *Company Law of the People's Republic of China.* On 26 October 2018, the 6th edition of the Standing Committee of the 13th National People's Congress amended the current version for the fourth time. The legislation on company law reveals a trend to loosen regulation on corporations for the purpose of stimulating market dynamic.

Latest changes to the company law[18] are as follows:

i/ Both the 'threshold' for setting up a limited liability company and a joint stock limited company are lower. The minimum registered capital of a limited liability company is reduced to RMB 30,000. The minimum amount of registered capital of a joint stock limited company has been reduced from 10 million yuan to 5 million yuan.
ii/ Shareholders own the right to decide the company to 'go or stay'. The revised company law stipulates under the condition that if the company's operation and management show serious difficulties, the continuity of survival will cause significant losses to shareholders' interests; and the difficulties cannot be resolved through other means, shareholders who hold more than 10% of the voting rights may request the people's court to dissolve the company.
iii/ A 'One-person limited liability' principle was officially written into the law. According to the new law, a natural person can set up a one-person limited liability company. The minimum registered capital of a one-person limited liability company is RMB 100,000.
iv/ The law also set up special sections to improve the governance structure of listed companies. In the chapter 'Establishment and organisation of a joint stock limited company', the law establishes a special section of 'Special Provisions for the Organisation of Listed Companies', which provides a governance basis for independent directors, secretary of the board of directors and related party transactions.

The new company law reduces parts of restrictions on corporations through adjusting access threshold. In the meantime, minority shareholders' interest obtains more attention. Shareholders gain stronger power

---

18 Company Law of the People's Republic of China (2018 Amendment).

on self-regulation. The form of corporations also become more flexible. Also, company governance structure steps towards rationalisation.

3. *The Foreign Investment Law of the PR of China:* 外商投资法

On 15 March 2019, the second session of the 13th National People's Congress voted and passed the brand-new *Foreign Investment Law*, which will implement on January 1, 2020. The purpose of this legislation is to further expanding foreign opening, attracting foreign investment, protecting the legitimate rights and interests of foreign investors, regulating foreign investment management. The new law, in this way, is expected to assist building a new pattern of comprehensive opening, and promote the healthy development of the socialist market economy.

The Foreign Investment Law mainly focus on five aspects:[19]

- i/ A pre-entry national treatment and a negative list management system are in process now in the PR China;
- ii/ Domestic corporate policy is equally applicable to foreign-invested enterprises, and vice versa;
- iii/ Foreign-invested enterprises participate in standard development work and government procurement activities in an equal way;
- iv/ A foreign-funded enterprise may conduct investment according to the law through different approaches, such as the public offering of stock, corporate bond, and other securities;
- v/ Local governments at various levels may formulate foreign investment promotion policies within the statutory authority. The local governments at all levels and their relevant departments shall further update services of foreign investment accordingly.

C. *Intellectual Property Law*

Since joining the World Intellectual Property Organisation in 1980, the Central People's Government of the People's Republic of China has successively enacted trademark law, patent law, technology contract law, copyright law, computer software protection, etc., thus forming a complete intellectual property legal protection system.

---

19 Foreign Investment Law of the People's Republic of China [Not Yet Effective].

The Trademark Law promulgated in 1982 is the first intellectual property law in China, marking the beginning of the establishment of China's intellectual property protection system. With the introduction of the Patent Law in 1984 and the Copyright Law of 1990, these three legislations indicated the initial formation of China's intellectual property protection system.

Presently, China domestic legislation devotes more efforts to protect intellectual property within the State and abroad. The government has introduced a series of laws and policies to stress the importance of intellectual property protection to economy development. Intellectual property is not only a foundation to technology innovation but also a potential approach to create the favourable business environment. Only when intellectual property gains lawful protections can foreign investors participate into domestic financial activities at ease.

D. Competition Law

1. Anti-monopoly Law of the People's Republic of China: 反垄断法

On 30 August 2007, at the Standing Committee of the Tenth National People's Congress of the People's Republic of China, the Anti-monopoly Law was adopted at the twenty-ninth meeting and implemented on 1 August 2008. The legislative purposes of Anti-monopoly Law[20] are: "to prevent and stop monopolistic behaviour, protect market fair competition, improve economic operation efficiency, safeguard consumer interests and social public interests, and promote the healthy development of the socialist market economy".

In this respect, mention can be made of the 'Qualcomm case'. In November 2013, the National Development and Reform Commission of China received reports from two US companies on Qualcomm's monopolistic behaviour of abuse of market dominance. The anti-monopoly investigation was initiated, based on the report. After 14 months of investigation, in February 2015, the National Development and Reform Commission announced the administrative penalty decision for Qualcomm's anti-monopoly case. The penalty amount was 8% of the total sales of Qualcomm in the Chinese market

20 Anti-monopoly Law of the People's Republic of China [Effective].

in 2013, totalling 6,008 billion yuan. Qualcomm did not appeal. Before China's penalty, the EU, Korea and Japan have launched anti-trust investigation against Qualcomm. The Qualcomm case in China reflects domestic authorities' attitude and determination toward giant international companies, misbehaviour. The enforcement of antitrust law is becoming one of the most useful tools to regulate competition on the market.

2. The Anti-Unfair Competition Law of the PR of China: 反不正当竞争法

The law was adopted at the 3rd meeting of the Standing Committee of the Eighth National People's Congress on 2 September 1993, effected on 2 December 1993, and revised on 4 November 2017, at the 30th meeting of the Standing Committee of the 12th National People's Congress. The legislative purposes of The Anti-Unfair Competition Law[21] are "to promote the healthy development of the socialist market economy, encourage and protect fair competition, avoid unfair competition, and protect the legitimate rights and interests of operators and consumers".

China is one of the few countries that enact anti-unfair competition law independently. The antitrust law or anti-unfair competition law value legislative core purposes in a different way. The latter focus more on fair trade, for instance what types of activities the sellers are forbidden to conduct, while the former pays more attention on creating an open atmosphere for competition.[22]

3. Law on the protection of consumer rights & interests: 消费者权益保护法

The consumer protection law was adopted at the 4th meeting of the Eighth National People's Congress Standing Committee on 31 October 1993, and implemented on 1 January 1994. On 15 March 2014, the second revision was officially implemented.

---

21 Anti-Unfair Competition Law of the People's Republic of China (2017 Revision) [Effective].

22 F. JIANG, "On the Ideological Foundation and Value Consensus of Competition Law", *Modern Law Science*, March 2019, 41(2), p. 146.

The legislative purposes of the law[23] are: "to protect the legitimate rights and interests of consumers, maintain social and economic order, and promote the healthy development of the socialist market economy".

Along with the antitrust law and anti-unfair competition law, a relatively comprehensive legal system on market order and participants' regulating and protection has been built up.

E. Criminal Law and Criminal Procedure Law

1. Criminal Law: 刑法

In 1979 and 1997, China successively promulgated two Criminal Laws. The Criminal Law of 1979 marked the transformation of conviction from following the administrative documents to abide which the law had completed; the 1997 Criminal Law showed the improvement of the criminal law legislation in China. Since 1999, China has issued 10 amendments to the Criminal Law.

The main modifications of the Criminal Law[24] are as follows. The revision of the general provisions of the criminal law is mainly reflected in the two aspects of reducing the death penalty and aggravating the imprisonment. i/ The reduction of the death penalty is mainly to abolish some parts of the death penalty. ii/ The aggravation of the imprisonment mainly refers to the actual execution period of the death penalty with suspension of execution and life imprisonment. The punishment for penalties, especially for the death penalty with suspension of execution, extended the actual execution period by limiting the commutation of sentences and setting up life imprisonment.

The revision of the Specific Provisions of Criminal Law is manifested in the revision of the old crimes and the addition of new crimes.

For forty years, criminal legislation constantly summarised practical experience and renewed legislative cognition accordingly. From the

---

23 Law of the People's Republic of China on the Protection of Consumer Rights and Interests (2013 Amendment) [Effective].

24 Criminal Law of the People's Republic of China (2017 Amendment PKULAW Version) [Effective].

enacting of the Criminal Law code to implementing the principle of *no penalty without a law* in the 1997 revision, and with more emphasis on human rights, the development path of criminal law shows characters of steadiness and practicability.[25]

2. *Criminal Procedure Law:* 刑事诉讼法

On 1 July 1979, the 2nd meeting of the Fifth National People's Congress voted and passed the Criminal Procedure Law, implemented from 1 January 1980. The sixth meeting of the Standing Committee of the 13th National People's Congress passed the third amendment on October 26, 2018.

The main points of the new revision of the Criminal Procedure Law[26] are as follows:

i/ The connection between the supervision system and the Criminal Procedure Law: the connection between the investigative power of the procuratorial authorities and the investigative power of the supervisory authorities is clarified, and the investigative power of duty crimes is transferred. The power to investigate the duty of public officials who exercise public power is attributed to the supervisory committee, but at the same time, the procuratorial authorities' partial investigative power is retained.

ii/ The revised law constructs the procedures for trials *in absentia.*

iii/ The revision also increases the criminal expedited procedures.

This time, the criminal procedure law revision mainly put emphasis on launching institutional innovation, which contains the related content of the procuratorial system and international anti-corruption.[27]

---

[25] M. GAO and D. SUN, "Retrospect and Prospect of China's Criminal Law Legislation. Commemorating the 40th anniversary of the third plenary session of the 11th CPC central committee", *Heibei Law Science*, 2019, 37(5), p. 4–7.

[26] Criminal Procedure Law of the People's Republic of China (2018 Amendment) [Effective].

[27] J. BIAN, "Discussion on the New Revision of Criminal Procedure Law", *Research on Rule of Law*, 2019(1), p. 3.

III. Summary of China's rule of law practice experience in the past 40 years

A. From the 'legal system' to the 'rule of law'

The rationale of the 'rule of law（法治）' is that law is at the supreme position when governing the State, which is equally to 'rule by law'. The 'legal system（法制）' merely represents the State institutional system. Compared with the 'legal system', the 'rule of law' means not only running a complete legal system and institution, but also establishing the authority of the law, ensuring the serious implementation of the law, and effectively governing the State and society in accordance with the law. Further, the 'legal system' is static, the 'rule of law' is dynamic. Thus, the 'rule of law' embraces the 'legal system'.

B. From paying attention to economic development to focusing on human rights protection

In the 3rd Plenary Session of the Eleventh Central Committee of the Communist Party of China, the development policy centred on economic construction was established. In parallel, China's legal system construction has also shifted its attention to economic construction. After the 18th National Congress of the Communist Party of China, the development thinking of 'people-centred' was more clearly put forward, and the construction of the legal system was inclined more to human rights protection.

C. The 'rule of law reform': an important part of deepening 'political reform'

Since 1978, the general formulation in the field of the rule of law has been the construction of the legal system, serving the overall situation of economic development. Since the 18th National Congress of the Communist Party of China, President Xi Jinping has pointed out many times that "a comprehensive promotion of the rule of law is a systematic project and a broad and profound revolution in the field of State governance".

In the present, some problems still exist in the political system, such as corruption and government neglect. Therefore, one of the purposes for the rule of law is to solve these problems through legal theoretical and institutional renovation.[28]

D. Organic integration of 'economic development', 'human rights protection' and 'political reform'

China's continuously deepening political reform is a powerful guarantee for China's remarkable achievements in its economic development for forty years, and it also provides strong support for the development of human rights protection in China. Human rights protection has always been the fundamental goal of China's economic development and political reform.

*

In conclusion, the construction of the Rule of Law over forty years has not only reached historic achievements but it also laid a solid foundation for realising the modernisation of the rule of law and building a strong socialist rule of law. As President Xi said,

> "History is the best teacher. Experience and lessons have made our party profoundly realise that the rule of law is an indispensable means of ruling the State. Benign rule of law leads the State to thrive, while declined rule of law brings chaotic. When attaching importance to the rule of law, the State is prosperous. When the rule of law is ignored and slack, the State is in chaos and people are discontent."

Main sources of Basic Laws in the RP China

1. Constitution of the People's Republic of China (Amended in 2018)
2. Property Law of the People's Republic of China [Effective]
3. Company Law of the People's Republic of China (2018 Amendment)
4. Foreign Investment Law of the People's Republic of China [Not Yet Effective]
5. Trademark Law of the People's Republic of China (2013 Amendment) [Effective]
6. Patent Law of the People's Republic of China (2008 Amendment) [Effective]
7. Anti-monopoly Law of the People's Republic of China [Effective]

---

28 G. NI and W. ZHANG, "The Theoretical Logic of China's Politic Development since the Reform and Opening-up", *Theory and Reform*, 2018(4), p. 15.

8. Anti-Unfair Competition Law of the People's Republic of China (2017 Revision) [Effective]
9. Law of the People's Republic of China on the Protection of Consumer Rights and Interests (2013 Amendment) [Effective]
10. Criminal Law of the People's Republic of China (2017 Amendment PKULAW Version) [Effective]
11. Criminal Procedure Law of the People's Republic of China (2018 Amendment) [Effective]

Development of the Eurasian Economic Union (EAEU) legal order by the practice of the EAEU Court

Ilya Lifshits
Russian Foreign Trade Academy, Moscow, Russia

The treaty on the Eurasian Economic Union (EAEU) established i/ a custom union and ii/ a single economic space for five post-soviet States.[1] The Treaty has equipped the EAEU with several attributes of an integration grouping: decision-making bodies, definition of their competence, the Court, notion of a Union law and direct application of certain legal acts. Yet the Union's legal order is not complete and it has to be complemented by the legal concepts which are essential for every effective association of the States purporting to create a supra-national legal order.

This chapter reviews the main legal concepts which the Court of the EAEU has introduced in the last three years since its establishment in 2015: the Union's exclusive competence, supra-national powers, direct application of the Treaty, primacy of the Union's law over national law, legal expectations. It argues that, despite limitations on the Court's competence and its young age, the Court has decisively begun to develop the Union's legal order. These developments contribute to integration but may result in certain resistance of the EAEU Members' national courts.

On 1 January 2015, entered into force the Treaty on the Eurasian Economic Union (hereinafter the Treaty or TEAEU),[2] signed in Astana. Currently, this integration grouping counts five members but already provides for the establishment of the Union's law-making bodies equipped

1 Republic of Armenia, Republic of Belarus, Republic of Kazakhstan, Kyrgyz Republic and the Russian Federation.

2 See English text of the TEAEU at the https://docs.eaeunion.org/en-us, last accessed on 1 May 2019.

with the authority to adopt legally binding acts. Moreover, the Treaty lays down the direct application in Member-States of the acts of one of the Union's bodies – the Eurasian Economic Commission (EEC).[3] This provision implies that the EEC acts create rights and obligations not only for Member-States, but also for individuals under their jurisdiction. Therefore, the Treaty initially reserved the quality of direct action and direct application for the acts of the Union. This suggests that, since the beginning of its existence, the Treaty claimed to create its own legal system and its own legal order, which are different from both the legal system of Member-States and from the international legal order.

Accordingly, article 6 of the Treaty defined the concept of Union law and included in it three types of international treaties (TEAEU; international treaties within the Union; international treaties of the Union with a third party), as well as decisions and dispositions (or orders) of the three following EAEU bodies: the Supreme Eurasian Economic Council, the Eurasian Intergovernmental Council, and EEC.

The existence of the legal system of this international integration grouping implies the establishment of judicial authority assigned to settle disputes and interpret the relevant international treaty. The TEAEU established the Court of the Eurasian Economic Union, the purpose of which, in accordance with clause 2 of its Statute (Annex 2 to the Treaty), was to ensure a uniform application of the Treaty and other acts of the Union law by Member-States and their bodies. The analysis of the Statute (paragraphs 39 and 46) makes it possible to say that the Court is vested with two types of jurisdiction: settling disputes between Member-States, Member-States with the Eurasian Economic Commission, disputes between economic entities and the Commission; and the competence of interpreting the Union's law.

The Court's decision in accordance with paragraph 99 of the Statute is binding (only) on the parties to the dispute. In paragraph 102, the Statute of the Court decisively limits its rule-making function: "No decision of the Court may alter and/or override the rules of the Union law and the legislation of Member-States, nor may it create new ones"; advisory opinions of the Court within the framework of the implementation of competence to clarify the Union law by the Statute are recommendatory (non-binding) in nature (paragraph 98). In addition, the Court's clarification of the Treaty does not deprive Member-States of joint interpretation

---

3 Article 13 of the Appendix 1 to the TEAEU.

of international treaties (paragraph 47). All these provisions clearly indicate that the parties to the Treaty sought to limit the activism of the Court, to give it the role of the body assigned to apply – but not make – the EU law. Different scholars also name such limitations of the Court's competence as the lack of jurisdiction to issue preliminary rulings at the request of national courts (such as the jurisdiction of the CJEU which is laid down in the article 267 of the Treaty on the Functioning of the EU); also the EEC does not have competence to sue the Member-States for the incompliance with the Union Law; damage and other material claims our also outside the scope of the Court's jurisdiction.[4]

Despite these limitations (deemed or real), in three years of its existence, the Court adopted a number of decisions and advisory opinions[5] substantially developing the legal order of the EAEU, not only explaining the rules of the Treaty, but also, in a certain sense, giving it a new content that was not originally contained in the international act, which established the Union. Prof. V.M. Shoumilov believes that supranational law "significantly matters since it changes the very substance of international law"[6]. To a large extent, the legal concepts formed by the Court resemble the practice of the EU Court of Justice[7] and, without doubt, grant to the

---

4 Z. KEMBAYEV, "The Court of the Eurasian Economic Union: An Adequate Body for Facilitating Eurasian Integration?", *Review of Central and East European Law*, 2016, 41(3–4), p. 342–367; M. KARLIUK, "The Eurasian Economic Union: An EU-Like Legal Order in the Post-Soviet Space?", September 23, 2015, *Higher School of Economics Research Paper* WP BRP 53/LAW/2015, available at SSRN: https://ssrn.com/abstract=2664519 or http://dx.doi.org/10.2139/ssrn.2664519; A. ROSANÒ, "Wrong Way to Direct Effect?: Case Note on the Advisory Opinion of the Court of the Eurasian Economic Union Delivered on 4 April 2017 at the Request of the Republic of Belarus", *Legal Issues of Economic Integration*, 2018, 45(2), p. 211–220; A. DI GREGORIO, "The Eurasian Economic Union: Origin and Development of a New Integration Format Compared That of the EU", in *The Eurasian Economic Union and the European Union Moving toward a greater Understanding*, The Hague, Eleven International Publishing, 2017, p. 11–14.

5 In total, as of 25 March 2019, the Court issued 29 court decisions, of which 16 were within the competence to settle disputes, and 13 – within the competence to clarify the provisions of the Treaty. See the official website of the Court: http://courteurasian.org/en/page-24521, last accessed on 30 March 2019.

6 V.M. SHOUMILOV, "Global normative system and its parts" (in Russian) "Global'naja normativnaja sistema i ee sostavljajushhie", *Gosudarstvo i pravo*, 2017(4), p. 75.

7 K. ENTIN and B. PIRKER, "The Early Case Law of the Eurasian Economic Union Court: On the Road to Luxembourg?", *Maastricht Journal of European and Comparative Law*, 2018, 25(3), p. 266–287.

Eurasian Economic Union the necessary qualities inherent in a developed integration grouping.

In particular, the Court formulated the concept of 'exclusive competence' of the Union, direct effect and the priority of the Union law, as well as legitimate expectations of the actions of the bodies of the Union, protection of the human rights, the rights and fundamental freedoms. Obviously, so far, the Court only cautiously 'defines' these concepts, merely announcing them, lacking deep elaboration of the corresponding legal positions. However, these approaches of the Court are worthy of analysis and comment, which will be done below.

I. The exclusive competence of the Union

The basic characteristic of any international grouping (international organisation or integration association) is the scope of its competence. The conferral of sovereign powers to the grouping implies an issue of competence-sharing between the grouping and its Member-States. The 2007 Lisbon Treaty introduced into the EU founding Treaties provisions regarding the categories of EU competences: i/ exclusive, ii/ shared, iii/ supportive (Articles 2-6 of the Treaty on the Functioning of the EU). Article 3 of the TEAEU states that the Union carries out activities within the competence (jurisdiction) granted to it by its Member-States, but the Treaty does not contain definitions of different types or categories of competences of the Union and its Member-States. The Treaty defines only a common (or single), agreed and coordinated policy pursued by Member-States. In accordance with article 2 of the TEAEU, a common policy assumes the use of 'unified legal regulation', agreed policy – the 'harmonisation of legal regulation', and coordinated policy – the 'implementation of cooperation of Member-States based on common approaches'. Therefore, the main criterion for distinguishing different policies is the degree of convergence of legal regulation. A few years before the signing of the Treaty, S. Aidarbayev pointed out that "harmonisation and unification of law are, first of all, a legal instrument of the integrated interaction of States, because it is through the processes of harmonisation and unification that integration solutions enter the legal system of States, into the system of its legislation".[8] It should be noted that this approach is fully reflected by the Treaty.

---

8 S. Z. AIDARBAYEV, "Integration processes in the post-Soviet countries in the globalising world: international legal aspects" (in Russian), "Integracionnye processy v

According to the degree of centralisation of powers at the Union level, a 'common' policy ranks first, and a 'coordinated' policy ranks last, but the Treaty does not specify what particular powers the Union has for each type of policies. There is also no list from which it would be possible to conclude to which type of policy a certain sphere of cooperation belongs. Parts two and three of the TEAEU describe different areas of cooperation of Member-States and the corresponding powers of the EU bodies. Article 25 indicates that, within the framework of the customs union of the Member-States, the Common Customs Tariff of the EAEU shall be applied as well as unified measures regulating the foreign trade with third countries and a common customs regulation. Article 45 establishes the powers of the Commission in the customs-tariff regulation (to establish the rates of import customs duties, tariff preferences and tariff quotas, etc.); the sections on technical regulation (article 51), sanitary and veterinary sanitary measures (articles 57, 58) also mention uniform requirements, although in the field of sanitary measures a 'coordinated' (not 'common') policy is carried out; in subparagraph 3 of paragraph 1 of article 31 of the TEAEU, the adoption of uniform rules in the field of circulation of medical devices is enshrined as a principle, although sub-paragraphs 1 of the same paragraph mentions only the harmonisation of the legislation of Member-States, not the unification, which is a sign of the common policy.

The term 'common' is also used in the areas of cooperation relating, for example, to macroeconomic policy: it mentions 'uniform principles for the functioning of the economies of Member-States and ensuring their effective interaction' (paragraph 2 (3), article 62), although in general this area of cooperation refers to coordinated policy. The above examples make it possible to conclude that the Treaty not only did not highlight the exclusive and joint competence of the Union and Member-States, but, moreover, it did not set the goal to consistently and clearly divide the areas of cooperation between the three categories of policy (common, agreed and coordinated) stipulated in the first part of the Treaty. Nevertheless, in one of its decisions, the Court of the EAEU found it possible and necessary to emphasise an exclusive competence of the bodies of the Union. Thus, in the Advisory opinion of 20 December 2018 on the clarification of the Regulation on social guarantees, privileges

postsovetskom prostranstve v uslovijah globalizacii mira: mezhdunarodno-pravovye aspekty", Monograph, Almaty, Kazak Univ., 2010, p. 293.

and immunities in the Eurasian Economic Union, the Court concluded that "Member-States of the Union transferred exclusive powers to the Commission and the Court in the areas of activities defined by the Treaty and international treaties within the Union".[9] This conclusion was made by the Court on the basis of 'systematic interpretation' of the general articles of the Treaty on the competence of the Union and its bodies, as well as the chapter of the Statute of the Court dedicated to its competence. Interestingly, the Treaty does not use the term 'exclusive competence' or 'exclusive powers'.[10] It neither states that Member-States have given up sovereign powers transferred to the bodies of the Union. In the absence of such indications, which constitute the essence of exclusive competence, the Court gave a new meaning to the provisions of the Treaty, effectively 'lifting' – from the sphere of activity of national authorities – all the powers transferred to the bodies of the Union. The judge of the EAEU Court K.L. Chaika, agreeing in the separate opinion with the findings of the Court on the transfer of exclusive powers of the Commission to Member-States, notes that "the Court should have concluded that the international officials of the Union bodies should perform the same functions that civil servants of Member-States of the Union carried out before their transfer to the supranational level".[11]

The Court's bold conclusion on the exclusive competences of the EAEU in certain areas (along with the introduction of the concept of 'supranational competence'[12]) undoubtedly contributes to the development of the EAEU as an integration grouping, although it may cause

---

[9] Advisory opinion of the Court of the Eurasian Economic Union of 20 December 2018, p. 7: http://courteurasian.org/page-25501, last accessed on 30 March 2019.

[10] Petrov and Kalinichenko argue that drafters of the TEAEU "intentionally avoided any references to the supranationality and supremacy of 'Union Law' and defined the EAEU as an 'international organisation of regional economic integration'": R. PETROV and P. KALINICHENKO, "On Similarities and Differences of the European Union and Eurasian Economic Union Legal Orders: Is There the 'Eurasian Economic Union Acquis'?", *Legal Issues of Economic Integration*, 2016, 43, p. 299.

[11] Separate opinion of judge K.L. Chaika regarding the application of the Eurasian Economic Commission on the clarification of provisions of paragraphs 53 and 54 of the Regulation on social guarantees, privileges and immunities in the Eurasian Economic Union (Annex n° 32 in the Treaty on the Eurasian Economic Union of 29 May 2014, p. 8). Available on the website http://courteurasian.org/page-25501, last accessed on 30 March 2019.

[12] *Ibidem*, p. 10, see also the Advisory Opinion of 10 July 2018, in which the Court indicated that "Member-States transferred the competence to establish uniform legal

a certain rejection by State bodies of some Member-States. In this case we should recall the Ruling of the Constitutional Court of the Russian Federation,[13] which emphasised its monopoly right to establish the scope and content of the constitutional rights and freedoms of the Russian citizens and its associations including the sphere of custom regulation.

II. Direct application

The provision of the Treaty (Article 13 of Annex 1) on the direct application of the Commission's decisions did not determine the effect and application of the Treaty provisions in the legal systems of the Member-States. Can the provisions of the Treaty be considered as the ones that are directly addressed to individuals? Do these rules give legal rights to citizens and organisations? Do they impose any obligations on them? In the absence of direct indications of the Treaty, this issue was to be decided by the Court of the Union.

It should be noted that the European Court of Justice indicated the direct effect of the provisions of the Treaty creating the European Economic Community five years after the establishment of the EEC in the well-known case *Van Gend & Loos*. The Court of Justice held that Community law not only "imposes obligations on individuals but is also intended to confer upon them rights which become part of their legal heritage" and can be invoked before national and Community courts.[14]

The Court of the Eurasian Economic Union took a similar position in the case of clarifying the provisions of the Treaty on the free movement of workers (cf. case on professional sportsmen). In the Advisory Opinion of 7 December 2018, the Court indicated that the legal norms of paragraphs 1 and 2 of article 97 on employment of workers are addressed not only to the States, but also to employers and employees.[15] The logical

norms for all Member States to the supranational level of regulation" (paragraph 2 of clause 2 of the Conclusions of the Grand Chamber of the Court).

13 Ruling of the Constitutional Court of the Russian Federation of 3 March 2015, n° 417-O. Available at http://doc.ksrf.ru/decision/KSRFDecision190708.pdf, last accessed on 30 March 2019.

14 Judgment of the Court of 5 February 1963, Case 26/62 *Van Gend & Loos*, ECR [1963] 12.

15 Advisory opinion of the Court of the Eurasian Economic Union of December 7, 2018 according to the statement of the Eurasian Economic Commission on clarification of the provisions of the Treaty on the Eurasian Economic Union of 29 May 2014, p. 5.

consequence of this conclusion was the generalisation that the relevant norms have the features of direct effect and direct application.[16] The Court of the Union has also given the quality of direct application and direct effect to the rules on the protection of competition on cross-border markets.[17]

III. Primacy

The interaction of different legal orders among themselves inevitably raises the issue of the legal force of legal norms relating to such legal orders. If such norms have a direct effect, then the resolution of the collision becomes particularly relevant. In associations of States, it is important to define the legal force of the norms of national legislation and the norms relating to the legislation of an integration association.

In the EU the principle of primacy was first proclaimed in 1964 in the case of *Costa/ENEL*[18] and then enshrined in the practice of the EU Court. This principle is reflected in the Declaration No. 17 concerning primacy attached to the Final Act of the intergovernmental conference that adopted the Treaty of Lisbon, which stated: "The conference recalls that, in accordance with well-settled case law of the Court of Justice of the EU and the law adopted by the Union on the basis of the Treaties have the primacy over the law of Member-States, under the conditions laid down by the said case law".

The priority of the Union's law over national legislations is proclaimed by the Court of the EAEU in the Advisory Opinion of 12 September 2017 in the case of clarification of the provisions of the Treaty on the filling of positions in the departments of the Commission on a competitive basis. In this act, the Court stated the following: "the national rules apply to labour relations involving the authorities of the Union within the limits established by the Union law. In this regard, the Grand Chamber of the Court rules on the priority of the norms of the Treaty".[19] In conclusion in the 'Case on the professional sportsmen', the Court ruled that "in the event of a contradiction between the Union law and the acts of

---

16 *Ibidem*, p. 6–13.

17 Advisory opinion of 4 April 2017. Paragraphs 1–2 of Clause 2.

18 Judgment of the Court of 15 July 1964. *Flaminio Costa v ENEL*. Case 6/64 ECR [1964] 1141.

19 See the advisory opinion of 10 July 2018, p. 7 of Section IV Conclusions.

national legislations... one should be guided by the provisions of the Union law".[20] These legal provisions of the Court gave grounds to Judge K.L. Chaika, in the dissenting opinion, to conclude about the primacy of the Union's law over the national law based on the 'settled practice of the Court'.[21] The 'primacy' results in the application of the Union's law in the event that such a rule is contrary to the national legislation.

IV. Other legal positions

Among other noteworthy legal positions of the Court, one should mention the principle of 'legitimate expectations', which is widely used in the practice of investment arbitrations in protecting the legitimate expectations of investors, as well as in the practice of the DSB of WTO.[22] In the Advisory Opinion on the clarification of the Social Security Regulations the Court indicated that "taking into account the clarity and certainty of paragraph 53 of Appendix No. 32 [to the Treaty] the officials and staff of the Commission and the Court relied on their legitimate expectations of getting the right to retirement benefits under the conditions determined in this legal rule, which sets the civil service work experience of employees at not less than 15 years".[23]

Judge K.L. Chaika, in the dissenting opinion, defines the principle of 'legitimate expectations' as a generally accepted principle of international law to be applied by the Court on the basis of Article 50 of the Statute.[24] The qualification of the principle of 'legitimate expectations' as a universally-recognised principle of international law causes doubt. It should

---

20 The last paragraph of Clause 7 of Section III Conclusions.

21 Special opinion of Judge K.L. Chaika regarding the application of the Eurasian Economic Commission on the clarification of provisions of paragraphs 53 and 54 of the Regulation on social guarantees, privileges and immunities in the Eurasian Economic Union (Annex n° 32 in the Treaty on the Eurasian Economic Union of 29 May 2014, p. 5). Available on the website http://courteurasian.org/page-25501, last accessed on 30 March 2019.

22 C. CARMODY, "Recalibrating the Embedded Liberalism Compromise: 'Legitimate Expectations' and International Economic Law", in G. MOON and L.TOOHEY (Eds.), *The Future of International Economic Integration*, Cambridge, Cambridge University Press, 2018, p. 58–78.

23 Advisory opinion of the Court of the Eurasian Economic Union of 20 December 2018, p. 8.

24 Special opinion of Judge K. L. Chaika regarding the application of the Eurasian Economic Commission on the clarification of provisions of paragraphs 53 and 54

also be noted that the Court of the Union applied this principle not to entrepreneurs, but to employees of the Union's body in relation to their labour relations.

In the absence of the 'Bill of Rights' of the Eurasian Economic Union, it is interesting how the Court deals with the issues of human rights and freedoms. For example, in the 'Case on retirement benefits', the Court indicated that "due to the commitment enshrined in the Treaty's preamble in relation to unconditional respect for the rights of man and national the level of such rights and freedoms guaranteed by the Union cannot be lower than in Member-States".[25]

*

In conclusion, this brief overview of the legal positions of the Court of the Union over the past three years suggests that the legal order of the EAEU has received a significant number of legal concepts necessary for the successful development of an integration grouping. The Court of the EU has been implementing these concepts for several decades and on the basis of the Treaty Establishing the European Economic Community (then the Treaty Establishing the European Community), which provided for a significantly higher level of integration than the EAEU. Such record periods coupled with the boldness of the Court contribute to integration, but can cause rejection of national law enforcement agencies, including the highest ones, as well as constitutional courts.

of the Regulation on social guarantees, privileges and immunities in the Eurasian Economic Union (Annex n° 32 in the Treaty on the Eurasian Economic Union of 29 May 2014, p. 10). Available on the website http://courteurasian.org/page-25501, last accessed on 30 March 2019.

25 *Ibidem.*

For a better functioning and integration of the European Union[1]

Michel BRUNO
Le Havre Normandie Université, LexFEIM, France

"Social art is the art of increasing the happiness of nations"

Abbé Sieyès, 1789.

Europe is perceived today by the majority of European citizens in Western Europe as going against their happiness. The idyll between 'Europe' and most of its populations is no more. The 'populist' parties benefit from this state of affairs. The European elections almost sounded the death knell for the construction of Europe by making possible the election of numerous Eurosceptics in the European parliament. In this case, the European Council and the Council of the EU might be in opposition to the European parliament. The European Commission would then fall into the hands of the 'populists' since European Commission is invested by the European parliament. In addition, most European legal texts – regulations and directives – are adopted by the European parliament and the Council of the EU, jointly proposed by the European Commission. The fact of a disagreement would lead to a break-up in the European marriage. Would it be "an evil for a good" (Leibniz)? There is a great risk that no benefit will be derived for the good of the peoples who make up the UE. An "evil often leads only to another evil", to paraphrase Voltaire criticising Leibniz.

1 Translated from the French by P. CHABAL.

The origins of this European falling-out or disenchantment come from both ambient ultra-liberalism combined with the last three enlargements of the EU. Indeed, since the 2004 enlargement of the EU, integrating most of the former Warsaw Pact countries, the functioning of the UE was negatively affected. In particular, the single market has suffered from an imbalance due to commercial competition of the new Member-States: i/ the States of Western Europe did not anticipate this competition to the detriment of their enterprises and their labour market, to that of their consumption and of their tax revenues. ii/ Since this enlargement, they have not been able to impose tax or social harmonisation on these new States. The latter want to preserve their competitive advantages. The solution was therefore for each State and particularly for France to review its social model downwards. Thus, French labour law has been unravelled, French public services go off the hook and social benefits are gradually revised downward. Other Member-States have suffered from the same difficulties. The relocation of many companies to eastern Europe and the arrival of eastern workers posted to Western Europe have destabilised national economies through the closure of businesses and the loss of jobs for national workers. Tax revenues have soared. Despite the recast of the 'posted workers' Directive of 1996 and the lowering of social security contributions by French companies and tax adjustments, the haemorrhage continues. It is further aggravated by the many free-trade agreements signed by the UE with third countries, which open up the Single market and therefore the European market to highly competitive products.

Today's Europe seems first and foremost a failure: The end of the protection of social rights and social *acquis* in some Member-States and of a form of democracy but without a European 'alternative democracy' (I). Europe must change this if it wants to survive. The EU can continue to progress only if it takes into consideration the happiness of the nations that compose it and there are solutions (II).

I. An assessment of democratic failure

The EU as a world defender of democracy and human rights has paradoxically undermined the democratic functioning of most Western European Member-States (A). The EU has mobilised more and more the populations of these countries against the European project because European democracy is limited (B).

A. National democracies in danger

De facto and *de jure*, the majority of western European democracies can no longer really exist or rather they 'stand on their head' by practising the maltreatment of their respective populations. They invoke the economic crisis and the competitiveness problems of companies within the EU, whose citizens are not responsible, for unwinding social *acquis*. They also invoke the public debt and have imposed upon themselves to respect the rule of the 3% public deficit of the European pact of stability and growth[2] to then adopt the Golden rule, that is zero public deficit.[3] This only increases the mistreatment of their populations. French democracy is an example of this. Formally, the democratic process is respected but materially the content of the legal texts in all areas goes against the interests of French citizens. The rights of French workers were rolled flat, as in Spain and Italy. Citizens are gradually losing rights and facing cuts in wages, but companies continue to relocate or close down. As a result, workers are losing more and more jobs, particularly in industry. But also everywhere in Western Europe, there were cuts in many positions of civil servants in order to reduce public expenses but then also the job offers. Thus, almost all European citizens in Western Europe have gradually lost faith in their own parliamentary democracy as in the European construction.

In the beginning of the Single market in 1993, the EEC/EU was roughly homogeneous fiscally and socially with certainly some 'poor' countries but that could be 'accompanied' towards social improvements. European populations were happy to be European before the ill-conceived 2004 enlargement. Since 2004, France and the most socially developed Member-States of the 'Europe of Fifteen' have suffered double jeopardy. These States i/ suffer from unfair competition on the social and fiscal fronts and ii/ finance the European budget, of which they are net contributors to the EU budget. These countries therefore finance their own low democratic and social deeds by financing common policies. These policies benefit the unfair competition of the countries of central and Eastern Europe, which have lower production costs than their Western European counterparts. As a result, the tax revenues of Eastern

---

2 Treaty of Amsterdam, 1997. But this rule existed already in the Maastricht Treaty as one of the criteria for the passage to a single currency. This rule was made permanent at the initiative of Germany, which whished a strong single currency.

3 Treaty on stability, coordination and governance, 2012.

European States are progressing more and more, while those of several Western European States are decreasing. In other words, social regression and bottom-up harmonisation have become established in all these countries that suffer from the most recent enlargements. Yet, democracy is one of Europe's leading values. France, the 'country of human rights,' is condemned to social regression… In a book on the common market, J.-Y. Deniau had warned that, in order to succeed with the common market, tax and social issues had to be prioritised, otherwise the common market would be a failure.[4] The Western European Member-States placed under this degree of competition are losing more and more tax revenue and must reduce their spending. Many public services disappeared, but even in 'regalian' public services, not only are jobs eliminated, but more and more activities are being outsourced. The European citizens of the most affected Member-States, including France, have lost a lot of social and tax benefits.

Poland, the largest EU Member-State in Central and Eastern Europe, has not experienced economic crisis thanks to its EU membership. EU policies finance about 10% of its budget. Poland receives the most aid under the common 'social and territorial economic cohesion policy'. It is also the country that benefits the most from the Single market with low production costs. Other European States of the former communist bloc also benefit. As a result, democracy operates well, in both formal and material terms, in most of the Eastern European Member-States, which benefit from the European financial windfall as from the European internal market. Since their accession to the EU, the GDP of most Eastern European countries in the EU has grown to the detriment of most Western European Member-States, except for Germany and Luxembourg.

As for migrations, the Member-States disagree and find no common solution among the 28. A migration quota system and the relocation of asylum-applicants have led to an objective failure. Some Member-States such as Hungary refuse any migrant on its territory. The reform of the 'Regulation on the Right of Asylum' is still in the hot seat. As for human rights and the evolution of morals, a similar gap exists between most of the States of Western Europe and certain Eastern European States. The differences are displayed: the European Charter of Fundamental Rights seems to have a 'variable geometry'. Moreover, the ecological urgency is taken into account more by the countries of Western Europe. Also,

---

4 J.-F. DENIAU, *Le marché commun*, Paris, Presses universitaires de France, 1958.

differences between members of the Euro-zone and non-Member-States add to the inequalities between the economies of those States and between their citizens. Finally, the abolition of border controls for individuals does not affect all Member-States.

B. A democracy and a European citizenship with disabilities

This democracy is incomplete. Indeed, the Council of the EU is an inter-governmental institution and still has a certain supremacy over other institutions, in particular the European parliament and the European Commission. Moreover, MEPs do not have the same prerogatives as national MPs because they do not have the right of initiative of legislative texts. In addition, control over appointments within the European Commission is limited. Recently 71% of MEPs voted against the choice made by the President of the European Commission Juncker. This legal battle goes back to 2018 and the highly-contested appointment of the new Secretary General of the European Commission by Juncker without taking into account the position of the European parliament that did not approve of that appointment. The European parliament therefore still appears to be in deficit with regard to the powers of a parliament worthy of the name.

European citizenship suffers from the partial application of the principle of equality of citizens before the law at European level. Indeed, Member-States have an obligation to apply existing regulations and harmonisation directives, creators of rights for European citizens. National courts and the Court of Justice of the EU enforce this application when they are seized. However, for all non-harmonised sectors, the practice is inequality between the citizens of the different-Member-States. This is not worthy of a true democratic system. In a 'community of law' or in an *État de droit*, this is an attack on one of the great democratic principles: the equality of citizens. It is true that the principle of non-discrimination on grounds of nationality and its corollary, the principle of equal treatment as with nationals, are present in the Treaty of Rome. But they only concern European citizens who use 'free movement of persons' in order to live in another Member-State. On this point, European citizens who settle in Member-States other than their own use the -free movement of persons – to choose a more lenient State for workers and in taxation, as well as in the in the field of freedom of establishment for companies.

The question of choosing the most attractive member-country for companies directly affects citizens who will either be able to access new jobs or lose their jobs depending on the policy followed by companies seeking the best taxation and/or costs of production. A further difference exists between European citizens regarding the crossing of borders as the whole territory of the EU is not affected by the abolition of border-controls of the Member-States.

European democracy and European citizenship are incomplete and it is therefore necessary to reform the EU.

II. Possible solutions and remedies

Most of the possible remedies can only be envisaged in a setting outside the EU, given the present institutional stalemate on the harmonisation of taxation and social rights, migration policy and respect for the fundamental rights of the human person. In addition, some Member-States are largely more integrated than others. A new treaty is needed to advance the integration of the Union (A). Within this new treaty, it will be necessary to complete European democracy and European citizenship (B).

A. A new treaty

With the announced departure of the United Kingdom from the EU as part of a 'hard' Brexit or even a 'soft' Brexit, the UK will no longer be included in the institutions of the UE and will no longer be involved in decision-making or impediment to decisions. Indeed, with a 'soft' Brexit, the UK will remain in the single market like Norway, Iceland or Lichtenstein without being a full member of the EU but a member of the European Economic Area.[5] With a 'hard' Brexit, a free-trade agreement will be at least negotiated. It is necessary to emphasise that the UK has been the main opponent to the development of a real European social policy and to a move towards greater political integration of the EU. It will therefore be easier for Member-States to move towards more integration without the UK.

---

5 Treaty of Porto, 1992, between the European Economic Community and the European Free-Trade Association, instituting the Single European Space.

It should be recalled that the 1986 'Single European Act', adopted by the 12 Member-States of the EEC, was to address the social question. During its negotiations, Germany and France proposed also an evolution towards a federal State. But the British vetoed both these developments which they did not want, barely agreeing that the Treaty mention an evolution towards an economic and monetary union of the EEC. With regard to the creation of a space without internal borders (article 12 of the Single Act), the British Government considered that the abolition of border controls thus induced only concerned goods, services and capital and could not apply to persons. This interpretation was adopted because it prevailed at the time in the EEC. Thus, the Schengen group initially composed of five Member-States[6] had secretly opened, in June 1985, negotiations that culminated in 1990 with the signature by the five States to the Schengen Convention. This agreement was gradually extended to most Member-States, then integrated in 1997 into the Treaty of Rome (Treaty of Amsterdam). Similarly, with the Maastricht Treaty establishing the EU, the social question and the federal question again put on the table by the Franco-German couple during the negotiations were victims of the British veto. The UK has, admittedly, accepted the possible evolution towards a single currency for States meeting economic criteria, provided that they wish it politically. Moreover, the UK made reservations on this point by specifying, in the appendix of the Treaty, that London would only participate in the single currency *after* a favourable vote of the British parliament or a referendum on this question. The United Kingdom has also accepted the concept of European citizenship, but knowing that this citizenship would not harm their sovereignty.

The 1997 Amsterdam Treaty and the 2001 Treaty of Nice also showed the limits of the European construction[7]. With regard to the Amsterdam Treaty, the introduction of the Schengen Convention into the legal corpus of the Treaty of Rome was seen as a success by many observers. However, while the UK accepted this 'community codification' of an agreement among some Member-States only, this codification was incomplete. One key point, dealing with the removal of border controls for people within the UE, is not applicable to the UK or Ireland. The

---

6 Germany, Belgium, the Netherlands, Luxemburg and France.

7 The Treaty of Nice, mainly, only just solved the institutional question relative to the entry of new Members anticipated for 2004, which the Treaty of Amsterdam had not succeeding in doing.

arguments put forward are the insularity of the two territories and their belonging to the 'Common area'.

From now on, two scenarios can be envisaged in case of the departure of UK from the EU. The first would encompass all Member-States but is seems illusionary due to the presence of populist governments in power in several Member-States or the presence of governmental coalitions in which populist parties participate, particularly in Hungary, Poland, Italy and Austria.

The second scenario was already used for the signing by five members of the 1990 Schengen Convention. President Chirac recommended it in June 2000 speaking to the German *Bundestag* indicating that a 'pioneer group' of Member-States could pave the way towards more integration with, at their helm, the Franco-German couple. Chirac incidentally used the idea of the German green minister for foreign affairs J. Fischer. The British government immediately rejected this initiative. This Franco-German initiative stirred no great enthusiasm at the time but is at the origin of the 2004 Treaty establishing a European Constitution, for which the political decision was taken by the 2000 European Council of Nice. Eventually, all Member-States signed this text, thus an *a minima* compromise with many imperfections and failures. Particularly, the social question is not addressed, nor the fiscal one. Moreover, it was legally-speaking a Constitution. Some opponents to this Treaty called for a no-vote on this ground of its no-legality, especially L. Fabius, whom later developments proved right. The French and the Dutch electors voted against this agreement and it had to be abandoned in its initial formulation. However, the 2007 Lisbon Treaty did little else but resume the main innovations of the 'European Constitution', with minor modifications. Yet, again, it comes well short of addressing the social and fiscal questions.

Today, without the UK, this second scenario is possible. The States that could move forward are most integrated Member-States that participate in both the Schengen area and in the single currency. However, among them, it will be necessary to exclude the populist governments and perhaps also of the Eastern European Members-States from the euro-zone, as these are little inclined to make social and fiscal concessions. The Franco-German couple could take on such an initiative especially in the event that the European elections turn into a nightmare for pro-European governments. The proposals by the French President and the President of the European Commission – to give Member-States of the euro-zone a clean budget – could therefore be taken up again. Reforms are needed to build a true European democracy and to rescue national democracies undermined by the 'Europe of competitiveness' and the 'Europe of political disunity'.

B. Physical and institutional reforms

The solution lies in an agreement between some States, just as for the Schengen agreements. However, if the content of the Schengen Agreements was feasible outside the European Community and as a complement, today the material and institutional reforms to be implemented are not of the same nature. They are necessary in the interest of the European citizens so that there is, on the one hand, a true European democracy and, on the other hand, a fiscal and social harmonisation and a harmonisation of the application of the fundamental rights of the human person and the respect for the rights of migrants. On these issues, the harmonisation is blocked and it will be even more so with populist parties winning European elections or at least strengthened in these elections. It is therefore almost irrelevant to reach an agreement outside the UE and, in addition, this would not change anything inside the UE. The abolition of border-controls provided by the Schengen Convention (and the correlative reinforcement of the Schengen Group's external border-controls) was a novelty that could be achieved in addition to the existing EU. But the questions now posed, and which cannot be answered, can only be resolved without the disruptive States of the UE. These States only wish to benefit from European aids and from a single market that favours the most 'competitive' members. They do not wish to leave it; only to enjoy the benefits they derive from the EU while criticising it and refusing harmonisation. The latter are nevertheless necessary for the proper functioning of the Single market. Some of them even refuse to respect fundamental rights and to prohibit certain forms of discrimination on their territory. It will thus be necessary for the main founders of the EU – Germany and France – to at least threaten to leave the existing EU and to create a new Union, healthier socially, fiscally and politically. This may help change the positions of uncooperative States.

It would then be necessary to use article 50 of the Treaty of the EU and leave the EU in order to create a new EU. Germany, France and other Member-States would thus be able to reach their purposes. They will leave the UE to re-found it according to similar provisions by making use of the current treaties with other Member-States sharing the same democratic and humanistic values. These States would complement the texts with common fiscal and social policies and will also respect the humanist values of 'the Europe of the founding fathers'. Among the 'pioneering' States that will follow Germany and France, one thinks of Belgium, Luxembourg, perhaps the Netherlands, that is the first Schengen group. Moreover, the European institutions are located on their territories. But why not the whole euro-zone, Italy included?

At the institutional level, it would be important to set up European elections with lists of candidates drawn at the European level with a single European constituency as advocated by some politicians. Indeed, this would make it possible to avoid, with national lists, that only national issues are at the heart of the electoral campaign. Or, to create a European constituency in addition to national constituencies as E. Macron and the President of the European Commission suggested in 2017. Each voter will have two ballots, one that (s)he would use at national level and one at European level. This proposal was rejected by the European Council and by the European parliament. It will also be necessary to perfect European democracy by transforming the Council of the EU into a real chamber representing European States or regions.

It would therefore be necessary to create a European Senate. This representation could be on an unequal basis. A breakdown of senators by Member-States based on the old qualified-majority voting-system could be applied. However, there should be a weighting close to that which existed before the Treaty of Nice. This treaty had indeed caused a loss of political weight to the large Member-States that financed the EU for the benefit of small Member-States. Each Member-State would have a number of senators equivalent or close to the number of votes cast with the weighted vote that was practised ever since the Single European Act. The voting system adopted with the Lisbon Treaty would therefore be abandoned: it would be impossible to implement[8] it in this new framework. European Senators would be elected by direct universal suffrage in each Member-State or in each European region. If the second option is chosen, then the Council of the European Regions could be abolished; or the powers of the Council of the EU given to the current European Committee of the Regions.

---

8 The vote is acquired only if a majority of States representing 65 % of the EU population adopts the text.

Concerning the MEPs, they would be granted the right of initiative of legal European texts in parallel to the European Commission. They would also obtain the opportunity to give their approval for the choice of European high officials. This power could also be entrusted to the European Senate as is the case in the USA. The European Council could be maintained initially but a gradual shift of its powers i/ to the benefit of the President of the EU will have to be planned or ii/ to the President of the European Commission. Here, it would be a question of choosing between a President without real powers, as in a parliamentary regime, or a presidentialist regime *à la française*. The President of the UE would have to be elected by all European citizens at the same time as the election of MEPs. The European Citizens' Initiative must be transformed into a fully-fledged referendum of popular initiative.

These are the transformations that will enable European democracy to be more complete and European citizenship to be more so. Other innovations may also be added.

*

In conclusion, the movement of 'yellow vests' in France displayed since the Autumn of 2018 the disarray of the most vulnerable populations as well as that of a large part of the middle-classes. This movement proves that the French people no longer want to undergo further tax-increases or new attacks on their social *acquis*. The people are unhappy. French support for this movement climaxed at 85% of the population. In other Western European Member-States, there is also great disappointment with governments that unravel all the social benefits and unstoppingly reduce reducing the purchasing power of their populations. The 'democracies' of the EU must put again democracy – in the etymological sense of the word – at the heart of their national concerns, but also at the heart of the European project, on pain of sanctioning their own policies.

A proposal for the constitutional reform of North Korea

Tai-Uk Chung
Law School, Inha University, South Korea

The peace process on the Korean peninsula is in progress. In 2018, North Korea declared the end of the parallel policy of nuclear arming and economic development, at the plenary meeting of the Worker's Party Central Committee, and decided to push for economic development. North Korea's leader, Kim Jong-un proclaimed the complete denuclearisation of the Korean Peninsula, and in return demanded a peace treaty and the lifting economic sanctions. Two summits of South and North Korea agreed to eliminate the war risks on the Korean peninsula and cease all hostilities against the other side. 'The Peace Federation of South and North' can be achieved in a foreseeable future.

However, the end of the war and the conclusion of a peace treaty are not sufficient conditions for a lasting and sustainable peace. Emmanuel Kant wrote that every State should have a republican constitution for the perpetual peace in the world, and John Rawls also wrote that each State should be a decent regime respecting basic human rights for the international peace. Without repeating the theory of 'democratic peace' which purports that international peace can only be sustained among liberal democracies, one can extend the peace project to non-liberal democratic regimes. Rawls also believed that peace and coexistence are possible between liberal and non-liberal societies. Rawls even suggested that a benevolent absolutism become a regular member of the international peace community.

In the same vein, one thinks of constitutionalism as a general condition of international peace. Constitutionalism is generally understood as a regime of the control of power, the division of power, and the guarantee of basic rights of the people. Liberal democracy is regarded as a representative of constitutionalism, even if it is a concept that has been shaped historically, as is the case with other political concepts. Constitutionalism has been developing from the ancient idea of 'mixed government' to the modern liberal idea of power separation and human rights. There exist various constitutional attempts or courses. There are constitutional monarchy and constitutional democracy, and also constitutional party-State, constitutional socialism, and so on.

From this perspective, what can be said about the constitutional future of North Korea? People talk about China and Vietnam as models for the future of North Korea. Indeed, these belong to the few countries on the planet that maintain a communist party-State system. However, it is necessary to pay attention to the difference as well as the similarity between those countries. As is known, North Korea has established one-person rule; the Communist Party (Workers' Party) of North Korea is not so strong or autonomous as the ruling parties of the other two countries. Instead, the status of the supreme leader is much greater. The North Korean regime is seen here formally as a party-State system, but in reality as kind of 'Principate' similar to that of the Ancient Rome. Therefore, the first step for improving the North Korean regime is to change from 'Principate' to 'Party-State'. North Korea needs such a structure division between 'dignified part' and 'efficient part' as in constitutional monarchy.

I. Introducing the development of the political and constitutional System of North Korea

A. The Origin of Korean Communism

After the Joseon Dynasty was forcefully brought to an end by Japan, monarchy was no longer a valued tradition for Korean people. As the 1911 'Republican Revolution – 辛亥革命' succeeded in China and the republican movement spread throughout the world, the republican ideology rose for the future of the Korean people.

Koreans placed high hopes in the 1919 Versailles Peace Conference ending World War I and in Wilson's doctrine of self-determination. There erupted a nation-wide protest against Japanese imperialism. Compatriots of Korean Peninsula, as well as Manchuria, Siberia and America joined the independence movement. This movement lasted for months with numerous of peaceful rallies and demonstrations, but

Japan used force to suppress them and thousands of people were killed. This 'March 1st Independence Movement – 3.1운동' marked the beginning of a new constitutional history in Korea. The aspiration to national liberation led to the demand for an independent national government. A couple of Korean provisional governments were proclaimed in the Russian Maritime Province, in Shanghai and in Seoul. Finally, an integrated one was formed in Shanghai: the Korean Provisional Government that declared itself as a 'Democratic Republic'. The idea of a democratic republic was represented by the US or France, and later Germany and Austria.

However, another idea of a democratic republic emerged: the soviet system. The Romanov Dynasty of Russia came to an end and Lenin carried out the communist revolution in the chaotic situation of the Kerensky interim government. It replaced 'bourgeois democracy' with 'soviet democracy' of working people. The soviets were led by a revolutionary vanguard party, that is the Communist Party. Soviet democracy eventually resulted in a 'party-State' with so-called 'democratic centralism'.

Colonised Koreans laid their hopes in the Western powers. The aspiration of President Wilson's national self-determinism resonated widely among them. Yet, the ideal of freedom and human rights proved useless for the oppressed peoples, ruled by the 'victors of World War I'. At the 1919 Paris Peace Conference, demands by Korea and Vietnam were completely ignored. At the 1921 Washington Arms Conference, the Korean issue was again completely disregarded. Instead, Japan was recognised as the world's third largest power in naval forces.

Koreans were greatly disappointed with 'Janus-faced' Western powers. At that moment, Lenin in Russia announced his 'Thesis on the Issue of Nations and Colonialism'. He promised support for the emancipation of colonial nations. This thesis was officially adopted at the Second Convention of the Komintern. Many Korean independence activists were impressed.

Ho Chi Minh of Vietnam had a similar experience. He had high hopes in the 1919 Peace Conference and wrote *Revendications du Peuple Annamite* to submit to the Conference, but in vain. After that, Ho Chi Minh participated in the debate over the Third International (*Komintern*) within the French Socialist Party and learned of the aforementioned thesis of Lenin's. He was uplifted and moved to tears.

China had some similar circumstances when it approached Russia. Though Sun Yat-sen had launched the Republican Revolution, it was not easy to establish a democratic republic, which was blocked by warlords of central Beijing. In particular, Western powers retained their rights through these Beijing warlords. Even in the 1919 Paris Peace Conference, Japan's encroachments on China were approved. The Chinese felt insulted. That was why the 'May Fourth Movement' broke out. The Russian government of Lenin was different: Lenin promised to renounce all privileges obtained by the Russian Empire. Sun Yat-sen joined hands with Russia and formed the KMT (Kuomintang)-CCP (Chinese Communist Party) Alliance.

With the Russian Soviet Revolution, communism flew into Korea's constitutional history. The early start of communism in Korea took place as Koreans lived collectively in the Maritime Province of Siberia. Koreans were great farmers. Rice-farming was introduced to the region by Koreans. The Russian government granted them the land to encourage their farming and induced their naturalisation. By 1919, the Korean population grew to as many as 200,000. Thus, the Maritime Province became an important base for the Korean overseas independence movement. Several communist organisations sprang up from 1918 to 1920. These movements were faster than China's and far faster than Vietnam's. Some of them joined the Korean Provisional Government in Shanghai. However, conservative nationalism was the mainstream of the Provisional Government, and Syngman Rhee, a pro-US diplomat and Princeton university, became the interim president.

Pro-soviet activists pursued independent war against Japan. They were supported by Lenin. Soviet Russia was the only power which financially supported the Korean independent activists. At the time, Russia was in the state of war with Japan, and the latter dispatched troops to intervene in the Russian civil war. Korean activists wanted an alliance with Russia and planned to form an alternative provisional government or nation-wide revolutionary party. But circumstances changed. Japan withdrew their troops and approved the Russian Soviet government. Thus, Russia did no longer wanted anti-Japanese Korean organisations in its territory. On top of that, Korean Communist fractions lacked integrative leadership. The Komintern did not endorse any political parties of the Korean people as an official Communist Party.

B. Origin of the Kim Il-sung's guerrilla unit

The communist movement was brought into the Korean Peninsula. The communist youth longed for national liberation and a new world. However, several attempts to construct a Korean Communist Party continued to fail due to repression by Japan. Since then, the communist movement in Korea was only fragmented among workers, peasants and students. In the end, Koreans were not able to have a consistent and unified communist organisation until their liberation in 1945.

Meanwhile, the aggression of Japanese imperialism increased. After taking Korea as a colony in 1910, the 'Taisho democracy (大正デモクラシー)' was introduced for a while but eventually turned to militarism. With the global economic crisis, Japanese chauvinism was heightened, and the 'Shōwa Restoration (昭和維新)' led by a radical military group destroyed the prospects of Japanese liberalism. Finally, in 1930, the Manchurian Kwantung Army (関東軍) caused the Mukden Incident by its own military action. And in 1932, the puppet government 'Manchukuo (満州国)' was established.

The anti-Japanese front then moved to China. Korean independence activists tried to co-operate with China to unite fronts. This proved uneasy. Chiang Kai–shek (蔣介石; Jiang Jieshi)'s government wanted to eliminate communists inside China rather than fighting against Japan. While Chiang Kai-shek continued its 'non-resistance' policy. The leadership of Manchuria's anti-Japanese front moved to the Chinese Communist Party. The Communist Party organised the 'Northeast Asian Anti-Japanese Militia' (thereafter 'Northeast Anti-Japanese United Army') by unifying various anti-Japanese forces. At that time, the majority of the communists of Manchuria were Koreans. Oppressed by Japanese imperialists, persecuted by the Chinese and exploited by landowners, more and more Korean youth longed for a communist revolution. Uprisings and arrests were repeated. Then, according to the Komintern's principle of 'one country-one party', Korean communists were admitted to the Chinese Communist Party and joined to the Northeast Anti-Japanese United Army. The most prominent Korean leader among them was Kim Il-sung, future founder of North Korea.

Kim's father was a nationalist intellectual, and his mother was a nationalist Christian. Kim Il-sung attended elementary and junior high schools in Korea and Manchuria. He had already participated in the anti-Japanese movement since his school days. After his parents' death, he joined the Communist Party and played a role as a young officer in the Northeast Anti-Japanese United Army. The Japanese military cited him as the most threatening figure along with Yang Jingyu (杨靖宇), the Chinese commander of the anti-Japanese forces in southern Manchuria. Kim Il-sung also undertook domestic operations. In 1937, the victory of the Battle of Pochonbo under Baekdu Mountain (长白山) was a small one, but the impact was so large that rumours of 'Kim Il-sung' spread over the whole country. In particular, the Dong-A Ilbo (one of the major newspapers then and now in Korea) reported it widely with issuing extra editions, and the myth of 'General Kim Il-sung' was thus formulated.

The Northeast Anti-Japanese United Army fought dozens of battles against the modernised Japanese Kwantongun in spite of the intense cold and harsh famine of Manchuria. However, most of them were killed, arrested and surrendered by the overwhelming forces of Japan. Meanwhile, Kim Il-sung kept his unit so that there were few who surrendered. The bonds of Kim Il-sung's unit were solid and the leadership of Kim Il-sung and his wife, Kim Jong-sook, was firm. There are many reminiscences that they shared food and hunger and orphan soldiers were taken care of.

Eventually, all Northeast Anti-Japanese United Army moved into Soviet territory. From 1940 onward, they crossed the border into Khabarovsk. They were reorganised by the Soviet army into the '88 Brigade'. They belonged to the Communist Party of China as well as to the Soviet Army as a military. Total numbers of the 88 brigades were reported to be about 600, among them Korean guerrillas of about 150. Kim Il-sung was their unshakable leader.

C. Establishment of the monolithic rule of Kim Il-sung

After liberation from Japanese rule in 1945, the Kim Il-sung's unit of the Soviet Khabarovsk '88 Brigade' came to North Korea together with Soviet troops. They became the major fraction of the North Korean Communist Party. Indeed, the Korean Communist Party was reconstructed in Seoul at the time of liberation. But the party could not develop properly under the regime of US military which controlled the southern half of Korea. Eventually the North Korean branch of the Korean Communist Party became the main body and changed its name to Korean Workers' Party. At its inception, the Communist Party was not a hegemonic one in North Korea. It had to compete with other parties.

Actually, the Joesun Democratic Party led by a renowned nationalist, Jo Man-shik, was more popular than the Communist Party. But Jo was ousted by the Russian military and his party became tributary to the Communist Party.

In 1948, North Korea proclaimed itself a 'People's Democracy', which is similar to Mao Zedong's 'New Democracy' of China. The leading principle of the party was nationalism, not Marx-Leninism. The State constitution referred to people's sovereignty, not the dictatorship of the proletariat. The ruler Kim Il-sung was merely the prime minister of the cabinet, and the supreme authority of the government was ascribed to the Supreme People's Assembly represented by elections of the people.

The so-called People's Democracy moved before long to the sole domination of the Communist Party (i.e. Workers' Party). After the 1950–1953 War, the various fractions of the party were purged and the monolithic regime of Kim Il-sung started. Marx Leninism was introduced in the party constitution of 1956 and Kim Il-sung's anti-Japanese armed struggle was adopted as the origin of the party in the 1961 Constitution. In the 1972 North Korea promulgated a 'Socialist Constitution', where the Juche (주체; self-reliance) idea of Kim Il-sung became the national ideology. And the Presidium of the Supreme People's Assembly became just a titular institution. Thus, North Korea shifted from a people's democracy to a party-State system and the one-person's rule of a 'supreme leader'. In the relations between the supreme leader and the party, the status of the supreme leader was overwhelming. Since 1980, no more Party Congress has been held. The Central Committee too was emasculated. Kim Il-sung abolished the chairmanship of the Central Committee and retained only the positions of i/ General Secretary and ii/ Chairman of the Central Military Commission.

This one-person rule was consolidated further under successor Kim Jong-il's era. The party's status was further demeaned. The motto of the Kim Jong-il's era was 'Military First'. As the North Korean economy and society collapsed in the late 1990s, the regional organisations of the Communist Party became paralysed. The military was instead in charge of maintaining social order and restoring economic productivity. Kim Jong–il elevated the government's National Defence Commission to be the sovereign apparatus and he ruled as Chairman of that Commission.

However, most of the key members of the Commission were too aged to be able to work. The circumstances of the Party's Central Military Commission were more serious. All other members retired or died, and

Kim Jong-il remained alone to lead the army. The military personnel appointments were issued in the name of commander-in-Chief, Kim Jong-il, only.

Kim Jong-il elevated his father, Kim Il-sung to be the progenitor of North Korea and defined him as 'Eternal President'. After Kim Il-sung's death in 1994, Kim Jong-il performed a 'Posthumous Rule' for three years of mourning. As ruling ideology, he declared the principles of 'Serving the People as Heaven' and 'Benevolence and Virtue', reminiscent of a Confucian kingship. North Korea was likened to a 'Socialist Grand Family', where the father is the supreme leader and the mother is the party. He named his son, Kim Jong-un, as his successor, only 27 years old when he was inaugurated as Supreme Commander Kim Jong-il's death in 2011. With no experience of statesmanship and an un-verified ability, the only reason for his succession was the bloodline.

After the power transfer to Kim Jong-un was stabilised, he seized the control of all – party, army, government – thanks to the dual legacy of Kim Il-sung and Kim Jong-il. Kim Jong-un got rid of potential competitors, had every party member, every soldier, and every citizen swear absolute allegiance to him as supreme leader. He set about institutionalising the hereditary succession of the Kim family. The revised party Constitution included 'the principle of leadership succession'. Moreover, the revised State Constitution stipulated both Kim Il-sung and Kim Jong-il as 'Eternal Supreme Leaders'.

II. Comparisons with China and Vietnam

China, Vietnam and North Korea are all communist countries with a party-State system. As is clear, a party-State system has a hegemonic party or a single party representing the people. All power is concentrated in that party. The government is not constituted by the people, but by the party. The legislative, executive, judiciary and military forces are not responsible to the people, but to the party. The Communist Party of China, Vietnam and North Korea are all in the same position. However, the status of the party in North Korea is relatively weaker.

The North Korean Communist Party was not the creator of the North Korea. During the process of establishing the North Korean government, the Communist Party was one of several political elements. It was the Kim Il-sung guerrilla forces and the Soviet authorities that built North Korea. Kim Il-sung's anti-Japanese armed struggle is in the founding legend of North Korea, not the Communist Party. The North Korean Communist Party was not created until the 1945 liberation from Japanese occupation.

China, on the other hand has a regime founded by the Communist Party. Since the latter was officially launched in 1921, it has been the leading force for making a new State. Indeed, the Chinese Communist Party was initially under the control of the Soviet Komintern, but later deviated from the Soviet influence under the guidance of Mao Zedong, who created China's own communism with land-reforms and peasant-communities. Also, the Chinese Communist Party displayed national power in contrast to Chiang Kai-shek's 'no resistance policy' against the Japanese invasion. In 1949, China's Communist Party defeated the Nationalist Party and succeeded in unifying China. Thus, Mao Zedong's personal worship operated but through the unshaken status of the Communist Party, the latter carrying out reforms and opening policy to drive the country to be elevated to the level of competing for global supremacy with the US.

The founder of modern Vietnam is also the Communist Party. Although the Communist Party of Vietnam began with the guidance of the Soviet Komintern, Ho Chi Minh, the founder of the Party, was the representative of the Komintern, and as such he was able to lead the Party to be the heart of national liberation movement. The Communist Party of Vietnam played a key role in the struggle against both French and Japanese imperialism. The party successfully constructed the 'League for the Independence of Vietnam' (Việt Minh). No sooner had the Japanese colonial rule collapsed than the Communist Party could succeed in controlling the whole country and proclaiming the establishment of a new democratic republic. After the division in South and North due to US intervention, the 'National Liberation Front' (Việt Cộng) in South Vietnam was also under the guidance of the Northern Communist Party.

North Korea differs from China and Vietnam also as to the status of the supreme leader. Kim Il-sung was the head of the Manchurian guerrilla unit, the only leader supported by the Soviet Union and the Chinese Communist Party. In addition, Kim Il-sung not only ruled the party, the military, and the government, but exercised power even in people's ordinary lives. Kim Il-sung was the head of State, a symbol of the people, and at the same time a practitioner of real government.

By contrast, Mao Zedong was not a leading character in founding the Communist Party of China, but only one of its founders. The leaders were two professors in Beijing University, Chen Duxiu (陈独秀) and Li Dazhao (李大钊), Mao being their assistant but not the head of the party until the 1935 Zunyi Conference (遵义会议). Even as the supreme authority in China, Mao was not the only leading figure. Mao Zedong purged Liu Shaoqi (刘少奇) and Peng Dehuai (彭德怀), but there were still outstanding leaders such as Deng Xiaoping (邓小平) and Zhou Enlai (周恩来). Although Mao wrote the first phase of Chinese communist history, it was not the whole story of Chinese communism. Before Mao, there was Sun Yat-sen's 'Three Principles of People' and after Mao Deng Xiaoping's 'Socialist Market Economy'.

In Vietnam, Ho Chi Minh had been the only leader since the foundation of the Communist Party and his personal worship has not cooled until now. He could thus be compared with Kim Il-sung. But there are differences. Ho Chi Minh created the 'Vietnamese Revolutionary Youth League' in 1925 and founded the Communist Party in 1930. However, Ho Chi Minh did not lead the party and the army directly. The party was led by successive general secretaries such as Lê Hồng Phong, Trường Chinh and Lê Duẩn, and the army by General Võ Nguyên Giáp. Ho Chi Minh remained a symbolic leader and acted just as an emergency authority. The Vietnamese Communist Party was under Ho Chi Minh's guidance, but not subordinate to Ho Chi Minh.

The North Korean People's Army is not an army of the Communist Party. It was not created as an army of the Party. There was no party organisation inside the army when the People's Army was founded. Instead, the Kim Il-sung's guerrilla forces gained control of the military command. Thereafter a party structure was established in the army. However, the status of the party could not exceed the status of Kim Il-sung. The North Korean People's Army became a 'palace guard' of the supreme leader.

III. A suggestion on North Korea's constitutional reform

Many refer to the Chinese and Vietnamese models as the future of North Korea. However, as we have seen, North Korea is actually forming the 'Kim Il-sung Dynasty' in the appearances of the Party-State. Therefore, even if North Korea should follow the models of China and Vietnam, it would be necessary to restore the genuine party-State system in the first place.

Therefore, some change in the monolithic rule of North Korea is necessary. A suggestion is to divide between the 'dignity part' and the 'efficiency part'. This is the distinction of W. Bagehot in *The English Constitution* of the Victorian era. Bagehot analysed the actual governance in Britain as carried out by the Cabinet – when people thought they were being governed by the Queen. The 'dignity part' guarantees the stability and continuity of the nation, and the 'efficiency' part guarantees the efficiency and accountability of the government.

The North Korean constitution does not know the dignity part. In the constitution, Kim Jong-un is just the Chairman of the State Council, thus head of the administrative branch of the government. There is another branch, the legislative body, composed by national election, namely the Supreme People's Assembly, and the Chairman of the State Council is elected by the Supreme People's Assembly. In terms of representation, the status of Chairman is lower than that of the Supreme People's Assembly. Also, Kim Jong-un is the chief executive officer of the Communist Party. In other words, he is not a transcendent entity.

In fact, Kim Jong-un is regarded as a god-like being. He transcends all government organisations, party organisations, and all factions and organisations of society. At the same time, he carries out all the affairs in the party and the government. He actually engages and directs in every aspects of the country's policy. In this way, the 'dignity part' and the 'efficient part' become intertwined in North Korea. This could cause the authority of the 'dignity part' to be vulnerable and the 'efficient part' to be helpless and irresponsible.

In this way, the dignity part should be elevated to a transcendental position and secure the national legitimacy through, possibly, a referendum. And the regular political affairs should be left to party-State apparatuses. They should be allowed real power and assume accountability. In particular, it would be good to revitalise the parliament and the cabinet constituted by national elections.

*

In conclusion, North Korea consists of both the Principate system and the Party-State system. The former overwhelms the latter, and the latter is trivialised. In the Kim Jon-un's era, a change took place. The functions of the party are being rebuilt. Since 1980, there had been no Party Congress in North Korea. However, with the succession of Kim Jung-un, the Representative Congress of the Party were held in 2010 and 2012 consecutively. In 2016, the Party Congress was held after 36 years.

The Central Committee of the Party is being held regularly now, and the Standing Committee of the Politburo has been normalised. The party's Central Military Commission has also been restructured. The function of the cabinet is also revitalised. The economist expert, Park Bong-ju, formerly demotion, returned to be Prime minister of the cabinet, and further entered the Standing Committee of Politburo and the Party's Central Military Commission. Recently, he was promoted as Deputy Chairman of the State Council. Legislative functions of the Presidium of the Supreme People's Assembly are becoming more active than ever.

Kim Jung-un seems to act towards a transition to a 'normal State'. Especially encouraging is that he declared the completion of the parallel policy of nuclear arming and economic development and switched to the single line of economic development. Yet, one cannot say that constitutional change has begun. Further genuine constitutional reforms are necessary for North Korea to become a 'normal State'. The first step is to turn the one-person rule into a constitutional one. North Korean Constitutionalism can be launched with the division of the 'dignity part' and of the 'efficiency part' according to the model of the British constitutional monarchy.

It is hoped that the dictatorship will be alleviated and the party and the government will become more responsible and representative through such a division. One can only wish that by doing so, ultimately, constitutional North Korea and South Korea can build a Korean Peace Federation.

References

Dae-Sook SUH, Kim Il Sung: the North Korean leader, New York, Columbia University Press, 1988.

Maurice MEISNER, *Mao Zedong: a political and intellectual portrait*, Cambridge, Malden, MA, Polity, 2007.

William J. DUIKER, *Ho Chi Minh*, New York, Hyperion, 2000.

Pierre BROCHEUX, *Ho Chi Minh: A Biography* (translated by Claire DUIKER), Cambridge, Cambridge University Press, 2007.

Immanuel C.Y. HSU, *The Rise of Modern China*, 6th ed., New York, Oxford University Press, 2000.

Charles K. ARMSTRONG, *The North Korean Revolution: 1945-1950*, Ithaca, NY, Cornell University Press, 2004.

Robert A. SCALAPINO, Chong-sik LEE, *Communism in Korea*, Berkeley, University of California Press, 1992.

Walter BAGEHOT, *The English Constitution* (edited by Paul SMITH), Cambridge, Cambridge University Press, 2001.

Part II

The Belt and Road Initiative: changes from Asia to Europe

Introduction

Kuralay BAIZAKOVA
al-Farabi Kazakh National University, Almaty, Kazakhstan

Part II of the book covers the strategic importance of China's 'One Belt, One Road Initiative' for Central Asia and Europe.

The modern Silk Road is a long-term and global strategy designed to be implemented over time. This strategic concept has a wide scope embracing the vast territory of Eurasia and reflecting the Chinese idea of mutually beneficial cooperation and joint development with Eurasian countries. China's new economic strategy directed at enforcing the role of the state in the global politics and governing in the regions suggests also new foreign policy towards other states, including Central Asia. To transform the Chinese economy and implement the reforms, cooperation with immediate neighbours is required. The Chinese leadership fully comprehends the importance of the struggle for the influence in Central Asia. OBOR provides new form of cooperation between China and CA countries, including the enhancement of investment activities. Beijing is also interested in the transport and transit potential of CA countries. Kazakhstan perceives as significant to participate in Chinese 'One Belt, One Road' initiative in order to use new opportunities and advantages of regional cooperation and to try to minimize the risks and challenges. The Chinese 'One Belt, One Road' and Kazakhstan's 'Nurly Zhol' new economic policy complement each other since both are set to develop infrastructures, mostly transportation and communications.

The chapter by Sagyngaliy Aidarbayev and Bakhyt Uderbayeva "The Chinese 'Belt and Road' and Kazakhstan's 'Nurly Zhol': legal and political aspects of cooperation within two initiatives" looks at the legal and political aspects of the cooperation within the framework of these two initiatives. According to Kazakhstani experts, thanks to the joint practical implementation of both combined strategic initiatives, the synergistic effect will be more significant and deeper for the economic development of Kazakhstan, which is not only one of the major members of the Eurasian Economic Union but also its founder. The question of how to combine OBOR and Nurly Zhol without getting into trouble with Russia and not to damage Kazakh-Russian relations remains quite a challenge.

Another chapter, "The 'Nurly Zhol' and the 'One Belt, One Road' projects: juxtaposition of an idea" by Duman Zhekenov, Askhat Darkenbaev and Zhassulan Zhunisov, also looks at these two projects. Authors compare the two initiatives, considering the ideas of the leadership of both China and Kazakhstan conclude that both projects open up unique opportunities. 'Nurly Zhol' creates new broad opportunities for transport development both in Kazakhstan and in the Central Asian region. At the same time, as part of OBOR, Kazakhstan is advancing its transport potential due to increasing international cooperation. This means that the country has every chance of becoming a leading transportation hub in the future.

In the chapter by Pierre Chabal "Theorising regional change, especially in the case of the 'Shanghai cooperation' ", the OBOR is considered through the prism of changes occurring in the 'New Asia'. The author concludes that multilateral sub-regional structures such as the SCO prolongs national dimensions based on the analysis of SCO development dynamics. The SCO as an instrument of cooperation between China and post-Soviet Asia also turned into a preparation stage for OBOR. The author makes serious conceptual conclusions that the Asian form of regional construction differs from the European one not only in details, but also in its origins and prospects, and at the present stage, geographical characteristics are turning into fully open and supporting geostrategic and geo-economic foundations of commercial domination. Practical implementation of the Chinese Silk Road Economic Belt may lead to the formation of a new architecture of the global economy around Eurasia, where Central Asia becomes the main link and Kazakhstan occupies a special, strategically important place.

The chapter "Kazakhstan-China strategic partnership under the 'Belt and Road initiative' " by Kuralay Baizakova, Fatima Kukeyeva and Zhulduz Baizakova tackles the strategic partnership of Kazakhstan and China within the BRI. Authors note that the main feature of a strategic partnership is complementarity, which involves taking advantage of one partner to unlock and develop the potential of another. This partnership promotes diversification, industrialization and modernization of the national economy of Kazakhstan. The advantages and possible benefits of taking part in the project are obvious. However, a question emerges as to the possible risks and challenges for Kazakhstan that may appear in the way of implementation of the BRI initiative. Hence the importance for Kazakhstan to have combined strategy concerning the BRI, just to be able to build its own agenda.

Migration between Kazakhstan and China has different dynamics and presents an important aspect to study from the perspective of sustainable development and international cooperation. Migration is also important in conjunction with the Eurasian Economic Union and the Silk Road Economic Belt. Two papers in this section are focused on it.

The chapter "Legal migration regulations of Kazakhstani-Chinese relations: prospects of the 'Belt and Road Initiative' and the EAEU" by Zulfiya Baimagambetova and Leila Delovarova looks at some aspects of the legal framework in the area of migration between Kazakhstan and China. Migration processes have become one of the vital aspects of the current transformation of international relations in the context of geo-economic and geopolitical relations. Kazakh-Chinese relations in this area remain of great interest.

The chapter by Yesbol Omirzhanov and Almagul Tusupova "Reforming Kazakhstan's migration legislation in light of the OBOR project" considers the issues of resolving labour migration within the OBOR. It discusses the issues associated with state control of Chinese business in Kazakhstan, as well as Chinese labour migration to Kazakhstan. The reader can discover the main BRI dimensions with Kazakhstan as an example. The New Silk Road, although beneficial to all participating countries, can become the foundation of a systemic shift in geopolitics.

The Chinese 'Belt and Road' and Kazakhstan's 'Nurly Zhol': legal and political aspects of cooperation within two initiatives

Sagyngaliy AIDARBAYEV
al-Farabi Kazakh National University, Almaty, Kazakhstan

Bakhyt UDERBAYEVA
Narxoz University, Almaty, Kazakhstan

The modern origins of the 'Belt and Road' project in the form of the idea of reviving the Silk Road first appeared in the early 1990s when the Central Asian countries gained independence after the collapse of the Soviet Union. According to J. Farchy, back in 1992, the proposal of the European Commission for the Central Asian countries as Kazakhstan, Kyrgyzstan, Tajikistan, Turkmenistan and Uzbekistan to re-create the new Silk Road was announced. The European vision of this project was to connect Europe and Central Asia through the International Transport Corridor (TRACECA). A little later, in 1999, the US adopted the Silk Road Strategy Act (updated in 2006) that was aimed at protecting the US long-term interests in Central Asia, the South Caucasus (later in Afghanistan) as well as strengthening regional security and cooperation (for example, through construction of a Turkmenistan-Afghanistan-Pakistan-India Gas Pipeline – TAPI).[1]

It should be noted that the initiators of the relevant projects as the EU and the US proceeded from their national interests. So, if the EU main interest was to close all the transport routes that enable exports of Central Asian resources to Europe, the strategic interest of the US was to withdraw export transportation routes of the region's resources

---

[1] J. FARCHY, "China seeking to revive the Silk Road", May 2016: https://www.ft.com/content/e99ff7a8-0bd8-11e6-9456-444ab5211a2f.

from dependence on Russia. Therefore, the US considered not only the Western (European) direction of transport routes, but also the southern direction. Thus, by the time the Chinese *Belt and Road* Initiative came to existence, there were already other Silk Road projects, which however have not been implemented in practice.

In September 2013, the Chinese President Xi Jinping in his speech to the Nazarbayev University students in the capital of Kazakhstan announced a new Chinese Initiative of the Silk Road Economic Belt, the main purpose of which is to create a new economic and investment space that will include China, the countries of the Asia-Pacific region, Eastern Europe, and the CIS.

As A. Vinogradov noted, initially the idea purported to create the transport corridors between the countries of the Asia-Pacific (hereinafter referred to as AP), first of all China and Western Europe as the main consumers of products manufactured in China and the AP countries. However, a little later in October 2013, during a summit of the Asia-Pacific Economic Community in the Indonesian island of Bali, the Chinese leader proposed another initiative – the 21st century 'Maritime Silk Road' – aimed at creating and expanding the existing maritime transport bridge from the southern provinces of China and South-East Asia to bring their products to world markets.[2]

Subsequently, the two projects were merged into one global project called 'One Belt, One Road', which became the main element of the foreign economic strategy pursued by Beijing. Thus, Beijing proposed a completely new approach and a new practice of cooperation.[3]

As for the Nurly Zhol (*shining path*), some thoughts are prompted by the chronology of the preparation of Kazakhstan's project. On 22 May 2012, the President of Kazakhstan N.A. Nazarbayev, officially launched a project entitled 'Kazakhstan – New Silk Road' at the 25th meeting of the Foreign Investors Council under the President of the Republic of Kazakhstan. The aim of the project is to revive the historical role of

---

2 Виноградов А. Что такое проект 'Один пояс, один путь' и каковы перспекти вы его 'сопряжения' с Евразийским союзом (5 сентября 2017): https://www.sonar2050.org/publications/chto-takoe-kitayskiy-proekt-odin-poyas-odin-put-i-perspektivy-ego-sopryajeniya-s-rossiyskim-proekt/.

3 БеляловА.А.Квопросуоказахстанско-китайскихотношениях//ВестникКазахского национального педагогического университета имени Абая, 2015: https://articlekz.com/article/19160.

Kazakhstan as the largest business and transit hub of the Central Asian region, a bridge between Europe and Asia. Six months later, in January 2013, the Government of Kazakhstan approved the Comprehensive action plan for the implementation of the New Silk Road Project.

On 6–8 September 2013, the President of the People's Republic of China Xi Jinping paid a State visit to Kazakhstan. After reviewing the project of implementing the New Silk Road Project, he underlined its importance and encouraged the relevant parties to remove barriers to facilitate trade and investment. He also notes that China and Kazakhstan need to create an 'economic corridor of the Silk Road'. During his speech at Nazarbayev University in Astana, the President of China identified five main objectives, which the 'Silk Road Economic Belt' (hereinafter the SREB) is intended to solve: i/ strengthening regional economic integration, ii/ building a unified trans-Asian transport infrastructure, iii/ eliminating investment and trade barriers, iv/ increasing the role of national currencies, v/ deepening cooperation in the humanitarian sphere. According to Chinese representatives, 67 States with 63% of the world population can connect to the SREB. The estimated project implementation period is 30 years.[4] During the State visit of Xi Jinping to Kazakhstan on 7 September 2013, a meeting of the Kazakh-Chinese Business Council was held, at which construction of the main Western Europe – Western China transport corridor, new roads and railways, marine terminals and logistics centres across the country – was launched.

On 29 May 2014, the Agreement on Establishment of the Eurasian Economic Union was signed in Astana. On 11 November 2014, the President of Kazakhstan N.A. Nazarbayev spoke to the people of Kazakhstan with his annual address entitled 'New Economic Policy of Kazakhstan – Nurly Zhol'. [On 1 January 2015, the Eurasian Economic Union (EAEU) began its official activity.] The 'Nurly Zhol' Project is based on another transportation and logistics project, 'Kazakhstan – New Silk Road', adopted 1.5 years before the announcement of the Chinese 'Silk Road Economic Belt Project'.

Considering that at the time of Xi Jinping's State visit to Kazakhstan, only a year has passed since he became a new leader of China's Communist Party and only six months since he took the highest post in China – the President of the People's Republic of China, it can be concluded that Kazakhstan's New Silk Road Project, with which Xi got acquainted in

---

4 Проект 'Один пояс, один путь'. Досье (3 июля 2017): https://tass.ru/info/4383152.

the capital of Kazakhstan, prompted him to the idea of the 'Silk Road Economic Project'. Such a timeliness requires more extensive research, but as a working version, it deserves consideration: such ideas may have long been hatched by a certain part of the Chinese intellectual elite but it was Kazakhstan's project that could have prompted in the Chinese leader that the time had come to announce it to the world.

The 'Silk Road Economic Belt Project' and the Eurasian Economic Union's Project bot were officially announced in Kazakhstan, which is a very symbolic factor for a State located in the centre of the Eurasian continent.

I. Political aspects of interaction between 'Belt and Road' and 'Nurly Zhol'

Most analysts agree that the two main domestic reasons for the adoption of the 'Belt and Road' Project are i/ the uneven development of China's eastern and western regions, causing a dangerous imbalance in the development of the country, and ii/ the problem of excess production capacity.

The imbalance in the development of China's eastern and western regions is clearly visible on this map of China's railways, where the western regions are poorly connected not only among themselves, but also with the rest of the country.

Map of China's Railways.

Source: A. VINOGRADOV, "What is the 'One Belt, One Road' Project and what are the prospects for its 'conjugation' with the Eurasian Union" (5 September 2017).

According to A. Vinogradov, in 2009–2012, after the global financial and economic crisis and contraction of global demand for Chinese exports, Beijing invested large funds in the development of domestic infrastructure. A high number of roads, houses, office buildings, ports and airports, etc. were built in the country, which led to a significant increase in the production capacity of construction materials, such as cement, steel structures, glass, etc. as well as production of rolling stock of railways, of cars, ships and their components. However, there was a limited demand for these products within the country, as it is unlikely to keep building continuously in such volumes. Soon problems would arise with the return on investments. Therefore, the Chinese OBOR initiative aimed at reducing pressure of excess capacity within China, while contributing to the development of the western regions of the country: the 'Silk Road Economic Belt' includes 12 western provinces and autonomous regions of China, 72% of its territory and 84% of its total borders. The idea of the 'One Belt, One Road' Project is to solve the problem of uneven regional development by dragging western regions into participation in the world economy and their entry into the world market via the construction of transport corridors to the West. In December 2016, as part of this 'expand abroad' strategy, the State Council of the PRC approved a programme for economic development of the western regions of the country 2016–2020. This is designed to ensure that they reach the level of 'moderate prosperity society'.[5]

According to the project's authors, the SREB will reduce delivery times of goods from China to Europe. While currently delivery time of container cargo by sea averages 45–60 days, in case of successful implementation of the SREB Project these goods will reach Europe in 10 days.[6] According to Wang Wen and Jia Jinjing, the economies of these regions are expected to represent about 29% of global GDP, and in the next 10 years, trade between China and countries along the 'Belt and Road' will double, thus increasing demand for passenger and cargo transportation systems. In this regard, the common space is designed to promote development of infrastructure and institutional framework, the creation of long-term international commercial projects with strategic partners of China.[7] Currently, the 'Belt and Road' Project involves 58 countries and its budget totals US$ 21 trillion, that is 29% of total international trade. Currently, more than 900 agreements worth over US$ 890 billion are being implemented.[8]

A key feature of the 'Silk Road Economic Belt' Project, which is part of the 'Belt and Road Initiative', that distinguishes it from previous initiatives of the EU and the US, is its multi-dimensionality, i.e. its relationship not only with transportation and comprehensive development of the road network, but also with some other important aspects.

---

5 Виноградов А. Что такое проект 'Один пояс, один путь' и каковы перспективы его 'сопряжения' с Евразийским союзом (5 сентября 2017): https://www.sonar2050.org/publications/chto-takoe-kitayskiy-proekt-odin-poyas-odin-put-i-perspektivy-ego-sopryajeniya-s-rossiyskim-proekt/.

6 Проект 'Один пояс, один путь'. Досье (3 июля 2017): https://tass.ru/info/4383152.

7 W. WEN and J. JINJING, "Silk Road Economic Development: Vision and Path", in ISPI Report (A. AMIGHINI, Ed.), *China Dream: Still coming true*, Renmin University of China, June 2016: www.ispionline.it/it/EBook/Rapporto_Cina_2016/Rapporto_cina_2016_Cap.6.pdf.

8 Каныбек Т.Н. Вовлечение Казахстана в проект 'Экономический пояс шелкового пути' // Известия Казахского Университета международных отношений и мировых языков имени Абылай хана, 2016: https://articlekz.com/article/19771.

Thus, T.N. Kanibek points to the following aspects of the 'Silk Road Economic Belt' Project[9] [6]: i/ link to political cooperation of the region; ii/ development of trade by eliminating trade barriers, reducing trade and investment costs, improving speed and quality of economic operations in the region; iii/ increase in foreign exchange flows through a move to payments in national currencies; iv/ strengthening the role of people's diplomacy, expansion of direct relationship between the peoples of the region.

Thus, while the historic Great Silk Road promoted exchange of goods and technologies, the new Great Silk Road in the form of the SREB Project interlinks not only economy, trade and infrastructure, but also politics, finance, and labour resources. This factor indicates that the PP project is more complex, diversified and multidimensional.

As part of the 'Belt and Road' Project, three main transport corridors are expected to be built: i/ the Northern Corridor (China – Central Asia (Kazakhstan) – Russia); ii/ the Central Corridor (China – Central and West Asia – Persian Gulf – Mediterranean Sea); iii/ the Southern Corridor (China – Southeast Asia – South Asia).

For the post-Soviet States involved in the 'Belt and Road' Project, participation provides great opportunities for implementing large-scale infrastructure projects, including building up international transit potential, modernising transport and logistics infrastructure, given the presence of a large strategic investor, China, ready to invest massively in them.

Reviving Kazakhstan's historical role as the largest business and transit hub of the Central Asian region, a bridge between Europe and Asia, in the framework of the initial 'Kazakhstan – New Silk Road' Project and then the 'Nurly Zhol' Project, and the main goal of China's SREB Project which aims at creating favourable conditions for the promotion of Chinese goods to foreign markets, harmoniously complement each other. Kazakhstan has a direct interest in having part of the Chinese exports redirected to Europe and the Middle East by transit through its territory. In addition, Kazakhstan is also interested in directly linking the east and the west of the country by railways and highways. In Soviet times, all transport routes in Kazakhstan were built in the south-to-north direction, towards Moscow, which was explained by the objective circumstances of the time. This aspect of the problem can be seen by studying the map of Kazakhstan's railways.

---

9 *Ibidem.*

The SREB Project is aimed at addressing similar challenges as the 'Nurly Zhol' Project, as long as it meets the goal of the SREB objectives such as: i/ simplifying customs, visa and other procedures to facilitate the activities of entrepreneurs and to expand the scope of cooperation; ii/ building an extensive transport and logistics infrastructure; iii/ increasing mutual trade and opening free trade zones in the regions through which the "economic belt" will pass; iv/ increasing volumes of mutual trade in national currencies with a view to turning *renminbi* into a regional currency which will be able to steal leadership from dollar and euro.[10] Thus, as K. Syroyezhkin states, the SREB concept is underpinned by concerns for intensive development of the western regions of China and their transformation into a transport and logistics, foreign economic and, in the future, financial hub of 'Big Central Asia'. At the same time, it is necessary to take into account that Central Asia has always remained for China a sales market for Chinese goods, a source of natural resources, and a transit territory.[11]

However, problems arise with the conjugation of the SREB and the Eurasian Economic Union (hereinafter EAEU) whose members are Kazakhstan, Russia, Belarus, Kyrgyzstan and Armenia. Without a

---

10 Сыроежкин К. Сопряжение ЕАЭС и ЭПШП // Россия и новые государства Евразии, 2016, №2. С.37–55: https://www.imemo.ru/jour/RNE/index.php?page_id=721&id=7526.

11 *Ibidem.*

conjugation of the SREB and the EAEU projects, it would be problematic for Kazakhstan to carry out harmonious interaction between the SREB and 'Nurly Zhol' Projects. The bottom-line is a conceptual contradiction between the SREB and the EAEU. While the EAEU aims at creating a well-protected integrated domestic market of five Member-States, the main goal of the SREB is to promote Chinese goods to foreign markets, including the EAEU market. Under these conditions, Kazakhstan faced a difficult task of ensuring conjugation between the SREB and the EAEU projects (that is, China and Russia) and only after that of determining all aspects of such conjugation between the SREB and 'Nurly Zhol' Projects.

Thus, the main political problem of the interaction between the 'Belt and Road' and 'Nurly Zhol' Projects is that of the conjugation of the Chinese Belt and Road Project (or, more precisely, SREB) and the EAEU.

II. Legal aspects of interaction between 'Belt and Road' and 'Nurly Zhol'

A breakthrough in the direction of the 'conjugation' of the Chinese SREB and the EAEU occurred, when the Joint Statement on *Cooperation for Conjugation of Construction of the EAEU and SREB* was adopted (Moscow, 8 May 2015).[12] This document contained several principal provisions: i/ mutual recognition of the two projects by China and Russia; ii/ definition of the main condition for conjugation of the two projects: conclusion of an agreement on trade and economic cooperation between the EAEU and the PRC (*de facto*, this is an agreement on division of spheres of influence between the two projects); iii/ introduction of a dialogue mechanism for conjugation of the EAEU and SREB in the format of a working group of the Foreign Affairs Ministries of Russia and China to coordinate cooperation. Progress towards an EAEU/China free trade zone was defined as a long-term goal.

One of the main conditions for conjugation of the two projects – the Agreement on Trade and Economic Cooperation between the EAEU and the PRC – was signed in Astana on 17 May 2018 during the Astana

---

12 Joint Statement on Cooperation for Conjugation of Construction of the EAEU and SREB (Moscow, May 8, 2015): http://kremlin.ru/supplement/4971.

Economic Summit[13] [9]. This Agreement is aimed at eliminating non-tariff barriers to trade, but it implies no strict obligations before each other and only defines a mechanism for cooperation based on setting various kinds of advisory committees and working groups. The document introduces the principle of transparency in making decisions that affect trading, and informing each other about new decisions. The agreement implies no significant measures towards increasing mutual investments. It contains a large number of references to WTO rules and agreements and many exemptions, including for the protection of public morality, people, animals, national security.

After the adoption of the Joint Statement of Russia and China on Cooperation for Conjugation of Construction of the EAEU and SREB (Moscow, 8 May 2015) and commencement of work on preparation of the Agreement on Trade and Economic Cooperation between the EAEU and the PRC, political and legal barriers to full-fledged interfacing of the SREB and 'Nurly Zhol' Projects disappeared.

In 2016, in the framework of the working visit of the President of Kazakhstan N.A. Nazarbayev to China (Hangzhou), a cooperation-plan for conjugation of the 'Nurly Zhol' New Economic Policy and the construction of the SREB was signed between the governments of Kazakhstan and China. Already on 31 August 2016, the Decree of the Government of Kazakhstan No. 518 'On Signing of the Plan of Cooperation for Conjugation of Nurly Zhol New Economic Policy and Construction of the Silk Road Economic Belt between the Government of the Republic of Kazakhstan and the Government of the People's Republic of China' was adopted [10]. This document contains a detailed mechanism for implementation of the two projects – Kazakhstani and Chinese – in Kazakhstan. Thus, the conjugation of the SREB and the 'Nurly Zhol' Projects occurred one year after the adoption of documents on conjugation of the EAEU and SREB projects. This means that Kazakhstan patiently sought first mutual conjugation of the EAEU and SREB projects. And only after that, the country signed the documents for conjugation of its national 'Nurly Zhol' Programme with the SREB Project.

*

13 Agreement on Economic and Trade Cooperation between the Eurasian Economic Union and its Member-States, of the one part, and the People's Republic of China, of the other part (Astana, May 17, 2018): https://online.zakon.kz/document/?doc_id=33755315#pos=1;-301.

In conclusion, the statistics of the rapid growth of Chinese investments in the economy of Kazakhstan testifies to how successful the interaction of the Chinese and Kazakhstan projects is.

The real breakthrough occurred in 2014–2015, when the volume of guaranteed Chinese investments in the economy of Kazakhstan tripled. Thus, at the end of 2012, the total volume of Chinese investments in Kazakhstan's economy amounted to $20 billion (of which $4.6 billion in direct foreign investment/DFI); at the beginning of 2014 – $22.6 billion (of which $5.68 billion in DFI). Following the visit of the President of Kazakhstan N.A. Nazarbayev to China in May 2014, the agreed amount of Chinese investment in the economy of Kazakhstan was $10 billion. During the visit of State Council Premier Li Keqiang to Kazakhstan in December 2014, contracts worth $14 billion were signed. During the visit of N.A. Nazarbayev to China in September 2015, the number of contracts signed totalled $24 billion. During the visit of Prime Minister of Kazakhstan K. Massimov in December 2015, the number of signed contracts totalled $10 billion. In other words, within the last two years, Kazakhstan signed contracts with China for $48 billion, and Chinese investments in the economy of Kazakhstan exceeded $70.6 billion.[14]

During these meetings, specific projects were discussed. For example, during a visit to China by the Prime Minister of Kazakhstan K. Massimov (December 2015), a total of 33 documents were reviewed on bilateral cooperation in the field of steel, non-ferrous metals, glass, oil refining, hydropower, automobiles, etc. totalling $23.6 billion. Additionally, in 2016, the volume of Chinese investments in the economies of the EAEU Member-States amounted to $25.7 billion. Of these: 82% ($21 billion) accounted for Kazakhstan, the share of Russia made $3.4 billion, the share of Kyrgyzstan $0.9 billion, the share of Belarus $0.4 billion.[15] These factors witness the successful promotion of the 'Belt and Road' Project in Kazakhstan and its harmonious interaction with Kazakhstan's 'Nurly Zhol' Project.

---

14 Сыроежкин К. Сопряжение ЕАЭС и ЭПШП // Россия и новые государс тва Евразии, 2016, №2. С.37–55: https://www.imemo.ru/jour/RNE/index.php?page_id=721&id=7526.

15 Кофнер Ю., *Матюхина*А., *Демидкина*О., *Мешкова*Т. Что представляет собой соглашение ЕАЭС – Китай: http://eurasian-studies.org/archives/9271.

References

FARCHY J., "China seeking to revive the Silk Road", May 2016: https://www.ft.com/ content/e99ff7a8-0bd8-11e6-9456-444ab5211a2f.

Виноградов А. Что такое проект 'Один пояс, один путь' и каковы пе рспективы его 'сопряжения' с Евразийским союзом (5 сентября 2017): https://www.sonar2050.org/publications/chto-takoe-kitayskiy-proekt-odin-poyas-odin-put-i-perspektivy-ego-sopryajeniya-s-rossiyskim-proekt/.

Белялов А.А. К вопросу о казахстанско-китайских отношениях //Вестник Казахского национального педагогического университета имени Абая, 2015: https://articlekz.com/article/19160.

Проект 'Один пояс, один путь'. Досье (3 июля 2017): https://tass.ru/info/4383152.

WEN Wang, JINJING Jia, "Silk Road Economic Development: Vision and Path", in ISPI Report (Alessia AMIGHINI, Ed.), China Dream: Still coming true, Renmin University of China, June 2016: www.ispionline.it/it/EBook/Rapporto_Cina_2016/Rapporto_cina_2016_Cap.6.pdf.

Каныбек Т.Н. Вовлечение Казахстана в проект 'Экономический пояс шелкового пути' // Известия Казахского Университета международных отношений и мировых языков имени Абылай хана, 2016: https://articlekz.com/article/19771.

Сыроежкин К. Сопряжение ЕАЭС и ЭПШП // Россия и новые госуда рства Евразии, 2016, №2. С.37–55: https://www.imemo.ru/jour/RNE/index.php?page_id=721&id=7526.

Joint Statement on Cooperation for Conjugation of Construction of the EAEU and SREB (Moscow, May 8, 2015): http://kremlin.ru/supplement/4971.

Agreement on Economic and Trade Cooperation between the Eurasian Economic Union and its Member-States, of the one part, and the People's Republic of China, of the other part (Astana, May 17, 2018): https://online.zakon.kz/document/?doc_id=33755315#pos=1.

Decree of the Government of the Republic of Kazakhstan No. 518 'On Signing of the Plan of Cooperation for Conjugation of Nurly Zhol New Economic Policy and Construction of the Silk Road Economic

Belt between the Government of the Republic of Kazakhstan and the Government of the People's Republic of China': https://online.zakon.kz/Document/?doc_id=39954788#pos=0;210.

Кофнер Ю., *Матюхина*А., *Демидкина*О., *Мешкова*Т. Что представляет собой соглашение ЕАЭС – Китай: http://eurasian-studies.org/archives/9271.

The 'Nurly Zhol' and the 'One Belt, One Road' projects: juxtaposition of an idea

Duman Zhekenov, Askhat Darkenbaev, Zhassulan Zhunisov
al-Farabi Kazakh National University, Almaty, Kazakhstan

Kazakhstan has high ambitions regarding the 'One Belt, One Road' initiative. Its territory represents the most comfortable area connecting China and the West. Kazakhstani interests in the initiative are clear: the country is already participating in the 'Nurly Zhol' programme, a plan to stimulate its economy with a budget of $9 billion for developing and modernising roads, railways and other transport systems. The economy of Kazakhstan has suffered from a fall in oil prices since the end of 2013, and the country's future economic growth depends on infrastructure development and regional trade. The country aims to become the largest business and transit hub in Central Asia, a bridge between Europe and Asia. It considers the Chinese initiative 'One Belt, One Road' as a means to achieve this goal. Kazakhstan is very important for the energy security of China. The country with its reserves of oil, gas, coal and uranium ranks tenth in the world. It has a strategic geographical position to control the flow of oil and gas from Central Asia to the East and the West. Its geographical proximity, safety of transport routes, as well as the absence of any hostile competitors in the region are the main advantages of Kazakhstan's energy sector for China.

According to the WTO, over 2013–2017, China's total trade with countries participating in the 'One Belt, One Road' project exceeded $5 trillion, and China's direct investment in these countries amounted to about $70 billion. Along the Belt and Road were built 82 zones for trade and economic cooperation. The 'Belt and Road Initiative' and its integral part, the 'Silk Road Economic Belt', will further strengthen mutually beneficial cooperation between China and Kazakhstan, China and the Central Asian countries. At present, China has become the largest investor and main trading partner of the countries of the CA region. The list of projects between China and Central Asian countries is increasing every year. The five republics of Central Asia – Kazakhstan, Kyrgyzstan, Tajikistan, Turkmenistan and Uzbekistan – reacted each differently to the Chinese initiative. The national strategic programme of Kazakhstan 'Nurly Zhol' has been connecting with the initiative 'One Belt, One Road' directly and reflects the desire of the country to become more than just a transit-zone between China and Europe.

The 'Belt and Road Initiative' has the opportunity to be implemented in Kazakhstan. Kazakhstan in the process of joint construction of 'One Belt, One Road' goes ahead of other countries and becomes an example of exemplary cooperation[1] (RPC General Consul in Almaty, Miao Hongbo). On 7 September [2018, editors' note], the Chinese-Kazakhstani business forum was successfully held in Astana to celebrate the fifth anniversary of the 'One Belt and One Road Initiative' in Kazakhstan. The holding of this event fully reflected the understanding, support and high interest of the Kazakh side to the 'One Belt and One Road Initiative'. China's Xi Jinping and Kazakhstan's N.A. Nazarbayev expressed their congratulations through a video message and highly appreciated the results achieved in the framework of the 'One Belt and One Road Initiative'. Over the past five years, with the joint efforts of both sides, China-Kazakhstan cooperation in the construction of 'One Belt, One Road' has achieved many results, to which one can say 'for the first time'. As a result of the successful matching of the 'One Belt and One Road Initiative' with the New Economic Policy 'Nurly Zhol', a list of projects in the industrial and investment sphere was created, including 51 projects totalling nearly $28 billion. The trade turnover between the two countries is steadily growing. Cooperation in the energy sector, financial cooperation is successfully promoted, the transport and communication interconnectedness continues to improve, cooperation in the agricultural sector, is

---

1 Speech at the opening of the scientific conference "One Belt and One Road Initiative": state and prospects – Almaty: Research Institute of International and Regional Cooperation of the Kazakh-German University, 2018.

gradually developing. Innovative cooperation is continuously growing for exchange in cultural and humanitarian sphere.

Kazakhstan has become China's largest trading partner in Central Asia and the second trading partner in the CIS. In 2017, the trade turnover between the two countries reached 10 billion US$, the growth rate 32%, and the number of freight trains crossing Kazakhstan exceeded 1,800 – a 50% increase in one year, which brought transit traffic to Kazakhstan to 3 billion US$. For the first time in history, based on cargo cooperation between China and Kazakhstan in the port of Lianyungang, Kazakhstan received access to the Pacific Ocean, turning from a land-locked country into a major transport and cargo hub of the Asia-Pacific region and continental Eurasia.

Cooperation in the framework of 'One Belt, One Road' brought both countries not only real economic benefits, but at the same time increased the number of new work places for local residents, improved the living conditions of peoples, increased financial revenues to the local budget, increased the technical level, accelerated the process industrialisation and stimulated socio-economic development. China is actively involved in the industrialisation of Kazakhstan, both countries jointly stimulate the development of the land port of Khorgos, the port of Aktau, the international highway Western China – Western Europe and other major infrastructure projects. One after another, a number of industrial investment projects are being implemented. China also plays an important role in the establishment of the Astana International Financial Centre. In addition, China and Kazakhstan are expanding further cultural and humanitarian cooperation, strengthening traditional friendship and strengthening mutual trust between our peoples.

In five years of joint construction of 'One Belt, One Road', many voiced doubts in the world. From the day of the initiative five years ago and to this day, these voices have not stopped but the people of the two countries see first-hand the benefits and potential opportunities of this 'One Belt, One Road'. These facts are replies to suspicions and doubts. There are naturally positive and negative sides: various kinds of problems arise in the process of developing initiatives but the current state of the project, beyond problems, opens the future.

I. Conceptual views on the issue

'One Belt, One Road' is widely discussed but this chapter reviews Kazakhstan's New Economic Policy 'Nurly Zhol' together with the Chinese 'One Belt and One Road Initiative'. In this analysis, the chapter draws from the research by colleagues from the Research Institute of International and Regional Cooperation of the Kazakh-German University. They have created an international experts club 'One Belt One Road' and organised an international conferences "'One Belt and One Road Initiative': state and prospects in 2018", from which were published materials used here, notably articles by B.K. Sultanov, "The initiative of the President of the People's Republic of China Xi Jinping is a breakthrough project of modernity"; by K.L. Syroezhkin, "Silk Road Economic Belt: success, challenges, and risks"; by A.M. Amrebaev, "One Belt and One Road Initiative: Kazakhstan's Participation"; by A. Arupov, "Interfacing of the One Belt and One Road Initiative and integration processes in Central Asia"...[2]

These pointedly complement other, more general views from all over the world in this field. Today numerous research works tackled the Chinese global project 'One Belt and One Road'. We can find different kind of statements. Some relate only indirectly to the present chapter. For example, T. Miller,[3] D. Shambaugh,[4] M. Clarke,[5] S. Peyrouse,[6] An-gang Hu.[7]

In order to understand the meaning of the OBOR and the Chinese foreign policy, it is useful to refer to speeches, conversations, official

---

2 Materials of the scientific conference "One Belt and One Road Initiative": state and prospects – Almaty: Research Institute of International and Regional Cooperation of the Kazakh-German University, 2018.

3 T. MILLER, *China's Asian Dream: Empire Building along the New Silk Road*, London, Zed Books.

4 D.L. SHAMBAUGH, *China Goes Global: the partial power*, New York: Oxford University Press, 2013.

5 M. CLARKE, "The Belt and Road Initiative: China's New Grand Strategy?", *Asian Policy*, 2017, 24, p. 71–79.

6 S. PEYROUSE, "The Evolution of Russia's Views on the Belt and Road Initiative", *Asian Policy*, 2017, 24, p. 96–102.

7 H. ANGANG, "Embracing China's 'New Normal': Why the Economy is still on track", *Foreign Affairs*, May-June 2015: https://www.foreignaffairs.com/articles/china/2015-04-20/embracing-chinas-new-normal.

announcements of the Chinese leader. *The Government of China*[8] comprises two volumes with information directly related to this chapter. The second volume of this book contains seventeen chapters, of which two of particular interest, entitled "Peaceful development and cooperation with other countries" and "The Belt and Road initiative". In these, Xi Jinping gives the direction of the development of the 'One Belt, One Road' project.

II. The 'Nurly Zhol' project and its developments

The strategic programme 'Nurly Zhol' was adopted on 11 November 2014. It aims at ensuring the sustainable development of the economy of Kazakhstan in the context of new global and regional challenges. The core of the 'Nurly Zhol' programme is the infrastructure development of Kazakhstan, in particular, the (re)construction of road-, rail- and air-lines, the creation of a logistics hub in the east of the country, and the maritime infrastructure in the Caspian Sea; the creation of industrial infrastructure, including the construction of new industrial zones; a balanced energy supply of all of Kazakhstan's regions; modernisation of housing and utilities infrastructure and water and heat supply networks; strengthening housing and social infrastructure; support for small and medium businesses.

The implementation of the 'Nurly Zhol' programme, which connects Kazakhstan's regions to intercontinental highways (Western China-Western Europe and China-Iran) will enable Kazakhstan to become the most important Eurasian transport and logistics hub connecting the North and South, the West and East of Eurasia, the countries of the EU, the Middle East and Southeast Asia. A prerequisite for the implementation of the 'Nurly Zhol' programme for Kazakhstan, which does not have direct access to the Baltic Sea or the Atlantic Ocean, the Persian Gulf or the Indian Ocean, or to the Pacific Ocean, is friendly and partnership relations with neighbouring States – China, Russia and Iran.

The leadership of Kazakhstan, supporting in general the conjugation of the Eurasian Economic Union (EAEU) and the SREB, put forward its own version of the linking of the 'Nurly Zhol' programme with the SREB, in which several other priorities are set. In particular, Kazakhstan,

---

8 XI, Jinping, *The Governance of China*, vol. 1, Beijing, Foreign Languages Press, 2014.

which is interested in diversifying its economy, initiates cooperation with China not only in the field of transit transport, but also in the processing industry, the creation of industrial and industrial parks, in the sphere of finance, agriculture…

Today, there exists a high level of political trust and mutual understanding between the leaders of China and Kazakhstan. Mutual relations are of a strategic nature, which is confirmed by a number of agreements: the bilateral Treaty of 13 June 2011 and the Joint Declaration of the People's Republic of China and the Republic of Kazakhstan on the further deepening of comprehensive strategic partnerships of 7 September 2013.[9] The countries support each other's initiatives at all international platforms, including the UN Security Council, the SCO and the CICA. Kazakhstan was the first to support the initiative of the Chinese leader to establish a SREB, as well as the creation of new political and economic institutions for interaction and transformation of the international order. Infrastructure links, being the central theme of the OBOR initiative proclaimed in Astana in 2013, currently cover more and more new areas.

Thus, starting from the construction of the Kenkiyak-Kumkol-Atasu-Alashankou oil pipeline as a 'breakthrough' project in the field of oil delivery to world markets, the 'infrastructural reserve' has now gone beyond the energy sphere. It includes railway-corridors in the direction of the EU through the territory of the Russian Federation and through the Caspian Sea to the Caucasus and beyond; as well as the railway line to the Persian Gulf through Turkmenistan and Iran from Kazakhstan.

As Chairman Xi Jinping noted at the First Forum *Belts and Ways* in May 2017, Kazakhstan is the 'champion' in the development of transit-transport potential.[10] At the same time, the existing transport arteries in the next five years can be 'built up' by connecting to the basic transport arteries from China to the EU, to the Mediterranean Sea and to the Middle East, and additional branches to the countries of the Central Asian and Caucasus region. The presence of confirmed intentions of the countries of these regions to participate in the *Belt and Roads* enables us to expect in the future that Central Eurasia can become a large transport and logistics hub, between East and West, North and South. That is, this

---

9 Договор о добрососедстве, дружбе и сотрудничестве между Республикой Казахстан и Китайской Народной Республикой (Пекин, 23 декабря 2002 года): https://online.zakon.kz/Document/?doc_id=1038954.

10 Xi Jinping noted at the First Forum *Belts and Ways* in May 2017.

region from itself a closed space, a kind of continental periphery (landlocked area) has all the opportunities to become a fairly dynamic centre of business activity in this part of the world, along with such world transportation and logistics hubs as Rotterdam, Singapore, Dubai.

At the same time, the role of Kazakhstan in this area can be a decisive one. To this end, it seems that the priority should be not the further construction of transport arteries, but the modernisation and construction of multimodal transport and logistics centres with a modern digital service infrastructure for coordinating and tracking the transportation of goods. Moreover, it is advisable to create these centres with a free transnational usage-status in the form of special economic zones favoured by the business and trade regime for business persons from different countries.

Yet, with regard to free trade between our countries, the prospects are not very bright. The principles and tariffs of the World Trade Organisation, of which both China and Kazakhstan are members, are today largely ignored in every way. Proposals for the creation of a Free Trade Zone between China and the EEU are blocked by Russia and Kazakhstan is forced to adhere to common rules of Eurasian integration. At the same time, a certain optimism is associated with the integration trends in Central Asia. The ideas of the presidents of Kazakhstan and Uzbekistan on the joint 'development' of the Chinese food market seem promising.

III. Legal hurdles along the new silk roads

In Kazakhstan, there may be some obstacles to China's foreign direct investment (FDI). A Chinese investor who plans to implement an energy project in Kazakhstan, as in any other developing country, may be faced with an unresolved legal and regulatory environment, an uncertain continuity of existing laws and the execution of contracts. Uncertainty about the enforcement of international arbitration clauses in disputes with sovereign persons and/or government bodies in connection with the recently adopted *Law on Arbitration*, among other things, creates particular risks for foreign investors.

The main Chinese direct investments in the energy sector of Kazakhstan are still highlighted by specific approaches used by Chinese investors with respect to obtaining additional legal protection in one form or another, which otherwise is not provided for by general law. For example, to ensure the profitability of the Kazakhstan-China oil pipeline and the Central Asia-China gas pipeline, unprecedented international agreements were signed and ratified between Kazakhstan and the PRC, which created a special legal framework for these two projects and which prevail over any contradicting Kazakhstani legislation.

However, such a unique model of foreign investment can be problematic and unacceptable for Kazakhstan if it covers all investments in the energy sector within the framework of the 'One Belt, One Road Initiative'.

The multi-vector energy policy of Kazakhstan: China already controls up to 30% of the oil industry in Kazakhstan. Since 2000, Kazakhstan has moved from complete dependence on Russia regarding oil- and gas-exports to greater diversification, but now there are fears that Kazakhstan is in a dangerous dependence on China. To solve this problem, Kazakhstan has developed legal instruments to prevent further expansion of control by China, Russia or any other country in its energy sector, if necessary, including the priority right of the State to acquire/permit the transfer of so-called 'strategic assets' and also the priority right of the State to acquire/authorise transfers in the field of sub-soil use. This may be an obstacle for some energy projects initiated by China in the framework of the initiative 'One Belt, One Road'.[11]

Kazakhstan has risen to the 35th place in the *Doing Business* ranking by the World Bank,[12] the latter also ranking the country among the 20 countries most attractive to investors. In order to promote industrialisation and diversification of its economy, Kazakhstan's legislation provides for a system of benefits and preferences (for example, exemption from tax and customs duties and duties, and even government reimbursement of up to 30% of the cost of building, installing and purchasing equipment), which promotes direct investment in certain areas, including transport infrastructure, agriculture, production of refined products, as well as production, electricity.

In 2013, feed-in tariffs and guaranteed deductions were introduced to facilitate the development of renewable energy projects, and in 2015, a law on public-private partnerships (PPPs) was adopted, providing a good legal basis for PPP projects in any sector of the economy. Therefore, Chinese FDI in the framework of the 'Belt and Road Initiative' should

---

11 S. CHIKANAYEV, "Kazakhstan and the initiative 'One Belt, One Road": http://www.gratanet.com/ru/ publications/details/cblj_kazakhstan_belt_road.

12 http://www.doingbusiness.org/en/reports/global-reports/doing-business-2019.

be implemented in Kazakhstan in accordance with the general legislative framework, which is already very favourable for investors.

Kazakhstan needs to reflect about growth alternatives through diversification and innovation, rather than relying solely on natural resources. The 'Belt and Road Initiative' provides a unique opportunity for Kazakhstan to attract Chinese funds and technologies, and become one of the largest transit hubs in Eurasia and export for natural products to China.

*

In conclusion, both the 'Belt and Road' and 'Nurly Zhol' projects offer a unique opportunity. Yet, they contain a great challenge with invisible and unpredictable factors. As the 9th largest State in the world (largest landlocked), Kazakhstan has not benefitted as much from the rise of post-industrial-revolution transcontinental-trade as other nations. The Soviet political ideology and southern borders offered little opportunity for commerce in the 20th century.

The rapid revival of the Silk Road and massive infrastructure spending over the next decade, however, lead to the re-emergence of Kazakhstan as a trading hub in Central Asia. With trade between China and Europe increasing yearly, and the clear trend of smaller, high-tech goods increasing in value, the balance of trade seems to be shifting towards faster, albeit costlier, railways. More than 90% of trade between China and Europe is shipped. Less than 5% passes by rail. Continuing political and financial investment can increase trade by rail to 10% by 2025. Kazakhstan is set to gain significantly as the spatial centrepiece of the land part of the 'New Silk Road'. Opportunities for trade and industry are numerous as local businesses can benefit from lower costs of exports/imports by providing services to freight forwarders and railway carriers.

Kazakhstan uses China's 'One Belt, One Road' as a means to light a firecracker under its own business and political class and really will combine this with its national programme 'Nurly Zhol' which opens wide opportunities for the development of transport potential, both in Kazakhstan and in the Central Asian region as a whole. The implementation of the international strategy for building the economic belt of the 'Silk Road' requires the creation of a modern transport and logistics infrastructure, throughout its entire length. Kazakhstan, as a participant of this project, thanks to the programme 'Nurly Zhol', increases its transport capabilities and, including through international cooperation, has every chance of becoming a major transport and logistics hub, which will positively affect the country's economy. The strategy of building the economic belt of the 'Silk Road' is supported by all countries involved in this project, as it can create a powerful push for development and thousands of new jobs.

Theorising regional change especially in the case of the 'Shanghai cooperation'

Pierre CHABAL
Le Havre Normandie University, LexFEIM, France
and Sciences Po Europe-Asia campus
Co-founder of the Kazakh-French-Korean law seminars

What is the status of the change that is invoked to characterise 'the new Asia' in the 21st century? Is it simply political change, for example under the form of regime change? To some extent, yes, and to be sure in the early 90s, change has meant the replacement of leadership priorities, of constitutions, of border-management and of societal transformation. But is the deep, underlying nature of that change not something else as well? For instance, a historical rupture, a breaking-away from tensions, misunderstandings, vertical dominations and even risks of war or at least of 'intervention' by one neighbour into the domestic affairs of another?

From this broader perspective, I believe we ought to envisage 'change' as a 'passage' from a former order to a new order,[1] which 'the new Asia' illustrates rather well. Here we find, not just one, but two kinds of such a deep change, a prescribed change (I) and an induced change (II)

I. Prescribed change, prescribed by the will of leaders

From a centripetal dynamic, what happened after 1991 is a 'construction': State-building, Nation-building, national identity-building. Following independence, priority was given to the domestic 're-sovereigntisation' but without closing-in, except for the possible

[1] With a certain 'irreversibility' to it, hence the powerful test (for the Europeanness) represented by the hypothesis of a British exit from the EU.

exception of Turkmenistan. This relates to both State-building (A) and region-building (B).

A. State-realism and transnational ground-work

The way in which after independence the regimes of the new Republics of Central Asia chose their course was that of an all-out priority. This priority was stability and security. Not just classic security but, broadly speaking, the security derived from a *capacity to manage change*. Classic security was ensured through stability at the borders and such fundamental decisions as giving-up nuclear technology and proliferation. This was finalised in 2006 by the signing of the Treaty of Semi-Palatinsk and the establishment of a Central Asian Nuclear-Weapon-Free Zone (CANWFZ).

But broader security was brought about, beyond domestic reforms and for Tajikistan after 1997 – the end of the civil clashes between government and opposition –, by the invention of a new and innovative mode of interaction with the neighbours. First the neighbours of China in the 1990s – before and after the work of the Group of the Shanghai Five. Then in the 2000s around the rapid and concrete steps taken by i/ the inter-State Cooperation launched under the form of a Shanghai Cooperation Organisation in 2001 with one more country, Uzbekistan, not contiguous with China, and ii/ its SCO Charter in 2002 and decisions to de-militarise borders as well as organise joint military exercises against terrorism.

This, again very quickly, led to economic cooperation, joint projects on energy issues and also cultural and educational priorities.

And so, clearly, the characteristic of the new Central Asia is not just the establishment of new republics and new presidential regimes, as many western observers are prone to contend with. The new Central Asia is a construction that 'paves the way', that conceives as possible and necessary the opening of the new borders with a view to turn them from rigid, sovereign State-delimitations into functional cross-border[2] facilitation.

---

[2] See the June 2018 conference in Bishkek on the topic "Cross-border exchanges: Eurasian views on logistics and diplomacy", the American University of Central Asia.

B. Presidential constructivism and regional affirmation

As for the presidents of the republics of the new Central Asia, the time has come for an appraisal of their historical mark. The recent transition in Kazakhstan in 2019, following that in Uzbekistan late 2016, and in Turkmenistan in 2006, with Kyrgyzstan having had five elected presidents, and Tajikistan having re-elected Mr Rahmon Nabiyev in 2013 (with 3 million votes) urge historians now to turn their attention to the legacies of these presidents over the middle-term, nearly 30 years. What have these presidents built since independence, nationally and regionally but going beyond stability? What has their diplomatic and regional effort been based on? Was it just based on vertical consensus, as it seems within the Shanghai Cooperation?

On the contrary, what has been achieved is a balancing-out and a levelling-off of political odds, that were thus avoided with China and Russia. Tensions were avoided and that led to a first, tangible 'result' of nearly 30 years of 'good neighbourhood'. By contrast, the period going from the 1950s to the 1980s had witnessed hard tensions between the URSS and China, and between India and China. Nothing of the sort since the mid-1980s between Moscow and Beijing and nothing of the sort since the turn of the centuries between Beijing and New-Delhi. Historians will study documents and explain this change.

Before they do, social scientists can suggest a few conceptual accounts. Simply put, the presidents of 'the new Asia', together with the leaders of China and Russia have placed State-reconstruction in Central Asia and State-transition in China and Russia under the common and subsuming ambition to build a region, not just to operate on parallel courses. Their courses converged towards region-building, as was demonstrated recently in June 2017 by enlarging the SCO to India and Pakistan and in November 2017 by holding the Samarkand forum among the 5 Central Asian States.

In conclusion of Part I, in a way, Turkmenistan was longer to join in (accepting in 2012 to be an invited participant in the SCO), but at the Samarkand forum, Ashgabat was represented by the highest-level foreign delegation in protocol. Another evolution of notable calibre is that Afghanistan and the Afghan relevance is turning the 5-country region into a 6-party dynamics, ever since the 2005 institutional SCO-Afghanistan contact-Group and 2012 when Afghanistan became an SCO observer-State.

II. Induced change, induced by the contextual elements

From a centrifugal dynamic, that of the Shanghai Cooperation Organisation (SCO), that is how a multilateral forum 'prolongs' national dimensions. Here, we find that very *quickly* after independence, as early as 1996–2002, a sub-regional system was established, that of the sino-postsoviet Asia. This relates to both the setting-up of the SCO (A) and the launch of the OBOR (B).

A. The meaningfulness of the SCO as an impact on foreign policies

Trans-nationalist views favour the setting-up by neighbours of new systems of interaction. This seems the best manner to qualify conceptually 'the new Asia' around Central Asia. Broadly speaking, the Shanghai dynamic, before and after 1996 and after 2001, consists of a change that took two forms. First, a strategy to turn *contiguity* (as a geographic given) into a *structuring* factor of coherence. Second, transforming that *coherence* into a subsuming cohesion able to structure *relations* in the region. Here, the 2002 Charter of the SCO adopted in Russia, in St-Petersburg, comes to mind. Among its principles (article 2) is *non-interference in domestic affairs*, that is non-interference by the Organisation or its members into the internal affairs of another Member or of other Members.

Here, non-interference is an allusion to what has been called in history 'intervention' into the affairs of an ally or of a neighbour. We take here this 'principle' as having had an impact on regional attitudes and inter-State attitudes. Neither in 2005 around the Andijan crisis in Uzbekistan, nor in 2010 during the Osh crisis in Kyrgyzstan, was this principle of non-interference breached. Neither the Uzbek leadership in 2005 nor the Kyrgyz leadership in 2010 called for foreign assistance, however serious the crisis and however tempting the foreign assistance. That assistance could have been suggested not from the SCO but from the CSTO and Russia, but it would have been near-intervention.

The point here is that the SCO principle impacted national decisions and even international opportunities. Either Uzbekistan or Kyrgyzstan and even Russia could have looked to the CSTO for keeping order – after all NATO troops have been deployed outside NATO territory, in Bosnia, Kosovo and Afghanistan – but the CSTO was not called upon.

Further, the SCO is most unlikely to intervene in Afghanistan, despite the fact that Afghanistan is not an SCO member (or not yet?).

B. The SCO as preparatory tool for New Silk Roads, 'Belt and Road Initiative'?

What is the ultimate logic behind the SCO dynamic? A number of hypotheses exist as to the real strategy, notably of China, behind the creation of a new manner to monitor the existence of a 'new Asia'.

i/ One hypothesis is *energy*. The new Asia would aim for an energy Club bringing together the contiguous producers *and* consumers with transport by *land*, no longer by shipping. Hence the possibility to 'detach' the new Asia from world energy markets.

ii/ Another hypothesis is the Sino-Russian *rivalry*. The new Asia would aim mainly at securing that this rivalry be *contained* within institutional mechanisms, avoiding tensions and escalation. Incidentally, this would concern also India and Pakistan, hence the enlightened SCO decision to admit in 2017 both together as members (avoiding the European 'mistake' in 1981 to admit Greece and not Turkey).

iii/ A third hypothesis is *OBOR*, suggesting an *a posteriori* reconstruction of the original aim. An original aim since when? 1978 and the Chinese modernisation? 1985 and the Soviet *perestroika*? 1992–1996 and the border-negotiations? 2002 and the principles of St-Petersburg (article 3)? 2006 and the Russian suggestion of an SCO energy Club? To be sure, the deciphering begins in 2013 and the Chinese president's speech at the Nazarbayev university, in the capital city of Nursultan/Astana. The rationale thus suddenly appears simple: first to secure good-neighbourhood as a *structing* reality; second to turn neighbours, SCO members as well as SCO affiliates, into investment-*partners* for massive transport-infrastructures; third, to design corridors across the *whole* continent of *Eurasia* by land that i) facilitate China's exports and ii) at the same time as they serve the interests of land-locked countries, especially in Central Asia.

Seen in this light, the Shanghai dynamic of the SCO could lead a complete change of the continent, turning China's export-routes from the sea into a combined mastery of both the sea and the land, and also turning the geographic situation from a handicap (being land-locked) into an advantage (being a land-bridge).

In conclusion of part II, the present historical period is no longer characterised mainly by being the post-cold war situation. It is a situation when geographical characteristics are being turned into fully open and fully supportive geo-strategic and geo-economic bases for commercial domination.

*

In conclusion of the whole presentation, what is clear is that in order to understand the *New* Asia beyond *old* western concepts, it is necessary to leave aside to a large extent *European* 'categories of the mind'. i/ The Asian form of region-building is different from the European one not only in details but also in origins and in perspectives. ii/ The aim of European region-building is integration, that is to say supra-sovereign integration. iii/ The aim of Asian region-building is cooperation, that is to say 'juxta-sovereign' dynamics. And so, without rejecting all forms of European and Western thought in/from International Relations, we must, in this 21st century, 'bring back' Asian thought, Asian 'ideas' of region into academic analysis.

Kazakhstan-China strategic partnership under the 'Belt and Road Initiative'[1]

Kuralay Baizakova, Fatima Kukeyeva, Zhulduz Baizakova
al-Farabi Kazakh National University, Almaty, Kazakhstan

On 16 September 2013 at Nazarbayev University in Astana Xi Jinping presented a comprehensive and ambitious 'Belt and Road Initiative' (BRI), which would extend across the entire Eurasian continent. The BRI went on to receive full support in Central Asian countries, in particular in Kazakhstan, where the search for economically effective corridors, market expansion, establishment of equal access to common infrastructure, and attracting investments in its economy are absolutely vital. Kazakhstan plays an important role in world economic processes thanks to its significant reserves of natural resources and its location at the intersection of major transcontinental trade and transportation routes.

Kazakhstan, with its enormous territory, small population and lack of sea access has always been located on the periphery of the global trade of goods. Participation in the BRI will enable the country to move away from its dependence on the export of hydrocarbons and to develop other sectors of its economy. Without the necessary transport infrastructure, Kazakhstan's vast open spaces would be a barrier, but with that infrastructure they would be an advantage. Consequently, Kazakhstan's interest in the success of this initiative is evident for a partnership with China (I) with benefits (II) out-weighing risks (III).

---

1 This article was prepared as part of a scientific project of the Kazakhstan Ministry of Education titled "The new trends of global and regional integration: the integration policy of the Republic of Kazakhstan as an essential part of the state's foreign policy", 2019.

I. Strategic partnership

The strategic partnership of Kazakhstan and China is based on the principle of 'mutual complementarity', that is, combining the advantages of two States, which will make it possible to form a modern large-scale 'development partnership': strengthening political contacts as prerequisite for effective interaction; development of communication as the basis for cooperation; removing trade barriers as the key goal, and financing as the guarantee, and people-to-people relations as the root of cooperation.

For effective initiative-realisation, intergovernmental cooperation should be strengthened, actively, promoting mutual contacts, freely sharing information on economic development strategies and measures taken, through consultations to jointly resolve problems in cooperation, in order to create favourable political support for the implementation of large-scale projects. Since 2012, 18 summits have been held within the framework of bilateral relations, which indicates a high degree of conjugation of the two countries' strategies in the field of implementing the BRI. Heads of State, prime ministers and deputy prime ministers of the two countries visited and met to study specific issues of mutually-beneficial cooperation, to ensure the continuous deepening of bilateral mutual trust and the strengthening of interaction.

Speaking at the Second Forum of International Cooperation *Belt and Road* in 2019, N. Nazarbayev stated the need to introduce three geopolitical dialogues that will give a powerful impetus to the development of countries and will accelerate the growth of economies of the participating countries.[2] Interconnection of the infrastructure of the two countries is the vital and priority direction for the BRI projects implementation, which includes not only facilitating international highways construction, but also coordinating participants of their plans for building infrastructure programmes. In an attempt to diversify its economy, the government of Kazakhstan has attached particular importance to the intensive development of transport infrastructure. Since 2015 the 'Nurly Zhol' programme, aimed at the modernisation of the country's

---

2 Мягкая сила Китая и проект 'Три Д' Назарбаева – итоги форума Один пояс и один путь: https://ru.sputniknews.kz/economy/20190427/9981680/odin-poyas-odin-put-itogi.html /04.2019.

transport assets, has been underway.[3] By 2020 projects totalling over 40 billion $ will be completed. Funds supplied by international banks will go towards the construction of highways from the centre to the south, east, and west of the country. Thanks to its geopolitical position as a transport link in the system of multi-levelled interactions between Asia and Europe, Kazakhstan announced its intention to become a regional transit hub.[4]

The creation of the Kazakhstan national transport programme 'Nurly Zhol' has enabled Kazakhstan to integrate effectively into the BRI. China reacted positively to the programme as many of its top priorities mirrored those of the SREB. One of the decisive factors in the success of this project will be Chinese investments, vital for the country's transit modernisation. Over five years now, a number of large infrastructure projects were put into operation, including the port of Lianyungang; the dry port of Khorgos on the border with China; the port of Aktau on the Caspian Sea; a new railway corridor 'Kazakhstan – Turkmenistan – Iran' with a total length of about 900 km, connecting the countries of Central Asia with the Persian Gulf and the port of Bandar Abbas in southern Iran; international transit corridor 'Western Europe – Western China', part of which passes through the territory of Kazakhstan. This makes possible to deliver goods from China through Kazakhstan to Europe in about 15 days, while delivery by sea takes 2–2.5 times more.

In addition to the infrastructure aspect, investment interaction is an integral BRI strategy component, viewed as a large-scale investment project involving the development of the participating countries in many areas. At present, China occupies one of the leading places in terms of foreign direct investment in the Kazakhstani economy. Over the past 10 years, more than $15 billion has been invested in Kazakhstan projects by the neighbouring State.[5] Within the BRI framework a joint programme for cooperation in the field of industry and investment

---

3 Государственная программа инфраструктурного развития 'Нұрлы жол' на 2015–2019 годы: https://www.baiterek.gov.kz/ru/programma-nurly-zol.

4 The Address of the President of the Republic of Kazakhstan 'Nurly Zhol – a Way to the Future': https://e-history.kz/en/contents/view/the_address_of_the_president_of_the_republic_of_kazakhstan_nurly_zhol__a_way_to_the_future__2647.

5 Казахстанско-китайское сотрудничество в рамках программы 'Один пояс, один путь' обсудили в Астане: https://primeminister.kz/ru/news/all/kazahstansko-kitaiskoe-sotrudnichestvo-v-ramkah-programmi-odin-poyas-odin-put-obsudili-v-astane-17096.

is working. According to this programme, 51 of the Kazakh-Chinese investment projects worth more than $27 billion are developing.[6]

In December 2016 the Silk Road Fund (SRF) was registered in Beijing. In 2018, the Fund and the National Company 'Kazakh Invest' signed a framework agreement on the establishment of a Kazakhstan-China production capacity fund – KCPCF) with a capitalisation of $2 billion. This will positively affect the development of investment activity in Kazakhstan.

The China CITIC Group actively supports the BRI construction and regards Kazakhstan as one of the most important countries participating in the route investment. The CITIC Group established cooperation with the relevant industries in Kazakhstan. Together with CITIC, Kazyna Capital created a CITIC Kazyna investment fund. This is the first fund created by two countries. Its total capital, $800 million, focuses on the Kazakh-Chinese non-resource sector. In 2016, the CITIC Group received the general contracting activities of two national projects on the reconstruction of highways in Kazakhstan.[7]

The energy sector remains the most important component of the Chinese strategy in Kazakhstan. The latter, using its resource advantages, stimulates economic development to protect its national interests. The cooperation in the oil sector that has developed over more than twenty years testifies to the established rules of mutually beneficial cooperation. The two countries are confident that the oil and gas sector is effectively integrated into the BRI. For example, the CNPC actively supports the modernisation of Kazakhstan's oil industry. The project to upgrade the Shymkent refinery is realised with the participation of Chinese investors. In Kazakhstan, the company paid more than $42 billion in taxes and fees and supported a social security project with $360 million, guaranteeing work for over 30,000 people. At the next stage, the CNPC is ready to continue cooperation in order to actively

6 Казахстан и Китай реализуют 51 совместный проект на сумму $27 млрд: https://eadaily.com/ru/news/2018/09/07/kazahstan-i-kitay-realizuyut-51-sovmestnyy-proekt-na-summu-27-mlrd.

7 Заместитель Генерального директора CITIC Group, председатель правления CITIC Securities Чжан Юцзюнь: https://primeminister.kz/ru/news/all/kazahstansko-kitaiskoe-sotrudnichestvo-v-ramkah-programmi-odin-poyas-odin-put-obsudili-v-astane-17096.

promote Kazakhstan-China oil and gas cooperation to a deeper level.[8] Kazakhstan has become China's largest trading partner. In 2017, foreign trade turnover between them amounted to $10.5 billion. Since the period of establishing diplomatic relations, the current bilateral trade has increased almost 40 times.[9]

Trade and economic cooperation between Kazakhstan and the China are characterised by complementarity. The two countries are trying to actively expand the areas of trade and economic cooperation in conditions going even further than the oil and gas sector, to make an effective locomotive for the development of the Kazakhstani economy. The BRI implementation could solve the problem of poor infrastructure, which creates difficulties for bilateral trade. It should be considered that a new era begins in the trade sphere – these are the transfers of spontaneous trade to new standards, the intensification of online sales by foreign retailers, and the development of master plans for cities with regard to trade.

Successful BRI implementation largely depends on mutual trust between the peoples of Kazakhstan and China. The Chinese authorities begin to better understand that Beijing meets the resistance to its influence in the economic, business and socio-cultural spheres. China has embarked on a concerted offensive of public diplomacy, focusing on people-to-people contacts in order to change its image in the region and interact with broader communities and stakeholders. Chinese influential political figures are taking decisive action to change the perception of the country that has emerged in the West and dominates the world. China wants to be seen as a reliable economic partner interested in mutually beneficial achievement of common objectives, but without any political goals. The strategy of Chinese soft power is promoting the image of Beijing as a reliable and pragmatic economic alternative to the West and Russia.

---

8 Казахстанско-китайское сотрудничество в рамках программы 'Один пояс, один путь' обсудили в Астане: https://primeminister.kz/ru/news/all/kazahstansko-kitaiskoe-sotrudnichestvo-v-ramkah-programmi-odin-poyas-odin-put-obsudili-v-astane-17096.

9 Внешнеторговый оборот Казахстана составил свыше 90 млрд долларов в 2018 году: https://bnews.kz/ru/news/vneshnetorgovii_oborot_kazahstana_sostavil_svishe_90_mlrd_dollarov_v_2018_godu.

II. BRI opportunities for Kazakhstan

Co-operation between Kazakhstan and China can contribute to the development of Kazakhstan's transit potential. The Chinese idea and the 'Nurly Zhol' programme have converging interests in the development of transport and logistical infrastructure on Kazakhstan's territory. This is what the 2016–2017 agreements between Kazakhstan and China and the issuance of credit lines from China are aimed at. A 'road map' to expand bilateral co-operation in all sectors of the economy, along with the creation of a joint working group on the integration of the SREB and 'Nurly Zhol' has been created.

According to the plans four areas of co-operation are anticipated.[10]

i/ development of a transit corridor, creation of logistical centres in Kazakhstan and simplification of procedures (customs, tax, financial, etc.) with the intention to expand bilateral trade. Kazakhstan's goal is to pick up part of the trade flow between China and Europe;

ii/ joint industrial projects. The first group includes 45 agreements, 25 of which are parts of signed contracts totalling 23 billion $. The overall co-operation programme in this area includes 51 projects with Chinese credits amounting to 50 billion $ in 2015;

iii/ co-operation in science-driven and high-tech sectors. Astana and Beijing are considering one to two areas in which Kazakhstan and China will collaborate at the level of scientific institutes, universities, as well as in the creation of joint enterprises. For the time being, discussions are underway about the areas in which Kazakhstan and China will collaborate, but neither institutes, nor universities where the collaboration would be carried out have been finalised;

iv/ co-operation in agriculture. Today Kazakhstan and China are working on 19 projects totalling more than 1.7 billion $. Recently, agreements have been reached about the creation of several more major joint projects in the agriculture sector. For example, the Chinese company *Rifa Holding Group* aims to invest in the construction of a meat-packing plant in Eastern Kazakhstan Region. 80% of the plants' production will be exported to China. The project is estimated at 7.9 billion *tenge*. The CITIC Corporation signed

10 Внешнеторговый оборот Казахстана составил свыше 90 млрд долларов в 2018 году: https://bnews.kz/ru/news/vneshnetorgovii_oborot_kazahstana_sostavil_svishe_90_mlrd_dollarov_v_2018_godu.

an agreement with the *Bayterek* holding company to undertake projects relating to feed lots and poultry farms. The Hong Kong financial group *Oriental Patron* plans to invest in the Kazakhstan company *Kazeksportastyk* to develop agricultural product processing with goods destined for the Chinese market. The investments total around 500 million $.[11]

All the afore-mentioned facts are proof that areas of integration between 'Nurly Zhol' and *SREB* have not only been selected, but have taken shape in the form of concrete projects. Even more importantly, they have already been funded. A major jump took place in 2014–2015 when guaranteed Chinese investments into the Kazakhstan economy grew threefold.[12]

III. Challenges and risks of Kazakhstan's BRI participation

In taking advantage of new opportunities and benefits of cooperation with China as part of the SREB, Kazakhstan must minimise possible risks and challenges. Clearly, when countries with considerable differences in potential are involved in joint projects, this inevitably creates contradictions not only economic in character, but also political, socio-cultural, environmental, etc.

While Kazakh authorities make claims about future prospects, there is increased anxiety in society around the consequences of such a shift. Many projects have non-transparent contract application procedures and financial terms that are not subject to public scrutiny. A part of the money invested is lost due to corruption and administrative dysfunction, and projects are evaluated mainly by their profitability rather than by meeting the standards of sustainable development.[13]

Although Chinese loans increase economic activity, and contribute to the growth of trade in Central Asia, the region risks becoming dependent

---

[11] Алибекова Р. ТНК из Поднебесной: интерес к Казахстану растет: www.kazpravda.kz/fresh/view/tnk-iz-podnebesnoi-interes-k-kazahstanu-rastet.

[12] Сыроежкин К. Геополитческие проекты в Центральной Азии и роль Казахстана: http://cabar.asia/ru/konstantin-syroezhkin-geopoliticheskie-proekty-v-tsentralnoj-azii-i-rol-kazahstana.

[13] "Один пояс, один путь" – это 'золотое дно' для коррупции: https://forbes.kz/massmedia/odin_poyas_odin_put_-_eto_zolotoe_dno_korruptsii.

on China's investments to maintain and develop the infrastructure built under the BRI. Beijing has gained control over individual infrastructure projects through equity agreements, long-term leases or multi-year contracts. For example, Tajikistan has already fallen into debt-dependence on Beijing, to which the Tajik authorities have transferred the gold deposit on account of the debt.[14]

The implementation of the BRI projects often suggests to use Chinese firms and labour, which does not involve local employment. The Chinese side is practicing complex agreements related to the interests of Chinese firms. Preferential loans for infrastructure projects provide that at least half of the materials, equipment, technology and services procured under the contract must come from China. Another key condition for easy lending is the involvement of Chinese companies, which enables Chinese State-owned enterprises to expand overseas by acquiring foreign contracts and resources.[15] Thus, from 2012 to 2015, the number of Chinese workers under contract increased from 5,000 to 15,000 people.[16]

In some cases, initiatives are realised without adequate environmental assessment or have caused serious damage to the environment. The Chinese government has launched a new political model 'Ecological Civilisation', that aims to minimise environmental pollution, to introduce 'green technology', etc. To this end, the question of which businesses China is relocating to Kazakhstan becomes relevant (operation of productions, environmental safety, outlook on product distribution, etc.). Importing businesses with 'dirty' technology threatens the development of 'yesterday's' resource economy in Central Asian countries while delaying their technological development in relation to China.

Much discussion has been dedicated to the question of integrating BRI with Kazakhstan's programme 'Nurly Zhol' and the Eurasian Economic Union (EAEU). Kazakhstan, along with Russia, was the founder of the economic integration bloc EEU in the post-Soviet space. It is possible that the EAEU and BRI will be able to integrate successfully despite the

14 Таджикистан расплатился с Китаем золоторудным месторождением: https://eadaily.com/ru/news/2018/04/16/tadzhikistan-rasplatilsya-s-kitaem-zolotorudnym-mestorozhdeniem.

15 Инициатива 'Пояс и путь' Китая и её влияние в Центральной Азии: https://caa-network.org/archives/12138.

16 National Bureau of Statistics of China: www.stats.gov.cn/english.

fact that their aims differ substantially: the EAEU aims to develop the domestic market, create new ones and modernise existing industries in alternative sectors of the economy. A significant potential for cooperation and the existence of areas of mutual interests within the framework will facilitate the integration of the EAEU and SREB.

For Kazakhstan, the harmonisation in relations between 'Nurly Zhol', the BRI, and the EEU is critical. The EEU and BRI are two of the most tangible projects that will lay the foundation for a Greater United Eurasian Economic Community. The integration of all three projects would become a model of the shift from competition to a level of inter-country, inter-continental economic co-operation. Between 'Nurly Zhol', BRI, and the EEU, Kazakhstan could act as a bridge in China and Russia's multi-dimensional relations.

Anti-Chinese sentiments are a serious roadblock in the implementation of BRI. While Central Asian elites welcome the flow of finance, Chinese businesses have been encountering xenophobia from the local population. One of the most widespread fears is that Chinese economic, demographic, and military expansion will, as a result, lead to a loss of sovereignty. Kazakh authorities unintentionally incited another wave of Sinophobia in 2010 when it was announced that Kazakhstan would lease farmland to China over the course of several decades which quickly prompted protests. Ultimately the deal did not go through.

The Kazakh side must raise the question of expanding cultural-humanitarian co-operation and building bridges between people (people-to-people bridges). This will enable Kazakhstanis to better recognise and understand Kazakhstan's strategic partnership with China. Favourable public opinion should become the foundation for co-operation in the 'Belt and Road Initiative'. Non-governmental forms of cultural exchange should be more diverse, and communication among business and cultural elites should be established. The rise of Sinophobia can be stopped with the help of the mass media, the internet, public diplomacy, a large-scale PR campaign that would clarify the goals and purposes of the SREB programme, its integration with 'Nurly Zhol', and the expected dividends for the local population and the State. It is essential to explain to the public questions associated with the transfer of excess Chinese manufacturing capacity to Kazakhstan, as well as joint projects in the agriculture sector. Easily available information would dispel speculation and rumours.

To foster constructive discussion and critique of the impact of BRI on the socio-economic landscape in Kazakhstan, it is important that there be a wide range of experts, including independent experts, who would not be restricted in preparing analytical materials for branches of government, and who would develop tools to influence public opinion. Building constructive relations with China must be based on cohesive expertise concerning the pluses and minuses in decision-making. The question of developing principles and framework for cooperation with China remains relevant. Experts must thoroughly analyse the objective benefits of each side, and correspondingly, clarify and adjust the agenda of bilateral co-operation. A lack of quality expertise on the Chinese *problématique* will make it impossible for Kazakhstan to form its own agenda in how bilateral relations develop further. Despite the expansion and deepening of co-operation and growth of China's influence in the world, there is in Kazakhstan a lack of demand for a 'think-tank on China'. These, among other factors, explain the absence of a school of Sinologists in Kazakhstan.

How to simplify customs and visa procedures so as to remove barriers for the expansion of trade and tourism is a question that remains open. People-to-people diplomacy brings the two societies closer together and reduces the level of fear relative to one another. One of the five main directions declared in China's partnership with the Silk Way countries is the 'bringing together of peoples' This consists of a wide range of areas for collaboration: cultural exchanges, scientific contacts, partnerships between mass media and volunteer organisations', and tourism among others.

*

In conclusion, at present, the BRI and its projects implementation has not yet become systematic and it is difficult to talk of the strategic partnership between RK and PRC that has been formed. The main characteristic of a strategic partnership is complementarity, which involves using the advantages of one partner for the disclosure and development of the potential of another. Despite the risks, participation in the BRI is more beneficial for Kazakhstan, as it helps realising the country's transit potential, thereby opening up Kazakhstan to new trade and economic opportunities. One of the main expected results should be diversification and withdrawal from a resource-dependent economy. For China, the strategic partnership with Kazakhstan is only a small part of the global policy under the BRI. Therefore, for domestic politicians and the expert community, it is very important to have a well-thought-out strategy for Kazakhstan's participation in the BRI in order to be able to shape their own agenda.

Legal migration regulations of Kazakhstani-Chinese relations: prospects of the 'Belt and Road Initiative' and the Eurasian Economic Union

Zulfiya Baimagambetova, Leila Delovarova
al-Farabi Kazakh National University, Almaty, Kazakhstan

Migration processes became one of the vital aspects of the current transformation in new geo-economic and geo-political relations. Global mobility covers practically every world-region and requires new and proper legal approaches. Chinese-Kazakhstani relations in this field are of great interests: migration processes between them display various dynamics and relevant aspects to study as to sustainable development and international cooperation.

The conjugation of the Eurasian Economic Union (EAEU) and Economic Belt of the Silk Road (EBSR) enhance this relevance of migration. China and Kazakhstan, strategic partners and good-neighbours, share a history of cooperation in the economic, political, cultural and educational fields. Kazakhstan's foreign policy concept sees the country as developing an all-round strategic cooperation with the PRC as part of a political dialogue at the highest level, developing investment in energy, technology, trade and cultural cooperation, cooperation, in particular the transit transport and cross-border water resources, rivers, agriculture and ecology.[1]

---

1 Foreign Policy Concept for 2014–2020 Republic of Kazakhstan: http://mfa.gov.kz/en/erevan/content-view/koncepcia-vnesnej-politiki-rk-na-2014-2020-gg.

Chinese-Kazakhstani diplomatic relations, established on 3 January 1992,[2] have formed in 25 years legal principles of a mutual development, signing about 300 documents on bilateral cooperation in the political, economic, security and cultural fields. China is one of the biggest investors in Kazakhstan, it supports and promotes cooperation with the Kazakhstan through the frameworks of the SCO and the CICA.

Migration processes are thus an important component of their bilateral relations. Mobility covers both directions and plays an essential role in the economic, political, cultural and educational fields. The factors fuelling migration processes cover historical and ethno-cultural ties as well as the revival traditions of the Silk Road. The two countries share geographical proximity of extended joint borders, the Kazakh diaspora in Xinjiang that underwent a repatriation programme and serves business, trade and the need for skilled personnel in Kazakhstan. These objective needs of the bilateral cooperation for labour resources for China's infrastructural projects in Kazakhstan connect with the New Silk Road.

I. Key migration trends and law base between Kazakhstan and China

Migration processes are an essential factor for Kazakhstan's development. This country was transformed from one of mass out-flow of migrants during the Soviet disintegration, into one that accepts migrants. As an actor of migration processes, it observes all types of migration: immigration, emigration, as well as transit corridors from Central Asia to Russia and Europe. From the years of independence of modern Kazakhstan, the regulation of migration processes has become a clear direction of State policy: ethnic migration (repatriation), import of foreign labour, refugees and internal migration of the population.

Its demographic potential is a defining aspect for the national development of migration. According to the Committee on statistics of the Ministry of National Economy, as of January 1, 2018, Kazakhstan's population was 18,157,078 people. Increasing and strengthening this demographic potential is one of the State's strategic tasks. Over the last quarter of a century, the balance in external migration has changed from negative,

---

2 Kazakh-Chinese relations at present stage: http://e-history.kz/en/conten ts/view/2162.

shortly after independence, to positive, then to negative again in recent years. According official agencies, during 1991–2003, the outflow averaged 225,000 people per year.[3] During 2004–2011, the balance was positive with an increase of 11,700 people per year and the volume of labour migration constantly increased. In the last five-year period, the migration balance again entered the negative zone.[4] What are the results of ethnic migration since 1991? A number of ethnic returnees over one million. Due to this demographic contribution of arriving repatriates-oralmans, the negative balance was reduced to –28%.[5]

Migration processes in Kazakhstan cover various dynamics and trends. At the present stage, the country is positioning itself as the destination for migrants from post-Soviet Central Asia – Kyrgyzstan, Tajikistan and Uzbekistan, but also as sending country to Russia, EU, UAE, etc. The role of Kazakhstan as a transit hub is increasing in the context of developing infrastructural projects as One Belt, One Road and the Eurasian Economic Union. The interregional, multidirectional migration, which covers the Eurasian space, South-East Asia, Europe and North America, is gaining in increasing dynamics.[6] This chapter attempts to look comparatively at demographic potential and migration processes of China, even if focusing on aspects of it referring to Kazakhstan.

As for China, as a demographic giant and one of the fastest growing economies in the world, its 2018 population was 1.42 billion, based on UN projections.[7] Highlighting selected aspects of Chinese migration to Kazakhstan, this chapter meets with the serious lack of statistical data on Chinese migrants of all categories in Kazakhstan. China and Kazakhstan are connected by intensive migration flows that mostly cover such types of migration as business migration, trade migration, labour migration,

---

3 The Government adopted the concept of a new migration policy (in Russian): https://kapital.kz/gosudarstvo/63101/pravitelstvo-prinyalo-koncepciyu-novoj-migracionnoj-politiki.html.

4 Qualified personnel actively leaving Kazakhstan (in Russian): https://forbes.kz/news/2017/11/14/159290/.

5 The Concept of the Migration Policy of the Republic of Kazakhstan for 2017–2021 has been approved: https://www.zakon.kz/4883043-utverzhdena-kontseptsiya-migratsionnoy.html.

6 L. F. DELOVAROVA, "Some migration aspects, trends and issues in the North and Central Asia: case of Kazakhstan": http://bulletin-ir-law.kaznu.kz/index.php/1-mo/article/view/748/728CTP 38-47.

7 China population 2018: http://worldpopulationreview.com/countries/china-population.

repatriation migration (from Xinjiang) and educational migration. According to experts, migration from China is less concerned by Han Chinese and includes mostly Kazakhs, Uyghurs, Dungans, Koreans, Uzbeks and other ethnic groups.[8]

The question of precise statistics of migrants from/to China remains acute for Kazakhstani scholars. Numerous myths also surround the flows of migrants, which affects the reliability of statistics. What is then possible is to refer to official sources from foreign representations such as the Embassy of the Republic of Kazakhstan. According to statistics provided by the RK Ambassador in China, Shakhrat Nuryshev, the number of visas issued in Beijing, Shanghai, Hong Kong and Urumqi as a whole can be cited.[9]

In 2015, a total of 118,321 visas were issued to Chinese citizens. Of these, 83,358 visas (more than 70%) were issued to ethnic Kazakhs residing in China, 19,000 were business visas, 10,000 served workers, 4,600 for tourists and 173 were educational visas.[10] In 2016 (first nine months), 86,203 visas were issued, of which 58,474 (about 68%) were issued to ethnic Kazakhs residing in the PRC. More than 15,000 business visas were issued, more than 6,000 for workers, 5,000 tourist and 299 for study, 322 for service, 23 to investors and 56 were transit visas.[11] This data from the RK Embassy Beijing, the consulates general in Shanghai and Hong Kong, and the passport- and visa-service in Urumqi, corresponds to reasonable estimates, according to which, about 500,000 Chinese arrive annually to Kazakhstan. Yet, this data on visas does not reflect the flows of irregular migration in both directions. It seems that this type of migration is the most problematic aspect for both countries to pay proper attention and to strengthen cooperation between responsible agencies at the State level.

---

8 Y. SADOVSKAYA, "China's Rise in Kazakhstan and Its Impact on Migration", Research Paper, 2016. MIRPAL, Regional Migration Program by the World Bank, IOM, UN Women, DFID, Moscow, Almaty, 120 p.

9 Kazakhstan's Ambassador to China, Shakhrat Nuryshev, commented on rumors about the mass entry of Chinese into the territory of the Republic (in Russian): https://365info.kz/2016/11/posol-oproverg-sluhi-o-massovoj-migratsii-kitajtsev-v-kazahstan.

10 *Ibidem.*

11 *Ibidem.*

II. Legal bases and legislation of migration

Coordination and regulation of migration processes is a key aspect of modern international law. Although international migration is a process in which at least two States are involved, the definition of conditions is the prerogative of each State. It is crucial that legislation be developed reflecting the main migration trends and realities not only at the national, regional level, but also taking into account the global context. The main problem here is the collisions that arise in the process of the operation of these laws. This is a common problem of modern international law.

Migration processes between China and Kazakhstan are based on the certain legislation. This chapter refers to some legislation migration coordination between two countries with the focus on Kazakhstan's law. The following key laws and regulations coordinate migration from China to Kazakhstan: General provisions include the Constitution of the Republic of Kazakhstan, 1995; the Law of the Republic of Kazakhstan 'On Citizenship' of 20 December 1991 No. 1017-XII; the Law of the Republic of Kazakhstan of 19 June 1995 No. 2337 'On the legal status of foreign citizens in the Republic of Kazakhstan'; the Decree of the President of the Republic of Kazakhstan 'On the procedure for granting political asylum to foreign citizens and Stateless persons in the Republic of Kazakhstan' of 15 July 1996, No. 3057; the Law of the Republic of Kazakhstan of 4 December 2009 No. 216-IV 'On Refugees'; the Law of the Republic of Kazakhstan 'On Migration' No. 477-IV of 22 July 2011 (as amended and supplemented as of 16 April 2018); the Resolution of the Government of the Republic of Kazakhstan of 29 September 2017 No. 602. On the approval of the Concept of the Migration Policy of the Republic of Kazakhstan for 2017–2021 and the Action Plan for the Implementation of the Concept of the Migration Policy of the Republic of Kazakhstan for 2017–2021; the Address of the President of the Republic of Kazakhstan, Nursultan Nazarbayev, to the People of Kazakhstan, 1 March 2006. Kazakhstan's strategy of joining the world's 50 most competitive countries; the Address of the President of the Republic of Kazakhstan, Nursultan Nazarbayev, to the People of Kazakhstan, December, 2012. Strategy 'Kazakhstan-2050'.

In the field of labour and business, relevant texts include: the Agreement between the Government of the Republic of Kazakhstan and the Government of the People's Republic of China on temporary employment of citizens of the Republic of Kazakhstan in the People's Republic of China and citizens of the People's Republic of China in the Republic of Kazakhstan, committed in Astana on 7 September 2013 (approved by the Resolution of the Government of the Republic of Kazakhstan dated 8 July 2014 No. 784).

In the field of tourism, legislation includes: the Memorandum between the Ministry of Investment and Development of the Republic Kazakhstan and the State Administration for Tourism of the People's Republic of China on the simplification of group tourist trips of Chinese citizens to the Republic of Kazakhstan (Beijing, 14 December 2015).

In the field of education, a selection of legislation includes the Agreement between the Ministry of Education and Science of the Republic of Kazakhstan and Ministry of Education of the PRC of 3 June 2003; the Agreement between the Governments of the Republic of Kazakhstan and the People's Republic of China on mutual recognition of documents on education and academic degrees from 20 December 2006; the Protocol on Amendments and Additions to the Agreement between the Ministry of Education and Science of the Republic of Kazakhstan and the Ministry of Education of the PRC on Cooperation in the Field of Education of 3 June 2003, dated 16 April 2009.

The existing legal framework is a good platform for the all-round development of bilateral relations. At the same time, it needs substantial strengthening, development and supplementation. It is the migration component that is the engine of progress in the contemporary international realities. Recognition of migration by the UN as an important component of sustainable development and the reflection of migration in the 17 Sustainable Development Goals[12] indicate the need for change, both at the national level and on a bilateral and multilateral basis. Law and legislation are the essential step for it. Business, trade and labour migration are vital fields to cooperate especially within the enlargement of transit potential usage, energy interaction, increasing turnover between two countries, investment and functioning of Khorgos checkpoint.

The sphere of education is very important for bilateral relations. Moreover, this trend is two-sided. According to some expert data (Syroezhkin), about 14,000 Kazakhstani students are studying in China. Most of the grants are from the Chinese side. In Kazakhstan,

---

[12] Sustainable Development Goals: https://www.un.org/sustainabledevelopment/sustainable-development-goals.

the Confucius Institute is active. Within the SCO, the SCO University is functioning for the Member-States and it has opened new aspects for the Organisation. The educational, business, trade and labour aspects of migration between Kazakhstan and China are very important in the context of enhancing comprehensive cooperation, especially in the process of implementing the mega-project 'One Belt, One Road'.

'One Belt, One Road' (OBOR) is a strategy of the PRC government, aimed at developing cooperation between countries, primarily on the Eurasian mainland. The strategy consists of two parts: the 'Economic Belt of the Silk Road' (EBSR) and the 'Sea Silk Road' (SSR). The project was first internationally announced by President Xi Jinping on 7 September 2013 at Nazarbayev University, Astana, Kazakhstan.[13] The concept is based on five principles: political convergence, infrastructure ties, free trade, circulation of capital, rapprochement of peoples. It aims at opening up transportation channels from the Pacific to the Baltic Sea and form gradually a transportation network connecting East Asia, West Asia, and South Asia.[14] All of its five parts should strengthen cooperation and friendship as it will open and realise great transit potential through the regions. Migration processes are thus mechanisms promoting the key principles of the OBOR.

'One Belt, One Road' (OBOR) initiative and the Eurasian Economic Union are also mixed, as are the bilateral level – Kazakhstan's 'Nurly Zhol' (Bright Road) programme and OBOR. Modern Kazakhstan, located in the heart of Eurasia, can be a stronger transit bridge in the system of multi-level interrelations of the countries of Asia and Europe. The development of internal transport and accessibility of international transport links form important components of any State's economic and political independence. Kazakhstan's government actively supports the OBOR initiative. Cooperation on it is already begun. According to experts, for Kazakhstan and other Central Asian countries, since independence, the role of international transport communications has been and remains particularly significant.[15] The project meets these expectations and strengthens cooperation with China.

---

13 President Xi Jinping Delivers Important Speech and Proposes to Build a Silk Road Economic Belt with Central Asian Countries, 2013/09/07: http://www.fmprc.gov.cn/mfa_eng/topics_665678/xpfwzysiesgjtfhshzzfh_665686/t1076334.shtml.

14 *Ibidem.*

15 S.K. KUSHKUMBAEV, "Prospects for the implementation of the project The economic belt of the Silk Road and the State programme 'Nurly Zhol'" (in

That President Xi Jinping's speech on OBOR was presented in Kazakhstan means for the latter that OBOR can realise the transit potential and improve internal infrastructure. The new economic policy of 'Nurly Zhol' declared by President N. Nazarbayev in November 2014, correlates with plans of an 'Economic Belt of the Silk Road'. Launched in recent years, sections of the international highway 'Western China – Western Europe', together with the railway 'Kazakhstan – Turkmenistan – Iran – Persian Gulf', can become an organic part of the modern routes of the Silk Road.[16]

The 'Nurly Zhol' programme aims at a comprehensive continuation of the course of reforms in the Kazakhstan's economy. The goal is to form a single economic market by integrating macro-regions of the country on the basis of building an effective infrastructure hub for long-term economic growth in Kazakhstan, as well as the implementation of anti-crisis measures to support specific sectors of the economy in the conditions on external markets conjuncture deterioration.[17]

Kazakhstan and China are actively cooperating in the field of industrialisation and investment: one such programme covers 51 projects worth $26 billion. Three projects have already been implemented, six projects are currently under implementation, other projects are actively working, and it is planned that they will be implemented consistently in the period 2018–2020.[18] The interaction is very tight is very at all governmental levels.

This programme is a key in the context of the development of national infrastructure of Kazakhstan for internal needs, social development, investment and realisation of external functions as a transport and transit hub. This vision fits with the implementation of OBOR and in turn connected with migration processes as inside the country as within the EAEU and China.

Russian): http://kisi.kz/ru/categories/geopolitika-i-mezhdunarodnye-otnosheniya/posts/perspektivy-realizacii-proekta-ekonomicheskij-poyas-shelkov.

16 *Ibidem.*

17 *Ibidem.*

18 The project is developing successfully. Exclusive interview of Shakhrat Nuryshev – Ambassador of the Republic of Kazakhstan to the PRC (in Russian): https://rg.ru/2017/05/29/posol-kazahstana-v-knr-rasskazal-o-dvustoronnih-otnosheniiah.html.

Some aspects of the OBOR initiative and of the EAEU relate to prospects for cooperation and more coordinated migration. The successful realisation of the OBOR correspond to most active and potential participants of the initiative including countries of Eurasian space. According to the President Xi Jinping's 2013 speech[19] "by strengthening the cooperation between the Shanghai Cooperation Organisation and the Eurasian Economic Community, we can gain a greater space for development". Regional and extra regional Organisations will promote the realisations of the project by the giving benefits to all parties. The Eurasian Economic Union is an integrative project covering main developing economies of the region. It was first offered in 1994 by President N. Nazarbayev in the Moscow State University. The EEU, established by the Treaty on the Eurasian Economic Union,[20] signed on 29 May 2014 by Kazakhstan, Russia and Belarus as founding members, was established on the basis of the EAEC Customs Union to strengthen the economies of the participating countries and to modernise and enhance the competitiveness of participating countries on the world market.[21]

The Eurasian Economic Union (EAEU) is an international organisation for regional economic integration. The Member-States of the EAEU are Armenia, Belarus, Kazakhstan, Kyrgyzstan and Russia. The EAEU provides for free movement of goods, services, capital and labour, pursues coordinated, harmonised and single policy in the sectors determined by the Treaty and international agreements within the Union.[22] The EAEU and the OBOR initiatives have common tasks and expectations. This gives grounds for more in-depth cooperation for the members of the Union and the participants in the project.

Coming to the migration field of the EAEU, its Common Labour Market begun on 1 January 2015 on the territories of the members of the Union, whereby the freedom of movement of labour started to be realised, regulated by section XXVI 'Labour migration' of the Agreement

---

19 President Xi Jinping Delivers Important Speech and Proposes to Build a Silk Road Economic Belt with Central Asian Countries, 2013/09/07: http://www.fmprc.gov.cn/mfa_eng/topics_665678/xpfwzysiesgjtfhshzzfh_665686/t1076334.shtml.

20 Treaty on the Eurasian Economic Union: https://docs.eaeunion.org/en-us/pages/displaydocument.aspx?s=bef9c798-3978-42f3-9ef2-d0fb3d53b75f&w=632c7868-4ee2-4b21-bc64-1995328e6ef3&l=540294ae-c3c9-4511-9bf8-aaf5d6e0d169&entityid=3610.

21 Eurasian Economic Union: http://www.eaeunion.org./#about.

22 *Ibidem.*

on the EEU.[23] This section provides for several norms aimed at the development of a stable labour-market and for the social and legal provision of labour migrants (articles 96-98). The term of temporary stay (residence) of working migrants and members of their families on the territory of the state of employment is determined by the term of the labour or civil contract concluded with the employer and working migrant.

A central point is the development of common legislation for the members of the Union regarding the social provision of migrants and members of their families, including education and health care. Mutual recognition of the documents on education received in one of the Member-States of the Union by other participating States without conducting any filtering procedures.[24] This gives the right to engage in professional activities in the specialty in any of the Member-States. But this rule does not apply to teachers, lawyers, pharmacists and doctors. Representatives of these professions with employment in another country of the EAEU must undergo the procedure for the recognition of the documents on education established by the legislation of the state of employment. Documents on academic degrees and academic degrees are subjected to the same procedure.[25] The Member-States of the EAEU can still restrict labour flows to establish and apply restrictions in order to ensure national security, including in sectors of the economy that are of strategic importance, as well as public order, with regards to workers' activities, occupation and territory (country) of sojourn. EAEU is an economic project in the Kazakhstani perception and, in this context, there are several types of activity yet to realise and work out. This experience and activity in the field of migration coordination could be important and applicable to the realisation of some parts of OBOR.

The conjunction of the OBOR and EAEU may significantly advance trade, economic, transport, energy and educational cooperation. This, in

---

23 Treaty on the Eurasian Economic Union: https://docs.eaeunion.org/en-us/pages/displaydocument.aspx?s=bef9c798-3978-42f3-9ef2-d0fb3d53b75f&w=632c7868-4ee2-4b21-bc64-1995328e6ef3&l=540294ae-c3c9-4511-9bf8-aaf5d6e0d169&entityid=3610.

24 L.F. DELOVAROVA, "Dynamics of migration processes within the framework of the EEU: a look from Kazakhstan" (in Russian): https://articlekz.com/article/16344.

25 Treaty on the Eurasian Economic Union: https://docs.eaeunion.org/en-us/pages/displaydocument.aspx?s=bef9c798-3978-42f3-9ef2-d0fb3d53b75f&w=632c7868-4ee2-4b21-bc64-1995328e6ef3&l=540294ae-c3c9-4511-9bf8-aaf5d6e0d169&entityid=3610.

turn, will further strengthen the mobility of the population. At the same time, this conjugation of OBOR and EEU can weaken the dependence of the economies of the Union and diversify the main types of economic, trade and energy activities. Multidimensional cooperation between China and Kazakhstan is a contributing factor in both directions.

*

In conclusion, global mobility has become an essential factor shaping the regional and global landscape of interdependent processes. Migration of the population is acquiring increasingly intricate and contiguous forms. Along with this, the problems remain and their main roots lie in the development of cooperation, harmonisation and unification of the legislation of national States.

Migration processes between the Kazakhstan and the China have historical roots and remain intensive for the development of bilateral relations, security and sustainable development at the regional and inter-regional level. At the bilateral level, a well-defined legislative framework has already been developed and active cooperation is under way in all fields including trade, economic, politics, security, transport and logistics, education and culture.

The initiative 'One Belt, One Way', proposed by the Chinese government is one such comprehensive integration initiatives of the present. The OBOR or 'New Silk Road', is based on cooperation, improvement of trade, transit-transport corridors, and most importantly – rapprochement of peoples. These components are closely related to migration processes. The conjugation of this initiative with the activities of the Eurasian Economic Union, in which the economic, social, trade and migration component is central, is promising for the successful interfacing mechanisms enabling the development of sustainable legal norms for effective implementation.

Reforming Kazakhstan's migration legislation in the light of the 'One Belt, One Road' project

Yesbol OMIRZHANOV, Almagul TUSUPOVA
al-Farabi Kazakh National University, Almaty, Kazakhstan

The situation of migration relates increasingly to the implementation of the project 'One Belt, One Road' (OBOR). The current migration legislation of Kazakhstan and the impact of the OBOR project on it need to be clarified. The present situation in the country in the field of migration thus calls for statistical data, review of relevant legislation and even reviewing the provisions of the Concept of Migration Policy of the Republic of Kazakhstan for 2017–2021. Research relies on the opinions of experts on the need to attract labour to Kazakhstan, emphasising questions of the State regulation of labour migration from China. To study the situation of Chinese labour migrants calls for facts with a negative impact on the implementation of the OBOR project in Kazakhstan. Re-education camps for Muslims in Xinjiang is an extreme such factor. There exists a clear necessity to reform Kazakhstan's migration legislation in the light of the OBOR implementation, as well as recommendations for improving State-participation in it.

Most States face the problem of active migration, Kazakhstan being no exception. In 1991, both out-flows and in-flows affected the country. Statistics indicate that during 1991–2018, almost 3,658,700 Kazakhstanis left and 1,542,500 people arrived in the country.[1] In the early 1990s, migrations were essentially *ethnic*: many ethnicities such as Russian, German, Ukrainian, Jewish, Polish returned to their historic homeland; and Kazakh nationals living in Mongolia, China, Uzbekistan, Russia, Turkmenistan and other States returned. Yet, with time, *internal*

---

1 A. YESENINA, "External migration for all years since independence", //сайт LS, 15 February 2019: https://www.lsm.kz.

migrations became urgent: rural residents began to move massively to large cities. Also, since the 2000s, the number of external *labour* migrants has increased in Kazakhstan. In recent years, Kazakhstan received numerous migrants from Turkey and China. Early 2019, their number reached almost 620,000 people.[2]

Two types of migrants come from China to Kazakhstan. i/ Ethnic migration of Chinese Kazakhs: since independence, about 140,000 people of Kazakh nationality returned home;[3] ii/ Labour migration of non-Kazakh population from China: while there were few migrants from China in the early 1990s, the number has surged since the 2000s, influenced by the expansion of business ties between the two countries and the implementation of major Chinese projects such as 'One Belt, One Road', the realisation of which requires efforts from both countries. The OBOR project focuses on improving connectivity and cooperation among Asian countries, Africa, China and Europe, thus on land- as well as maritime-routes, a policy helping China also to boost domestic growth. The OBOR is also a part of China's strategy for economic diplomacy.[4]

Yet, with time, the implementation of this project may affect the policy of Kazakhstan in the field of migration. Already the country, within OBOR, realises more than 50 joint projects. Their implementation requires the involvement of foreign labour from China, as each needs skilled service personnel who know the techniques of working with the necessary equipment. In addition, qualified staff need technical specialists who understand Chinese. Thus, a legal analysis of the conditions and the possibility of the impact of the project OBOR on the migration legislation is needed for Kazakhstan as a whole.

I. Approaching a complex issue: concepts and results

This chapter is based on statistical data for elaborating conclusions. The method is system analysis, as well as the historical analysis in order to

---

2 "How many people moved from China to Kazakhstan in a year", website of newspaper *Our Kostanay*, 16 April 2018 : http://top-news.kz.

3 "Reference materials in the field of migration", official website of the Ministry of Labour and Social Protection of RK: http://www.enbek.gov.kz/kk/taxonomy/term/521.

4 "What is China's One Belt One Road (OBOR) project?", *The Indian Express*, 14 May 2017: https://indianexpress.com.

probe into the time-development of Chinese-Kazakh economic relations and the causes of Chinese migration to Kazakhstan. Complementing this data, materials cover the media of Kazakhstan and foreign countries for an assessment of the existing situation.

The implementation of the project OBOR relates to labour migration from China as Kazakhstan cannot fully provide large international projects with qualified personnel. As a result of this emigration and brain drain, Kazakhstan faces a shortage of qualified staff in education, science, healthcare, industry, agriculture and other sectors. Another challenging issue for the country's labour market (and throughout Central Asia) is the decreasing quality of higher (university) technical education and the collapse of the system of secondary vocational education, resulting in a severe shortage of engineers and skilled workers. This shortage of skills at the graduate level necessitates the recruitment of foreign (in particular Chinese) specialists and workers to implement joint China-Kazakhstan projects.[5]

In this regard, at the present stage of development, external labour migration came in first place in the Republic of Kazakhstan. This chapter thus analyses the legal acts related to external labour migration. Kazakhstan's current migration legislation includes the Law of the Republic of Kazakhstan "On the Legal Status of Foreigners" dated 19 June 1995; the Law of the Republic of Kazakhstan "On ratification of the Agreement on cooperation to combat illegal labour migration from third States" dated 28 June 2011; the Law of the Republic of Kazakhstan "On Migration" dated 22 July 2011; the Law of the Republic of Kazakhstan "On employment" dated 6 April 2016, as well as many subordinate acts.

According to article 34 of the Law of the Republic of Kazakhstan of 22 July 2011 No. 477-IV "On migration", immigrants arriving for the purpose of employment are divided into the following categories: foreign workers; business immigrants; seasonal foreign employees; labour immigrants. Article 36 of this Law defines the conditions for issuing entry visas to foreign workers, according to which entry visas for foreign workers are issued by the Ministry for foreign Affairs and foreign institutions of the Republic of Kazakhstan in coordination with the national security bodies on the basis and for the duration of the permit issued to a foreign

---

5 Y. SADOVSKAYA, "China's Rise in Kazakhstan and Its Impact on Migration", Research Paper, MIRPAL, Regional Migration Program by the World Bank, IOM, UN Women, DFID, Almaty-Moscow, 2016, 120 p., p. 43.

employee for employment or an employer to attract foreign labour, including within the framework of internal corporate transfer.

A work permit is issued to employers who attract qualified foreign specialists for a specific job, or for the implementation of specific projects for a period of one year, with right to extend it. In accordance with article 14 of the "Rules for entry and exit from Kazakhstan for foreign nationals", as well as their departure from the Republic of Kazakhstan approved by the decree of the Government of the Republic of Kazakhstan of 21 January 2012, No. 148, attraction of foreign labour force, as well as employment of temporarily staying immigrants in the Republic of Kazakhstan shall be carried out on the basis of permission of the local executive body or internal affairs bodies, unless otherwise provided by the legislation of the Republic of Kazakhstan in the field of migration and/or international agreements of the Republic of Kazakhstan.

For further regulation of this sphere, there were adopted the Rules for establishing quotas for engagement of foreign labour force in the Republic of Kazakhstan and its distribution among regions of the Republic of Kazakhstan, identifying persons whose work does not require permission from local executive bodies to attract foreign labour, and recognising as declared to be no longer in force of the Government of the Republic of Kazakhstan, approved by the Resolution of the Government of the Republic of Kazakhstan No. 802 dated 15 December 2016.

According to these rules, quotas for engagement of foreign labour force are established as a percentage of the labour force and includes: i/ quota for engagement of foreign labour force by economic activity; ii/ quota for attracting labour immigrants; iii/ quota for engagement of foreign labour force in the countries of origin in the presence of international treaties on cooperation in the field of labour migration and social protection of migrant workers ratified by the Republic of Kazakhstan. The quotas for attracting foreign labour by type of economic activity for the coming year determine the maximum allowable amount of foreign labour, allowed to attract employers and to carry out labour activities in the territory of the relevant administrative-territorial unit.

State authorities try to create favourable conditions for qualified foreign workers and top managers. For this purpose, the Decree of the Government of Kazakhstan dated 13 April 2018, added amendments to these Rules according to which, the following categories of employees do not require permission of local Executive bodies: i/ working as the first heads of branches or representative offices of foreign legal entities, as well as the first heads of Kazakhstan legal entities and their deputies with one hundred percent foreign participation in their authorised capital; ii/ working in the national management holding positions not lower than the heads of departments with higher education as *per* confirmed documents in accordance with the legislation of the Republic of Kazakhstan; iii/ attracted to work as members of the Board of Directors of the national management holding. Moreover, the Majilis (parliament) approved the draft Law "On ratification of the agreement between the government of the Republic of Kazakhstan and the people's Republic of China on exemption from taxation of certain types of income of the Kazakhstan-China Cooperation Fund of production facilities, carrying out direct investments in Kazakhstan". This law exempts the Fund from taxation of dividends.[6]

Although, Kazakh authorities try to control external labour migration in this area, currently there are many problems in this matter. Thus, the Concept of migration policy of the Republic of Kazakhstan for 2017–2021 and the Action Plan for the implementation of the Concept of migration policy of the Republic of Kazakhstan for 2017–2021, approved by the Government of the Republic of Kazakhstan dated 29 September 2017, No. 602, provides a complete analysis of the current situation in the field of migration. This Concept states that migration policy is devoid of consistency and each direction of migration policy works separately, without an obvious interrelationship with each other. This leads to an imbalance in the use of foreign and local labour, which worsens the imbalance in the national labour market. Kazakhstan faces the risk of ineffective recruitment of foreign labour, because i/ there are already relevant specialists in the labour market in Kazakhstan and ii/ foreign labour can have insufficient qualifications.[7]

Labour immigration occurs in two forms in Kazakhstan: the official attraction of foreign labour force and spontaneous labour immigration: the attraction of the unregulated labour migration to the country primarily connected with the low cost of services rendered by migrants, the absence of social packages, and other conditions.[8] According to

---

6 "To free some Chinese projects from taxes agreed Mazhilis", newspaper *Vremya*, 5 December 2018: https://time.kz.

7 "Formation of an effective migration policy in the framework of improving the investment rate cite of the Federation of Labour Unions of the Republic of Kazakhstan", website of Federation of Labour Union, 7 December 2018: http://fprk.kz.

8 S. N. ALPYSBAEVA and others, *Volumes of Labour Migration in the Republic of Kazakhstan. Studies on Russian Economic Development*, 2015, 26(5), p. 510–516.

experts, illegal labour migration in the country is manifold that of legal labour migrants and norms of the labour legislation of the Republic of Kazakhstan are not observed with regard to illegal labour migrants.

II. Discussing current trends and challenges

The 7 September 2013 speech by Chinese President Xi Jinping at Nazarbayev University officially put forward an initiative for the joint construction of a 'Silk Road Economic Belt' (SREB), which received prompt support from the President of Kazakhstan. In turn, this influenced the development of Chinese business in Kazakhstan. In 2014, the number of Chinese labour migrants to Kazakhstan increased by 100% according to statistics released by the Committee of Labour, Social Protection and Migration (CLSPM). That year, Kazakhstan issued about 31,000 work permits to attract foreign labour, of which 11,860 for Chinese. The CLSPM cannot give exact number of Chinese people living in Kazakhstan, as they come both official and unofficial ways. Currently, in the country, Chinese companies control from one fifth to a quarter of oil production and in the implementation of general projects, the Chinese side provides maximum returns to their own workers.[9]

Kazakhstan has since 1993 been attracting foreign labour. Statistics show that 2,100 arrived in the in the 1990s, of which 26.6% from China. In the 2000s, on account of the signing of Agreements on economic partnership and the construction of oil pipeline, the immigration of Chinese specialists and workers increased. Noteworthy, the spread of Chinese migration is not only attracted legally but also follows spontaneous unregulated flow of labour migrants, repeatedly exceeding the first. Some legally enter Kazakhstan but then use all the opportunities for illegal employment and become migrants with 'unregulated status'.[10]

According to the CLSPM, the number of foreigners violating the migration legislation is increasing every year. In 2017, 139,000 people from distant foreign countries illegally entered the country, most of them

---

9 K. KLEMENKOVA, "The Turks leave, The Chinese come. New trends of Labour Migration in Kazakhstan", 10 November 2015: https://365info.kz.

10 Y. SADOVSKAYA, "Chinese migration in Kazakhstan: causes, main trends and prospects", *Central Asia and the Caucasus*, 2015: https://cyberleninka.ru.

are citizens of China, Turkey, India and Mongolia.[11] In recent years, criminal groups have organised illegal transportation of people from China to Kazakhstan. In 2018, two transnational criminal groups were detained, which organised a channel of mass illegal entry from China to Kazakhstan through 85 registered Kazakhstani companies.[12]

According to the Department of Migration Police of the Ministry of Internal Affairs of the Republic of Kazakhstan, the peak of Chinese migration was 1993–1994, when about 40,000 to 50,000 Chinese traders permanently lived in Almaty. At that time, the concentration of Chinese citizens in certain areas of business caused great concern, particularly in trade and catering and in some areas of large cities, mainly Almaty and Astana, with threats of prototypes 'Chinatowns'.[13]

The mass media published a lot of materials, including about the growth in numbers of Chinese people in Kazakhstan. In 2014–2015, the official Chinese edition of *Huangqiu Shibao* (*The Global Times*) reported that 400,000 ethnic Chinese live in Kazakhstan. In general, 38% of labour migrants in Kazakhstan are Chinese and their salary is five times higher than that of Kazakhstani citizens.[14] Sociological research suggests that the attitude of respondents to migrants from China, which used to be generally indifferent (average score: 2.9 points out of 5) begins to vary greatly from less to more tolerant regions. Currently, some groups of the urban population have a negative attitude towards Chinese migrants and growing concerns about the consequences of Chinese migration for Kazakhstan: 24% of respondents are afraid of serious competition in the labour market and 18% have a negative attitude towards Chinese migrants. There is less tolerance towards Chinese migrants in the Western and Central regions compared to other regions.[15]

---

11 Z. URANKAYEVA, "The Number of foreigners illegally entered the Republic of Kazakhstan was named in the Ministry of internal Affairs", *Kazakhstanskaya pravda* newspaper site, 3 November 2017: https://www.kazpravda.kz.

12 "Mass entry of Chinese into Kazakhstan organised by criminals", website *Kazday*, 16 April 2018: https://kazday.kz.

13 A. MUMINOV, "Migration in Chinese. How many residents of China in Kazakhstan?", site *Exclusive*, 10 August 2016: http://www.exclusive.kz.

14 K. MATREKOV, "Chinese in Kazakhstan: is there a threat?", 30 March 2017: https://365info.kz.

15 Y. SADOVSKAYA, "Chinese migrants in Kazakhstan: the attitude of Kazakh citizens (according to the results of sociological research)", *Demoscope Weekly*, 367–368, 2–15 марта 2009: http://www.demoscope.ru.

The attitude of local populations to the Chinese has changed in the recent years in a negative way, due to the following factors:

i/ an increase in Kazakhstan's foreign debt to China. The total external debt of Kazakhstan at the beginning of 2018 exceeded 168 billion $ (119% of GDP). Two-thirds of this fall on five large creditors: the Netherlands (49.8 billion), the UK (27.7 billion), the US (13.2 billion), China (12.3 billion) and France (11.9 billion).[16] There is growing alarm to the debt to China, as other neighbouring countries (Tajikistan, Kyrgyzstan…) have already become hostages of China.[17]

ii/ since 2017, ethnic Kazakhs are being persecuted on religious belief in China, where authorities wage a campaign against 'separatists' in the western Xinjiang Autonomous Uyghur Region, blaming recent attacks on the Uyghurs and apply to Kazakhs the same restrictions as on Uyghurs.[18] In August 2018, a court in eastern Kazakhstan declined to deport an ethnic Kazakh Chinese citizen who had illegally crossed the border, fleeing from a position working as a teacher in one of the re-education camps. "In fact, it is a prison located in the mountains", Sauytbay said, whose testimony was widely covered and closely watched, as a first-hand account of the camps.[19]

The public of Kazakhstan requires the government to intervene in the affairs of ethnic Kazakhs in China. At the same time, The PRC Minister of Foreign Affairs, Wang Yi, after a meeting with Kazakhstan's Minister for Foreign Affairs of Kazakhstan, B. Atamkulov, confirmed his 'appreciation' of the 'support' of Kazakhstan in the fight against 'extremism' in the Xinjiang Uighur Autonomous Region.[20]

---

16 S. SMIRNOV, "External debt of Kazakhstan: what is it and what we risk", сайт Informburo, 28 February 2018: https://informburo.kz.

17 A. YURIEV, "Tajikistan's debt hole threat: why China lends the Central Asia", website Sputnik, 7 June 2018: https://sptnkne.ws.

18 B. PANNIER, "China's New Security Concern: The Kazakhs", Radio Free Europe/Radio Liberty, 8 August 2017: https://www.rferl.org.

19 C. PUTZ, "Kazakhstan and the Xinjiang Problem", *The Diplomat*, 11 September 2018: https://thediplomat.com.

20 "China thanked Kazakhstan for understanding China's position on combating extremism in XUAR", website Informburo, 29 March 2019: https://informburo.kz.

iii/ year after year, the Chinese presence in Kazakhstan is felt. Over the past 10 years, China invested over $15 billion in Kazakhstan's projects. Chinese companies are actively involved in the industrialisation of Kazakhstan and the implementation of major investment projects. Foreign trade turnover between Kazakhstan and China in 2017 increased by more than 30% at 10,5 billion US$.[21] Negative attitudes of ordinary citizens towards Chinese people are caused by recognition of Chinese as one of the ethnic groups of Kazakhstan and the inclusion of their associations in the Assembly of peoples of Kazakhstan, as well as the opening of the first Chinese school *Hope* in Almaty, etc.

Some civil society activists intensively oppose Chinese expansion and publish open letters. Thus, a group of public activists appealed to the President of Kazakhstan. Their letter noted the current share of Chinese companies as 22% of the annual production of oil and gas condensate in Kazakhstan, and that Chinese investors own the rights to develop almost all the largest resource fields. A separate concern is the plan to sell land to the Chinese under the guise of building joint ventures.[22]

Kazakh official authorities have tried to maintain friendly relations with the Chinese side in recent years, openly promoting the Chinese language. For example, then President Nazarbayev urged young people to learn Chinese,[23] and Dariga Nazarbayeva, current Speaker of the Senate, recommended at a meeting with Almaty's youth to learn Chinese: "Learn Chinese. I insist. I am scolded by the national patriots for this, but I believe that this is the future".[24] Kazakh authorities openly began to persecute activists working against the interests of China. Serikzhan Bilash, head of the advocacy group *Ata Jurt*, was accused of "inciting ethnic hatred" and placed under house arrest in Astana. Bilash's group has been actively supporting relatives of detained Uyghurs, Kazakhs and

---

21 "Kazakh-Chinese cooperation in the framework of the programme 'One Belt, One Road' was discussed in Astana", 7 September 2018, official website of the Prime Minister of the Republic of Kazakhstan: https://primeminister.kz.

22 "China and the UK share of Kazakhstan", website News.ru, 9 August 2018: https://news.rambler.ru.

23 V. VODNEV, "Nursultan Nazarbayev told students why it is necessary to learn Chinese", website Sputnik, 1 December 2018: https://ru.sputniknews.kz.

24 "'Learn Chinese': D. Nazarbayeva addressed to youth", website of NUR KZ, 16 October 2018: https://www.nur.kz.

other ethnic minorities in Chinese internment camps.[25] And at present, most of the Kazakh population is opposed to the deepening of Chinese-Kazakh relations and Kazakh authorities remain between i/ the growing influence of China and ii/ the growing anti-Chinese mood of the local population.

The implementation of the 2013 project OBOR in Kazakhstan is carried out at a rapid pace, but after five years, specific problems can be associated with this project. Sinologist K. Syroezhkin identifies five problems associated with such as the implementation. One of them, he highlights, is "the inevitable prospect of getting [participating] countries in debt bondage of China".[26]

*

In conclusion, as to the implementation of the OBOR project, Kazakh authorities have created a maximum of favourable conditions. This leads to an increase of Chinese companies that would need labour force. The Kazakh side would have to reform its policy in the field of regulation and control of external labour migration. Since Chinese companies prefer to employ workers with knowledge of the Chinese language, the Kazakh side has the right to require Chinese companies to hire ethnic Kazakhs from China who speak Chinese. This, in turn, would solve the problem of shortage of workers with knowledge of the Chinese language. It would also contribute to the decline of anti-Chinese sentiment in society.

In the coming years, Kazakhstan's presidency and government will face numerous linked to the implementing of the project OBOR in the country. In order to successfully realise this project, it is necessary to revise existing, signed bilateral agreements for their direct connection with the project OBOR. It is also necessary to update the composition of the migration service, replacing the personnel who were bribed by representatives of Chinese business. In addition, it is necessary to tighten up control over Chinese citizens who cross the border of Kazakhstan on an inappropriate visa, in order to prevent their employment in Kazakhstan.

---

25 N. VASILYEVA, "Kazakh Activist Complains of Pressure by Authorities", *The Diplomat*, 15 March 2019: https://thediplomat.com.

26 R. IVANOV, "5 problems of the project 'One Belt, One Road'", website 365info, 22 September 2018: https://365info.kz.

Part III

Regional and national changes: sectoral cases

Introduction

Remus Titiriga
Law School, Inha University, South Korea

In Part III of the book, chapters can be grouped in two broad categories. Three chapters examine the interactions of challengers for the agents of change impacted onto the Eurasian space or arising from the Eurasian space.

Foreign to the Eurasian space, the USA, the main super power, initiated a new foreign trade policy under the leadership of D. Trump, with tremendous impact globally and in Eurasia. This is the subject of "Globalisation 2.0? Legal implications for Eurasia of the new US trade-policies" by Remus Titiriga. The paper determines, first, a pattern by analysing the declarations of D. Trump himself and the actions of his Administration (such as over-the-border-measures' concerning aluminium and steel tariffs, or the renegotiation process of NAFTA or KOREUS. That pattern is then employed in understanding the US trade actions in relation to China and the US forthcoming acts in relation to the EU, Japan and, eventually the WTO. The US trade war with China would undoubtedly disrupt the latter's 'Belt and Road Initiative' (BRI) and the 'Maritime Economic Cooperation' (MEC). The US is acting as a global challenger of the regional challenger – China.

In the same direction is the chapter about "The implications for South Korea of China's Belt and Road Initiative (BRI) and of the Maritime Economic Cooperation (MEC) in East Asia" by Seok-Woo Lee. The US is the main defense and security partner of South Korea while China became, in the last years, South Korea's main economic partner. This situation imposed a delicate balance for South Korea especially now, when the US, under the Trump Administration is disengaging from its liberal trade policies. South Korea has shown its capacity to rise to the demands of sustaining an autonomous position equidistant from the two super powers and competitors.

Another chapter, "Why, like other African States, does Mali like China?" by Éloi Diarra, provides an overview of the relations between Mali, a developing African state and the Asian superpower, China. It evaluates positively both China's participation in Mali's industrialisation and the building of various infrastructures and China's discretion in regard to the internal affairs of Mali.

Still in Part III of the book, two other chapters focus on the legal challenges imposing change in the legal frame, structures or remedies within the context created by Chinese investment initiatives.

A first chapter in this direction, "Legal aspects of trade cooperation in the framework of the 'Belt and Road initiative' " by Zhuldyz Sairambaeva and Gulmira Mashimbayeva, examines the Silk Road Economic Belt initiative which, in its initial stages, was based on separate independent agreements, memorandums and programmes concluded by China with each Central Asian country. It further analyses the prospect of an institutionalisation of cooperation between China and the regional integration initiative of the Eurasian Economic Union, a cooperation grounded on joint establishments.

The next chapter, "The 'Most-Favoured-Nation' principle in recent investment arbitration involving Eurasian countries" by Chan-Mo Chung, analyses the investor-State dispute-settlement (ISDS) procedure rising in Eurasia, where investment treaties usually include a most-favoured-nation (MFN) treatment clause which guarantees a no less favourable treatment to investors from a contracting party than that which the party provides to investors and investments from a third party. The author evaluates the diverse jurisdictional practice concerning whether the complaining investor from an investment treaty party may rely on an MFN clause to resort to the dispute settlement mechanism of other investment treaty which the investor deems more favourable (in relation, for example, to the possibility of bringing a case directly to arbitration without recourse to the required negotiation or local procedure).

Part III is thus a valuable insight into the economic aspects of the challenge to Eurasian systems.

Globalisation 2.0?

Legal implications for Eurasia of the new US trade-policies

Remus TITIRIGA
Law School, Inha University, South Korea

The chapter examines the trade policies of the new US administration in their relation to Eurasia. It begins by assessing the goals and the tools of this new US trade policy through open declarations of President Trump. Then a first part identifies the strategies/tactics of the trade policy by analysing actions of the new US administration as to, for example, aluminium and steel tariffs or to the re-negotiations of KOREUS or USMCA agreement (I). A second part uses the frame identified in the first part in order to apprehend the forthcoming trade actions of the US Administration in regard to Eurasian actors, such as the EU, Japan, China; striving to determine possible outcome of such actions, that will have a disruptive impact on the globalisation process of the last 3 decades (II).

Identifying the goals and the tools of the new US trade policy through declarations – In his presidential campaign the then candidate Trump announced that he would pursue an economic programme of reconstructing the industrial might of US in order to strengthen the economic position of the American middle class ('America first'; 'Make America great again'). That required new economic policies for creating first-rate environment for the US manufacturing, and reverse the last three decades' trends which made industrial investment outside the US more attractive.[1]

---

[1] During the 2 years in power, the Trump administration have followed this goal within a multi stage economic approach which included: assisting and improving the US abundance of free and cheap energy (resulting from the shale gas revolution) accompanied by bold initiatives such as the withdrawal of Paris Agreement; deregulation;

The silver lining in President Trump declarations seems to be the car industry. He often focuses on the gap between the 2.5% levy charged by the US on imported passenger-cars[2] and higher tariffs in the EU[3] or in China.[4] His message was clear-cut: "We will soon be starting reciprocal taxes so that we will charge the same thing as they charge us, $800 Billion Trade Deficit-have no choice!"[5]

In his book *Art of the deal*, future President Trump provided some key elements he considered essential in concluding business deals[6]. Among the most relevant one is the rule 5 about using own leverage: "The best thing you can do is deal from strength, and leverage is the biggest strength you can have. Leverage is having something the other guy wants. Or better yet, needs. Or best of all, simply can't do without."

During negotiation, leverage is the power that one side of a negotiation has to influence the other side to move closer to their negotiating position.[7]

Trump, with his business background, seems to adopt a new, more transactional attitude in international trade, with a market-oriented approach based on actions considered from a cost/benefits perspective. The conceptual filter is less ideological/political and more economical.

Even security aspects seem to be considered within such a cost/benefits economic perspective. The clearest example is the discussions about the costs of the NATO pact and the uneven contribution to it by the European allies. It seems that the economy and military defence/strategy are not distinctive fields and there are no limits, no segmentation

---

the reduction of internal-corporate taxation through a massive reform of fiscal/tax regulation; and, last but not least, new and transformative trade and commercial policies.

2 One must notice that US auto industry currently enjoys a crucial protective tariff, namely the 25 percent tariff on imported pickup trucks.

3 For example the tariffs for customs clearance set up at the EU level are of 22 percent for trucks and 10 percent for passenger cars.

4 China has 25 percent tariffs on US cars.

5 https://twitter.com/realdonaldtrump/status/969572374977839106?lang=en.

6 See chapter 2 of Donald Trump *Art of the deal*, Random House, 1 November 1987.

7 Positive leverage is a negotiator's ability to provide things that his opponent wants. The power from positive leverage comes from the opportunity to provide or withhold a needed item or action. Negative leverage is a threat-based form of leverage that represents one side's ability to put the other side in a worse position. Cf. Wikipedia.

between actions/instruments and goals, since military instruments can be put in the service of the US economy and its growth and vice-versa.

I. The tactics and strategies of the US Administration in international trade trough illustrative actions

Words can be used to understand the trade strategy of US administrations and its announced goals but actions taken are even more significant. Sometimes, in trade negotiation, words are used to deceive by design and to hide real intentions. In other occasions, the words have a rhetorical function, persuading and pushing the other side to understand their weak positions in future negotiations. The way of getting the 'common thread', among these trade declarations, by separating real objectives from noise is to focus on the measures designed to achieve the purpose outlined by President Trump, the re-industrialisation of the US, and the recovery of blue- and white-collar jobs for the American middle class.

A. First, de-entanglement from multinational agreements: withdrawal from TPP

President Trump withdrew the US signature on the Trans-Pacific Partnership (TPP). He used an executive order since the ratification process by the US Congress had not yet started. One can understand his intentions by examining the TPP from the perspective of a re-industrialisation focusing on the reconstruction of the auto industry within the US.

In this respect, trade relations with Japan, resulting from the TPP are highly relevant. The US has put in place car tariffs of 2.5% and truck tariffs of 25%, while for auto-parts the US tariffs are fixed at 2.5% to 5%. The higher tax on trucks has forced the foreign car-makers, (including Japanese ones) to build truck and SUV plants in the US, within a market dominated by Chrysler, Fiat, and General Motors.

Before the TPP negotiations, Japan had no tariffs on cars and trucks from the US, but US auto-makers claimed that Japan, which imports among the fewest vehicles of any major auto market, has closed its market to American cars out with non-tariffs barriers. The TPP included a 30-year phase-out of US tariffs for trucks. The tariffs on auto-parts, had a more complicated phase-out schedule, of 12 to 15 years. All that seemed to be a 'win' for the US.

Nevertheless, the rules-of-origin criteria for autos in the TPP required that only 45% of a passenger car or light truck's net cost to originate in a member-country. This threshold was lower than in the original NAFTA agreement, seen as a bad deal within the Trump administration.[8] Key members of the Trump administration seemed convinced that the US could have obtained better terms by 'one on one' negotiations with other partners, notably with Japan.[9] Hence, the TPP withdrawal gave liberty of movement (and leverage) for the US in future bilateral trade negotiations.

B. Over-the-board measures

1. US tariffs on imports of solar panels

Section 201 is a part of the 1974 Trade Act that permits the US President to grant temporary import-relief, by raising import duties or imposing non-tariff barriers on goods entering the US that harm or threaten to harm domestic industries producing similar goods. The criteria for import-relief under section 201 are based on article XIX of the GATT (as defined by the WTO Agreement on Safeguards) referred to as the escape-clause since it permits a country to 'escape' temporarily from its obligations under the GATT.

In April 2017, *Suniva*, a US solar module manufacturer declared bankruptcy, and within a week filed a trade complaint using Section 201 as its primary basis. On 22 January 2018, President Trump announced 30% US tariffs on imports of solar panel in the name of protecting the few remaining US solar cell and module manufacturers.[10] The 'over the board' safeguard measure were needed because foreign producers, mainly from China, were evading American restrictions on imports from specific countries by spreading their factories around the globe.[11]

---

8 See below the renegotiation of NAFTA.

9 https://thehill.com/policy/.../314846-ross-prefers-inking-bilateral-trade-agreements.

10 The president approved solar tariffs for the next four years, starting with levies of 30 percent that will ultimately fall to 15 percent.

11 After two rounds of US Anti-dumping and countervailing duties were imposed on Chinese solar products, in 2012 and 2014, many Chinese solar cells makers build cell and module factories in Southeast Asia, and the direct imports from China slowed down.

The solution, complying with the re-industrialisation interests of the US administration, is for the Chinese producers to move their factories within the US.[12]

2. US tariffs on imports of washing machines

The US has been pursuing the foreign washing-machines makers with anti-dumping duties since 2011. On 23 January 2018, in conjunction with the tariffs placed on solar panels, the Office of the US Trade Representative announced new tariffs on washing-machines. Trump was responding to a recommendation by the US International Trade Commission to raise import duties after Whirlpool accused Samsung and LG Electronics of selling the appliances in the US below fair-market value.[13]

The 'over the board' safeguard measure was necessary because foreign producers (mainly from South Korea but also from China) were likewise evading American restrictions on imports from specific countries by spreading their factories around the globe.

As a solution, Samsung and LG, which are among the top exporters of washing-machines to the US, will circumvent these import taxes by starting to produce washers in their new US-based plants.[14]

3. US tariffs on foreign steel and aluminium on grounds that imports undermined US national security

China has half of the world's steel production capacity, much of which is excessive. That has led to a situation where Chinese steel production had to be exported to the rest of the world at very low prices, considered by many, including the US, as dumping.

On 27 April 2017, Trump ordered a review of the aluminium and steel imports grounded on the Section 232 of Trade Expansion Act of 1962, which enables the president to act unilaterally if national security

---

12 For example First Solar and Jinko Solar are constructing factories in the US. First Solar will make thin film modules from raw materials in Ohio and Jinko says it will import cells from Malaysia for its Florida facility.

13 https://www.wsj.com/articles/whirlpool-wanted-washing-machine-tariffs-it-didnt-plan-for-a-trade-war-1531757621.

14 LG is building a washing-machine factory in Tennessee and Samsung's home-appliances plant in South Carolina steeped up its production of washing machines.

is at stake. Such an act seems to be out of reach of WTO because the WTO's charter includes an exemption for such cases (article XXI of GATT 1964). The section has rarely been used under GATT regime, and was never invoked since the creation of the WTO.

On 8 March 2018, the US administration moved to impose tariffs of 25% on foreign steel[15] and 10% on aluminium on grounds that the imports undermined US national security. The tariffs were imposed to prevent the overflow of steel products that originated mostly from China and which attempted to bypass anti-dumping measures by trans-shipping.

Later on, Trump announced that the Administration has reached final agreements (permanent exceptions) with South Korea on steel imports and with Argentina, Australia, and Brazil on steel and aluminium.

C. Renegotiation processes

1. Renegotiation of KORUS

The US trade deficit in goods with South Korea increased after the original KORUS pact took effect in 2012. The US and South Korea have agreed in principle to a renovation of their bilateral trade agreement. Koreans agreed to improve American firms' access to Korea's automotive and pharmaceutical markets while restricting their own exports of steel to the US by nearly one-third.

The US seemed to settle for less than expected. However, from the perspective of a US re-industrialisation interest, there was a breakthrough. According to the new agreement, South Korea will extend the phase-out of the 25% US tariff on trucks until 2041 (which was scheduled, according to original KORUS, to be phased-out by 2021). As a result, the greatly expanding truck market of the US will be protected from South Korean competition for another 20 years.

2. Renegotiation of NAFTA

The US trade with Canada and Mexico within NAFTA in 2017 was almost twice of its trade with China and 10 times that with South

---

[15] President Trump also told steel company executives that a global tariff was needed to prevent transshipping through other countries. Cf. https://www.ft.com/content/42fa0906-c4f5-11e8-8670-c5353379f7c2.

Korea ($1.1tn). In his first 100 days, Trump threatened to withdraw from NAFTA if Canada and Mexico refused to renegotiate. Thereafter NAFTA re-negotiations began on 16 August 2017.

One of Trump's core complaints about the NAFTA is that it has helped Mexico to emerge as an auto-making powerhouse.[16] Besides that, NAFTA has not deepened economic links among its signatories, and has encouraged third countries to ship auto-parts to Mexico and Canada, and to assemble products there so that they would qualify for the rules-of-origin criteria of NAFTA, and enter the US with no tariffs. NAFTA created a loophole for autos[17] that reduced American-made components not in favour of Mexican or Canadian components, but instead of Chinese and German components (Mexico and Canada being both in the FTAs with EU).

At the start of renegotiation, the US solution was to update NAFTA's rules-of-origin criteria, and introduce a 5-year sunset provision into the agreement, allowing all three signatories to revisit and update NAFTA regularly. After 13 months of negotiation, an initial agreement between the US and Mexico was reached before the final agreement, including Canada, was signed under the name of USMCA.

Two group of provisions are important from our perspective. According to new rules of origin, auto companies must manufacture at least 75% of the car's components in Canada, Mexico, or the US. Also, at least 30% of the car must be made by workers earning at least $16 an hour. That increases to 40% in 2023. That amount is three times greater than what the average salary of Mexican auto workers. Autos that do not meet these requirements will be subject to tariffs, a change that should create more U.S. jobs for autoworkers.[18]

---

16 Trump had asked Mexico to end the maquiladora programme which allows U.S. companies to set up low-cost factories across the border in Mexico to assemble finished products. They then export the goods back to the US. As a result, maquiladoras became responsible for 65 percent of Mexico's exports and employ 30 percent of its workforce. Cf. https://www.thestar.com › News › World.

17 Under current NAFTA rules, at least 62.5 percent of a car needed to be originated from the three countries in order for it to be traded tariff-free.

18 As an example of downstream consequences the German auto-maker BMW recently built a $2 billion assembly plant in Mexico. Most of their core parts were coming from the EU (steel/aluminium casting components) and/or Asia (electronics). From now the assembly plant will have to source 75 % of the auto-parts from the US and Mexico, with 45 % of those parts from facilities paying $16/

The agreement also allows the US to impose future emergency tariffs of up to 25% on cars and car parts on grounds of national security (using the same Section 232 of the Trade Expansion Act of 1962 that was employed for tariffs on aluminium and steel). Exports of cars and SUVs or auto-parts from Mexico or Canada to US would face a 25% US tariff if they exceed a certain specific volume and value. Below this threshold, vehicles that comply with the new regional content requirements could enter the US duty-free.

Not yet ratified, the agreement produces already its effects. Ford, Fiat Chrysler, and Volkswagen have all expanded their production of trucks in the US in anticipation of USMCA passage.[19]

II. Prognosis for current and future actions of the US Administration

A. China

1. *Trade measures adopted in relation to China*

There is a clear unbalance in trade relations between the US and China. The US trade deficit in goods was $375 billion in 2017, and China accounts for nearly half (43.6%) of America's total trade deficit with the entire world.

Section 301 of the 1974 US Trade Act authorises the US President to take all appropriate action, including retaliation, to obtain the removal of any act, policy, or practice of a foreign government that violates an international trade agreement or is unjustified, unreasonable, or discriminatory, and that burdens or restricts US commerce. On 22 March 2018, the US released details of its 'Findings of the investigation into China's acts, policies, and practices related to technology transfer, intellectual property, and innovation under section 301 of the Trade Act of 1974' underlining and proposing retaliation for product-dumping, lack of reciprocity on market access, and intellectual property theft.

---

hr. As a result BMW will need to modify their supply chain and build auto parts in the US and Mexico. Cf. https://theconservativetreehouse.com/2018/08/27/preliminary-details-of-u-s-mexico-trade-deal/.

19 *Cf.* http://fortune.com/2018/10/29/nafta-fiat-chrysler-mexico-production/.

On 15 June, Trump declared in a White House statement that the US would impose a 25% tariff on $50 billion of Chinese exports. American tariffs on $34 billion of Chinese goods came into effect on 6 July 2018. China imposed retaliatory tariffs on US goods of a similar value. By 23 August, the US implemented a further 25% of tariffs on $16 billion of goods as promised, which was reciprocated by China.

On 17 September, the US announced that its 10% tariff on $200 billion worth of Chinese goods would begin on 24 September, increasing to 25% by the end of the year. China promptly retaliated on 18 September, with 10% tariffs on $60 billion of US import. At that moment, China has either imposed or proposed tariffs on $110 billion of US goods, representing most of its imports of American products.

2. *Negotiations with China and their breakup*

The cease of trade escalation came in December 2018 when the US postponed the increase from 10% to 25% tariff on $200 billion worth of Chinese for 90 days, and allowed further negotiations. These negotiations have produced some advancements and the 1 March deadline for raising tariffs was delayed once more.

However, beginning in May, the US-China trade talks collapsed. The US side has focused heavily on the enforcement mechanisms within the trade talks. Apparently, when the 150-page draft agreement (negotiated in proportion of 90%) was presented to the Chinese politburo, Beijing backtracked at allowing the US to hold controlling enforcement over the trade agreement terms. It seems that, in each of the seven chapters of the draft trade deal, China had cancelled its commitments to change laws and resolve essential complaints of the US: theft of US intellectual property and trade secrets; forced technology transfers; competition policy; access to financial services; and currency manipulation: "[…] The stripping of binding legal language from the draft struck directly at the highest priority of US Trade Representative Robert Lighthizer – who views changes to Chinese laws as essential to verifying compliance after years of what US officials have called empty reform promises".[20]

20 https://www.reuters.com/article/us-usa-trade-china-backtracking-exclusiv/exclusive-china-backtracked-on-nearly-all-aspects-of-u-s-trade-deal-sources-idUSKCN1SE0WJ?utm_medium=Social&utm_source=twitter.

As a result, on 10 May 2019, the US raised tariffs on $200bn of Chinese products from 10% to 25%. China retaliated but officials say the countries are still talking.

Then, the US has started the process for hitting an additional $300bn of Chinese *goods* with tariffs, which means that all Chinese imports could be subject to tariffs. On the Chinese side all the US imported goods were already submitted to tariffs, and China run out of options (in regard of tariffs). The American trade posture has broad bipartisan support in the US. Depending on the position adopted by China, this can become a protracted trade war whose relative winner will be the US.

B. Negotiations with Japan and EU and eventual new over-the-border measures on cars

In 2017, the US Trade Representative announced plans to negotiate new trade deals with the EU and Japan, which collectively accounted for $350 billion of American exports in 2017. However, no real advancements were achieved with any of them yet.

i/ Japan's trade imbalance is the third largest among all major US trading partners, behind China and Mexico. The $54 billion trade deficit in automobiles and parts accounts for three-quarters of the overall figure. Negotiations with Japan might be far easier than those with the EU as they will be a one-on-one basis compared with the multilateral dimensions existing in the EE. However, the US-Japan deadlock persists.

The Trump administration tried to create leverage and launched a national security investigation into car and truck imports in May 2018, under section 232 of the Trade Expansion Act. Higher tariffs could be particularly harmful for Japanese automakers including Toyota, Nissan, and Honda, which count on the US as a major market. However, analysts at Geopolitical Intelligence firm *Stratfor* said that Japan could be insulated to some extent from US trade action because of the many Japanese production factories in the US.[21]

ii/ The EU agreed, at last, in March 2019, to start negotiations with the US[22] to prevent the trade dispute brandished by Trump. The decision

---

21 *Cf.* https://worldview.stratfor.com/article/2019-annual-forecast-geopolitics-intelligence-global-risk.

22 *Cf.* http://europa.eu/rapid/press-release_IP-19-2148_en.htm.

to launch negotiations comes after Trump threatened in 2018, as for Japan, to hit the EU with punitive tariffs, especially on the export of cars mainly from Germany, a country that has a trade surplus with the U.S. Ministers of the EU authorised the European Commission to work with the US on two deals in order to eliminate tariffs on industrial goods and to recognise each other's conformity assessments. However, the US Congress is now insisting that the deal should also cover farm products.

Tariffs on cars as leverage or as protective measures?

The US is threatening to push tariffs up to 25% on imported cars and parts. In February 2019, the US Commerce Department sent a report to Trump that could release steep tariffs on imported cars and auto parts[23] based on another 'Section 232' of national security.

Trump had 90 days to decide whether to act upon the recommendations. It was anticipated that its recommendation options would include broad tariffs of up to 20% to 25% on assembled cars and parts, or narrower tariffs targeting components and technologies related to new energy cars, autonomous, internet connected and shared vehicles. But its fate was intimately linked to the conundrum of security exception within the frame of WTO, which is explored below. An added consideration was the protracted trade war with China and the need of allies for the US administration.

Hence, on 17 May 2019, the Trump administration decided to delay for six months auto tariffs in order to facilitate (leverage) the continuing negotiations with EU and Japan.

C. Security exception and the legal conundrum at WTO

Trump's use of 'over the border' steel and aluminium tariffs has frustrated not only competitors but allies across the globe. Canada, Mexico, the EU, Turkey, etc., have challenged Trump's tariffs at the WTO, pretending that their aluminium and steel export pose no threat to America's national security. They have adopted their own retaliatory tariffs, pushing the Trump administration to bring its own WTO complaints against those countries.[24]

---

23 D. LAWDER and D. SHEPARDSON, "U.S. agency submits auto tariff probe report to White House", *Washington (Reuters)*, 17 February 2019.

24 See A. SWANSON and J. EWING, "Trump's National Security Claim for Tariffs Sets Off Crisis at W.T.O.", *New York Times*, 12 August 2018.

At the centre of the legal conflict is whether the US claim that its steel and aluminium tariffs are necessary to protect national security or whether they are simply a mechanism to protect American metal manufacturers from global competition.

Any decision could seal the fate of the WTO. Agreeing with the US claim of national security could alter the organisation's authority and push other countries to begin invoking their own national security interests. And that will also open the door for the US to apply future over the border tariffs on cars based on national security reasons. A ruling against the Trump administration could prompt the US to leave the WTO or to immobilise it.

In fact, the US withheld the appointment of new members for a WTO appeals body, a decision that threatens to paralyse the group's ability to settle disputes. The Trump administration claims that the WTO is over-reaching its mandate, especially in its opposition to trade charges that the US uses to combat unfair external trade competition.

From September 2018, the appellate body, which normally has seven members, operates with just three, the minimum needed to issue rulings. If the US continues to deny the approval of new appointments when members' terms expire, by the end of 2019, there may be only one panel member left and the appellate body (and the WTO as such) will stop functioning.

*

In conclusion, what are the possible outcomes? The US has options, since it possesses enormous leverages, greater than any trade partner. A great free-trade agreement with China will be signed, if ever, only after China is seriously affected economically. An eventual trade agreement with the US will be on the lines of the initial draft rejected by China and will contain enforcement measures, required by the American side.

If negotiations with Japan and EU stall, the US might adopt new 'over the border' tariffs on cars based on Section 232 and the national security clause. Further, it might propose to Japan and EU some exceptions to such tariffs based on quantitative measures similar to those adopted in relation to steel and aluminium.

But such tariffs might be still postponed if the trade war with China continues. Such tariffs can initiate a global recession and created two new fronts on a global trade war that US could win, only as a Phyrical victory. Such a measure will also tremendously amplify the 'legal stress" within the WTO. If the conundrum of the security exception is solved in a way that the US Administration consider unsatisfactory, the WTO might be *de facto* abolished.

However, this might be just a temporary paralysis of the organisation, as a step in creating and using leverage for renegotiating the WTO statute, which, everybody agree, is in great demand of being reformed. Maybe the Trump administration is not trying to demolish the multilateral economic system of today but pushing its partners to conclude new deals closer to US interests and to reform the WTO *en passant*, thereby creating the condition for a globalisation 2.0 (within the frame of a reformed WTO).

The 'Most-Favoured-Nation' principle in recent investment arbitration cases involving some Eurasian countries

Chan-Mo Chung
Law School, Inha University, South Korea

Investment disputes rising in the region – Eurasia has attracted increasing foreign investment as countries of the region have paid more attention to economic development since the end of the cold war. China's 'One Belt, One Road' initiative accelerated this trend by adding up investments in infrastructure of the regional developing countries.[1] Although investment in the transitional economies in the region is currently experiencing temporary fluctuation,[2] the long-term prospect of growing inbound and outbound investment is unwavering.

Not all investment projects proceed as planned and satisfy all the parties concerned. In fact, many investment projects embroil disputes in implementation, payment and profit—sharing, etc. Some of those disputes may be resolved in domestic court proceedings or commercial arbitration. However, in some cases where the disputes were claimed to be caused by action or inaction of the State that receives investment from an investor with whose home country the recipient country made bilateral or regional investment treaty, investor-State dispute settlement (ISDS) procedure may be the preferred option for the investor to resort to in that the procedure is more neutral and, once win the case, remedies are more secure to obtain as States seldom go bankrupt.

The regime of investment treaty and investor-State arbitration revealed strength as well as weakness, and those treaties especially adopted by

---

1 UNCTAD, *World Investment Report*, 2018, p. 45–46, 48–49.

2 *Ibidem*, p. 56–59, 70–72.

Eurasian countries have plenty of room to improve in terms of clarity, transparency and scope of coverage. States in the region have not been keen on the issue of improving the ISDS system. Developments in recent years, however, suggest an awakening of the regional States. For example, Asia-Pacific regional meeting on ISDS reform was held in Incheon, Korea, 10–11 September 2018.[3] This may be explained by the rising number of investment arbitration raised by and against the countries in the region. During the past thirty years, Eurasian countries have been more or less passive participants to the ISDS system. Winning rate as a participant of the regional States was also lower (28%) than global average (37%). Although the winning rate of regional investors was higher (38%) than global average (25%)[4], considering the small number of cases initiated by regional investors, this data would rather show regional investors' low awareness about the ISDS system than their better performance at arbitration battle. Enhanced awareness of the States and investors of the region will bring the score closer to the global average.

The MFN clause in the middle of controversy – Bilateral investment treaties (BIT) and investment chapters of free trade agreements usually include a most-favoured-nation (MFN) treatment clause which guarantees no less favourable treatment to investors and investments from a contracting party than the party provides to investors and investments from a third party.[5] Although the MFN principle is adopted in most of international trade and investment agreements, it has yet to gain the status of customary international law. The hurly-burly over the scope of MFN clause testifies the lack of consistent State practice.

The most frequent controversy concerns whether a complaining investor from a BIT party may rely on an MFN clause to resort to the dispute settlement mechanism of other BIT which the investor deems

---

3 Summary of the intersessional regional meeting on investor State dispute settlement (ISDS) reform submitted by the Government of the Republic of Korea, UN Commission on International Trade Law, Working Group III (Investor-State Dispute Settlement Reform) Thirty-sixth session, Vienna, 29 October-2 November 2018, UN, A/CN.9/WG.III/WP.154.

4 M.F. FERRACANE, "Investor-State Dispute Settlement (ISDS) Cases in the Asia-Pacific Region: The Record", in J. CHAISSE *et al.* (Eds.), *Asia's Changing International Investment Regime: Sustainability, Regionalization, and Arbitration*, Singapore, Springer, 2017, p. 229–242.

5 As shown in the *Caratube II* below, national investment laws in a less frequent occasion incorporate MFN and/or ISDS.

Number of cases involving some selected States, as of December 2018. Source: https://investmentpolicyhub.unctad.org/ISDS/FilterByCountry.

	Cases as Respondent State	Cases as Home State of claimant
China	3	5
Czech	38	5
France	1	49
India	24	5
Kazakhstan	19	5
Korea	7	5
Kyrgyzstan	14	0
Romania	15	1
Russia	24	22
Turkey	14	33
Turkmenistan	13	0
USA	16	174
Uzbekistan	8	1

more favourable. For example, some bilateral investment agreements require the complainant to take domestic administrative and/or court procedure before the investor bring the case to investor-State arbitration. Tribunals have offered diverse views over the possibility of bringing the case directly to arbitration without recourse to the required negotiation or local procedure. The *Maffezini* decision allowed avoiding an 18-month local procedure required to have gone through prior to submitting a case to investor-State arbitration by invoking other investment treaty without a local remedies condition, by means of an MFN provision of the basic investment treaty.[6] Arbitral decisions after *Maffezini*, however, diverged. Some in favour,[7] some against.[8]

All tribunals pay respect to the text of agreements. Difficulties arise when the text is vague. One approach is to distinguish the issues of jurisdiction and admissibility. Some tribunals took the local-remedy-first

6 Emilio Agustín Maffezini v. The Kingdom of Spain (Jurisdiction), ICSID Case No. ARB/97/7, January 2000.

7 Among others, Siemens v. Argentina (Jurisdiction), ICSID Case No. ARB/02/8, 3 August 2004.

8 Among others, Wintershall v. Argentina (Award), ICSID Case No. ARB/04/14, 8 December 2008.

requirement as an admissibility condition which may be overcome through MFN clause of investment agreement.[9] Other tribunals, however, see it as a jurisdictional condition that cannot be skipped over via MFN clause.[10] The lack of consistency in the jurisprudence threatened the stability of international investment protection and the ISDS system. Hereunder, we discuss recent ISDS cases involving some Eurasian countries (I) and draw implications (II).

I. MFN Applied in Recent Investment Disputes in the Region

A. *Kılıç, Sehil, and İçkale against Turkmenistan*

1. Kılıç *v. Turkmenistan*

Kılıç, a Turkish construction company, tried to resolve its disputes with Turkmenistan through an International Centre for Settlement of Investment Disputes (ICSID) arbitration. Article 7 of the Turkey-Turkmenistan BIT,[11] which the complainant relied on, however, required a foreign investor to first go through domestic dispute resolution procedure for one year. To evade the seemingly time-wasting local remedies requirement, the complainant resorted to MFN treatment clause, Article 2.2 of the basic treaty, which reads:

> "Each Party shall accord to these investments, once established, treatment no less favourable than that accorded in similar situations to investments of its investors or to investments of investors of any third country, whichever is the most favourable."

---

[9] Among others, Hochtief v. Argentina (Jurisdiction), ICSID Case No. ARB/07/31, 24 October 2011.

[10] Among others, Daimler v. Argentina (Award), ICSID Case No. ARB/05/1, 22 October 2012.

[11] "1. Disputes between one of the Parties and one investor of the other Party, in connection with his investment, shall be notified in writing, including a [*sic*] detailed information, by the investor to the recipient Party of the investment. As far as possible, the investor and the concerned Party shall endeavor to settle these disputes by consultations and negotiations in good faith. 2. If these desputes [*sic*] cannot be settled in this way within six months following the date of the written notification

The *Kılıç* tribunal put priority on the letter of agreement and recognised the distinction between jurisdiction and admissibility. It, however, regarded the local-remedy-first requirement as a jurisdictional condition. The tribunal nevertheless proceeded to assess whether the MFN clause or futility argument may provide grounds for the recognition of jurisdiction. From the structure of the basic BIT in which the MFN clause is located just before the substantive provisions, it found that the MFN clause applies only to the substantive provisions excluding dispute-settlement provisions which come next. It also found that the non-inclusion of local remedies requirement in some prior BITs that Turkey made and inclusion of local remedies requirement in every prior BITs that Turkmenistan made suggest Parties' intention not to apply MFN principle of the basic BIT to dispute settlement. Otherwise, the dispute settlement provision would lose effectiveness and fairness.[12]

The tribunal also found that the wording of Article 2.2 is not as extensive as the MFN provisions that have been interpreted by preceding tribunals as applying to dispute settlement. Subsequent State practices that when the parties made BITs with the UK they explicitly included dispute-settlement within the coverage of MFN clause were recognised as supporting the tribunals finding that the MFN clause of the basic treaty which lacks such explicit wording does not apply to dispute settlement. Finally, the tribunal found that the complainant failed to prove futility of local remedies provided by the respondent State.

Therefore, the Tribunal dismissed all the claims of the complainant on the ground that it lacks jurisdiction as the complainant did not fulfil the precondition of local procedure and was not exempted from this condition.

---

mentioned in paragraph 1, the dispute can be submitted, as the investor may choose, to: (a) the International Center for Settlement of Investment Disputes (ICSID)… (b)… (c)…, provided that [if] the investor concerned has brought the dispute before the courts of justice of the Party that is a party to the dispute and a final award has not been rendered within one year."

12 Turkey's effort in later negotiations to include local remedies requirement would be useless and there would be imbalance of rights and obligations between the Parties and their nationals.

2. Muhammet & Sehil v. Turkmenistan

In contrast to the *Kılıç* decision, the *Sehil* tribunal decided that the local remedies in Article 7(2) of the Turkey-Turkmenistan BIT is optional and an investor can bring dispute before arbitration directly.[13] While the *Kılıç* tribunal gave priority to the Russian version of the BIT, this tribunal gave priority to the English version.[14] The tribunal understood Article 7(2) of the BIT as a 'fork in the road' provision to prevent duplicate local and international proceedings. Therefore, it was not necessary for the claimant to rely on the MFN clause in this case.

3. İçkale İnşaat Limited Şirketi v. Turkmenistan

The *İçkale* tribunal swung back to side with the *Kılıç* decision holding that Article 7(2) of the Turkey-Turkmenistan BIT is mandatory.[15] Still this tribunal regarded the local proceedings as a matter of admissibility not of jurisdiction. In this case, the tribunal acknowledged the existence of local proceedings initiated ironically by Turkmenistan authorities. MFN provision was invoked by the complainant to import from other investment treaties concluded by Turkmenistan substantive standards of protection such as fair and equitable treatment, full protection and security, non-discrimination and umbrella clause protections which were not included in the basic treaty. The tribunal rejected such a claim, holding that as the relevant MFN clause includes the term "similar situations" the clause must be restrictively interpreted to apply to a "factually" similar situation.[16] The tribunal dismissed the claimant's claims in their entirety for lack of merits.

B. A11Y v. Czech

Article 8 of the Agreement between the U.K. and the Czech Slovak Republic for the Promotion and Protection of Investments of 10 July 1990, under which the complainant brought this arbitration provides:

---

13 Muhammet Çap & Sehil Inşaat v. Turkmenistan (Jurisdiction), ICSID Case No. ARB/12/6, 13 February 2015.

14 *Ibidem*, paras. 273–274.

15 İçkale İnşaat Limited Şirketi v. Turkmenistan, ICSID Case No. ARB/10/24, 8 March 2016.

16 *Ibidel*, paras. 329, 332.

> "8.1 Disputes between an investor of one Contracting Party and the other Contracting Party concerning an obligation of the latter under Articles 2(3), 4, 5 and 6 of this Agreement in relation to an investment of the former which have not been amicably settled shall, after a period of four months from written notification of a claim, be submitted to arbitration under paragraph (2) below if either party to the dispute so wishes."

The complainant wanted to add the breach of Article 2(2) concerning fair and equitable treatment and full protection and security and Article 3 concerning national treatment as causes of claim for the arbitration. For that purpose, the complainant tried to invoke Netherlands-Czech BIT which allows all disputes to be resolved through arbitration by way of MFN clause of the basic treaty, which reads:

> "3(1) Each Contracting Party shall ensure that under its law investments or returns of investors of the other Contracting Party are granted treatment no less favourable than that which it accords to investments or return of its own investors or to investments or returns of investors of any third State.
>
> 3(2) Each Contracting Party shall ensure that under its law investors of the other Contracting Party, as regards their management, maintenance, use, enjoyment or disposal of their investments, are granted treatment not less favourable than that which it accords to its own investors or to investors of any third State."

The tribunal for this case at the beginning conceded that MFN principle applies not only for substantive treatment but also for procedural treatment.[17] The tribunal, however, recognised limitations of the MFN principle in cases (i) it contravenes public policy of the recipient State, such as creating consent to arbitration itself; or (ii) the basic treaty explicitly confines the scope of MFN clause.[18] In this case, the Tribunal found that Article 8 of the basic treaty explicitly limited the scope of consent to arbitration to disputes concerning specific provisions, and an MFN clause cannot extend it.[19] The tribunal also recognised the principle of severability (autonomy) of arbitration clause as a rationale supporting its decision.[20]

---

17 A11Y LTD. v. Czech Republic (Jurisdiction), ICSID Case No. UNCT/15/1, 9 February 2017, paras. 96–97.

18 *Ibidem*, paras. 98–100.

19 *Ibidem*, paras. 102–104.

20 *Ibidem*, para. 102 quoting Plama v. Bulgaria (Jurisdiction), 2005, para. 212.

Then, the tribunal proceeded into merit stage for claims over which it recognised jurisdiction, but dismissed the claims as the claimant failed to evidence that the business loss was due to unfair discrimination against it and not to legitimate policy change of the host State.[21]

C. *Ansung Housing v. China*

A Korean construction company, *Ansung Housing*, brought an ICSID arbitration against China based on the Korea-China BIT after it suffered severe losses in the investment for developing golf courses and condominium, claiming unfair treatment by a Chinese provincial government.[22] The first hurdle for the claimant was whether *Ansung* brought the arbitration within three years since it knew or should be able to know the loss, as required by Article 9(7) of the basic treaty.

In case the argument that the three-year period has not elapsed would not be accepted by the tribunal, the claimant imported better provisions from China's BITs with third countries which do not include similar limitation period by way of the MFN provision of the basic treaty, which reads:

> "Each Contracting Party shall in its territory accord to investors of the other Contracting Party and to their investments and activities associated with such investments by the investors of the other Contracting Party treatment no less favourable than that accorded in like circumstances to the investors and investments and associated activities by the investors of any third State (hereinafter referred to as 'most-favoured-nation treatment') with respect to investments and business activities, including the admission of investment." (Article 3(3))

The claimant argued that the limitation period to arbitration is substantive by nature and the MFN provision is broad enough to cover the limitation period. On the other hand, China argued that the limitation is procedural and the scope of MFN clause is limited by the words 'in its territory' and 'investments and business activities'.

The tribunal found that 'investments and business activities' is defined as "the expansion, operation, management, maintenance, use, enjoyment, and sale or other disposal of investments" in Article 3(1) and

---

[21] A11Y LTD. v. Czech Republic (Award), 29 June 2018.

[22] Ansung Housing Co., Ltd. v. People's Republic of China, ICSID Case No. ARB/14/25, 9 March 2017.

does not extend to the limitation period for investor-State arbitration.[23] The tribunal also noted that while Article 3(5) offers specific MFN protection in relation to an investor's access to domestic courts of justice and administrative tribunals and authorities,[24] Article 3(3) does not refer international dispute resolution. From those considerations the tribunal found that the wording of the MFN clause in Article 3(3) of the Treaty clearly does not cover dispute settlement including arbitral consent and conditions to arbitration.[25]

The finding of the tribunal that "the expansion, operation, management, maintenance, use, enjoyment, and sale or other disposal of investments" does not include dispute settlement is supported only by some of previous arbitral awards and opposed by others.[26] Nevertheless, other contextual elements may justify the tribunal's finding.

D. *Caratube v. Kazakhstan (Caratube II)*

After its first arbitration filing based on Kazakhstan-USA BIT (1992) failed,[27] *Caratube* brought again an arbitration case this time based on the Foreign Investment Law of Kazakhstan. The tribunal this time recognised the occurrence of an expropriation without compensation.[28] Annulment procedure is pending.

In this proceeding, the complainant relied on the MFN clause, Article 4(1) of the Foreign Investment Law to invoke the more favourable treatment in the BITs that Kazakhstan has entered into with third countries. Kazakhstan, however, reminded that Article 4(2) of the Law stipulates that MFN "does not apply […] to the benefits that the Republic of

---

23 *Ibidem*, paras. 137–138.

24 "5. Treatment accorded to investors of one Contracting Party within the territory of the other Contracting Party with respect to access to the courts of justice and administrative tribunals and authorities both in pursuit and in defense of their rights shall not be less favourable than that accorded to investors of the latter Contracting Party or to investors of any third State."

25 *Ansung* award, paras. 139–140.

26 ILC, Final Report of the Study Group on the Most-Favoured-Nation clause, 2015, paras. 198, 206.

27 Caratube International Oil Company LLP v. Republic of Kazakhstan, ICSID Case No. ARB/08/12, 5 June 2012 (*Caratube I*).

28 Caratube International Oil Company LLP and Devincci Salah Hourani v. Republic of Kazakhstan, ICSID Case No. ARB/13/13, 27 September 2017 (*Caratube II*).

Kazakhstan provides to individuals or legal entities from other countries under the international treaties concluded with these countries or joint participation with these States in international conventions". The tribunal upheld Kazakhstan's position on this issue.[29]

II. Generalising Recent Trends in the Application of MFN Clauses

From the analysis above, we find that in no case since the *Kılıç* decision, the tribunals decided in favour of the invocation of an MFN clause. It is not only true for importation of procedure such as direct recourse to arbitration without local-remedy-first requirement but also for importation of substantive protection. The *Kılıç, A11Y, Ansung Housing*, and *Caratube (II)* decisions delivered clear and consistent opinions on the topic. An MFN clause cannot widen the scope of arbitration consent. The judicial dictum that cases along the line with Maffezeni supported, i.e. an early filing of arbitration may be enabled through shortening procedural conditions on the basis of MFN clause in the basic treaty and more favourable procedure in the comparable treaty, was either formally contradicted or practically ignored.

In detail, *Ansung* tribunal ruled that it may not extend the limitation of the period for the submission of a dispute to arbitration and MFN clause cannot change the scope and conditions of arbitral consent.

The *A11Y* tribunal recognised limitations of the MFN principle in cases where (i) it contravenes public policy of the host State, such as creating consent to arbitration itself; or (ii) the basic treaty explicitly confines the scope of MFN clause.

The *İçkale* tribunal went further to reject the tradition dichotomy contrasting procedural against substantive provision and declined to recognise neither substantive standards of treatment, nor procedure of dispute settlement. These lines of decisions based their rationale on the principle of autonomy of arbitration consent.

The *İçkale* tribunal's disallowance of the invocation of MFN clause to import substantive investment protection standards from a comparable treaty, unless there is actual treatment to similar investment under the comparable treaty, is a deviation from the established WTO case-law on MFN

---

29 *Ibidem*, para. 821.

that the aim of the principle is to guarantee equality of competitive opportunity and it does not require actual existence of trade effect.[30] The *İçkale* decision seems to be influenced by some recent investment treaties which explicitly require existence of measures adopted in order to actualise substantive obligation of the comparator treaties.[31] Although there is no reason that the investment law should always follow trade law principles, deviation without explanation should be discouraged.

Recent trends in arbitral awards correspond with increasing State practices in making investment treaty. Many countries explicitly excluded dispute-settlement provisions from the scope of MFN application when they enter into new BITs or FTAs.[32] Although most of the States maintained old treaties intact, new practices might have affected the way tribunals interpret even old treaties.

It is currently not certain whether this new wave of cases represents an emerging consensus or a recoil against aggressive decisions such as *Maffezini*. It seems that decisions discussed here pursued a short-term goal of a strong State's sovereignty but lost the long-term agenda for a good governance of the global economy. For a reconstruction of the destabilised legal theory in this area, a new set of tests, which balance the effects of MFN application on the interests of investor on the one hand and those of host State on the other, should be found.

In order to find an equitable balance between the opposing arguments and theories, efforts are needed to focus on drawing of fine boundaries rather than digging trenches for one's position. In this regard, the *Kılıç* decision may be reappraised as a step forwards for finer classification of local procedures which are required to be taken prior to arbitration. For instance, a waiting period should have different legal value from the requirement to bring a case first to a specific local court. The *Kılıç* decision should be better understood as meaning that the MFN clause cannot replace an explicitly specified local procedure, yet can replace a generally described local procedure.

*

In conclusion, it is a good thing that the veil of MFN clause has been lifted to some extent through recent investment arbitrations. There is

---

30 WTO Appellate Body Report, EC-Seal Products (2014), para. 5.82.

31 Articles X.7 of the CETA 2016.

32 CPTPP Article 9.5(3); Revised (2018) KORUS FTA Article 11.4(3).

some concern, however, that the recent MFN-aversive case trend would distort the whole picture of the MFN principle. The value of MFN as an equaliser at the higher level of protection should be preserved. Exceptions to the MFN should be utilised rather than the principle itself be put in peril.

Some of the recent arbitral decisions discussed in this paper are located at the minimalist end, while the *Maffezini* stands at the maximalist end. Hopefully, the median can be found soon. Swaying along the direction of political winds is not something expected from a neutral dispute-settlement body. No destruction but reconstruction of old legal doctrines on the application of MFN, such as dichotomies of 'substantive/procedural' obligation and 'admissibility/jurisdiction', are requested for practicing lawyers as well as for academic lawyers in the field of investment arbitration.

Legal aspects of trade cooperation in the framework of the 'Belt and Road Initiative'

Zhuldyz SAIRAMBAEVA, Gulmira MASHIMBAYEVA
al-Farabi Kazakh National University, Almaty, Kazakhstan

On 7 September 2013, during his first State visit to Kazakhstan, the Chinese President Xi Jinping delivered a speech at Nazarbayev University and officially launched an ambitious initiative to jointly build the 'Silk Road Economic Belt', which received support from President Nazarbayev and an active response from various communities in Kazakhstan. Subsequently, Kazakhstan became one of the first States to take part in international cooperation in the framework of the initiative 'One Belt, One Road'.

The concepts of the 'Silk Road Economic Belt' and the 'Sea Silk Road' of the 21st century laid the foundations of a new external strategy for China in the near historical perspective. The implementation of these projects, which were united under the common title 'One Belt, One Road', became one of Beijing's most important tasks in optimising the spatial structure of the economic development of the entire Eurasian region.

Both concepts put forward by President Xi Jinping in the fall of 2013 initially caused ambiguous interpretations in political and scientific circles. This was followed by the development of the initiative at the expert level, and gradually it began to take on more specific forms. The principles, structure, as well as priority areas and cooperation mechanisms under the 'One Belt, One Road' initiative were clearly formulated in March 2015 during the Boao Forum for Asia. The document published, in the development of which the State Committee for the Development and Reforms, the Ministry of Foreign Affairs and the Ministry of Commerce of the PRC took part, was called the "Concept and Action Plan to Promote the Joint Construction of the Silk Road Economic Belt and the Sea Silk Road of the XXI Century". The stated goal of this large-scale project is the creation of new mechanisms for economic development that will contribute to a more efficient allocation of resources in the region and strengthen market integration between Europe, Asia and Africa.

The 'Silk Road Economic Belt' is considered as a large-scale economic project aimed at expanding ties with foreign countries, especially with the countries of Central Asia. Its essence is the creation of the Trans-Eurasian land bridge and the development of three economic corridors: the Northern (China – Mongolia – Russia), Central (China – Central Asia – Middle East) and Southern (Bangladesh – China – India – Myanmar, and also China – Pakistan).

The published Action Plan for the joint construction of "belts and roads" calls for the coordination of political efforts, the development of infrastructure cooperation, free trade, commercial integration and the strengthening of connections between people. In the field of infrastructure construction alone, which includes the creation of roads and railways, the laying of oil pipelines and power lines, the construction of bridges and ports, enormous financial opportunities are emerging. Experts of the Asian Development Bank predict that by 2020 the need for investment in this area will be 8 trillion US $.

The document notes that this project, open to all States, international and regional organisations, creates significant inclusive platform for uniting the Chinese economy with the interests of the countries involved. As President Xi Jinping stated, speaking before the participants of the Boao Forum for Asia in March 2015: " 'One Belt, One Road' Initiative is not a Chinese solo, but a symphony of interested parties".[1] China, noted by the authors of the concept, is ready to work with other countries to improve the content of the initiative, to develop project schedules and multilateral cooperation formats, and also calls for multi-polarity and equal negotiations on international issues.

According to experts of the Eurasian Economic Cooperation Organisation (EECO), at present in China and other fast-growing countries of Southeast Asia a new, more efficient socio-economic system is being formed compared to the traditional American-European

---

1 K.U. BIEKENOV, "The Great Silk Road as the key to the creation and development of a new model of social infrastructure", *KazNU Bulletin. Series of Psychology and Sociology*, 2018, 67(4).

social economic system, which is adequate to the requirements of the new technological order. The PRC is becoming the world leader in such promising areas as alternative energy sources, biotechnologies, new generations of information technologies, production of high-quality equipment, modern materials, vehicles on alternative fuels, energy-saving and environmentally friendly technologies, technologies for increasing energy efficiency and ensuring security of energy supply, etc.

The peculiarity of the initiative is the fact that the States involved in this process did not initially rely on any single legal platform, there was no goal of creating some kind of organisation, an economic bloc with appropriate international legal support. China concludes separate independent agreements, memorandums and programmes with each country, on the basis of which it is prepared to invest money, technology, labour, etc. in the economy of these countries.

As S.G. Luzyanin notes, the Chinese initiative is unlikely to ever become an institutionalised project – it will likely remain a tool for the economic, investment, transport and humanitarian development of the Eurasian space[2].

The economic convergence between the States of Eurasia, the harmonisation of various integration projects can give a powerful impetus to the development of the economies of a number of States – ultimately – to form new sources of growth in the global economy.

I. The need for legal analysis

It is from this point of view that it makes sense to analyse the current state of the many-sided work on the conjugation of the SREB and the EAEU. This term entered the lexicon of diplomatic meetings in 2015 since the meeting of Putin and Xi Jinping in Moscow. The use of this word indicated the need to solve non-trivial political tasks. The primary one is to find a format in which the long-term strategic initiative of transcontinental scale, formulated in fairly general terms, could be combined with already functioning structures and mechanisms of the regional economic integration association (EAEU).

---

2 S.G. LUZYANIN, "Absorption, conjugation or conflict? SCO, Chinese Silk Road Project and EAEU: Options for Cooperation in Eurasia", *Final expert and analytical report on RFBR project,* No. 16'07'00024: http://www.ifes'ras.ru/images/stories/2018/report_2018_luzyanin_s_g.pdf.

Beijing met the capitals of the EAEU States, expressing its readiness to transfer the regulation of a number of significant issues to the level of interaction with the integration structures of post-Soviet regionalism. These issues include cooperation in the development of infrastructure, industry, transport, stimulation of investment activity, regulation of access to financial markets, services market, etc.

On 17 May 2018, within the framework of the Astana Economic Forum, an Agreement on Trade and Economic Cooperation between the Eurasian Economic Union (EAEU) and the People's Republic of China (PRC) was signed. Negotiations on the signing of this agreement had been going on for two years.

Thanks to the agreement reached, additional tools will also appear to level out the existing imbalances in trade and economic relations between China and the EAEU countries.

The current stage of interfacing is characterised by gradual adaptation of the EAEU States to the peculiarities of the promotion of the Chinese initiative 'One Belt, One Road' (OBOR), uniting the 'Silk Road Economic Belt' (SREB) and the 'Sea Silk Road of the XXI century' project. However, it is too early to say that all difficulties have been overcome. Among the remaining problems is a kind of 'blurring' of a number of key parameters of cooperation within the OBOR, expressed in Beijing's readiness to define these parameters *ad hoc* each time, taking into account the specific circumstances and interests of a particular partner with whom the dialogue is conducted. In this context, the successful completion of negotiations on the preparation of trade and economic agreement between the PRC and the EAEU is a very important stage in the process of determining the specific conditions and format of interfacing.

The development of the transport and related infrastructure of the Eurasian continent, capable of ensuring reliable supply of resources and expanding the export opportunities of the Chinese economy, is the most important task of the 'One Belt, One Road' initiative. Accordingly, this aspect will inevitably come to the fore in the process of pairing the SREB with the EAEU. It is the qualitative renovation of the transport and logistics infrastructure, which reliably connects the largest markets of Eurasia – China and the EU – that will ensure the process of interconnection of truly transcontinental significance. Trade and economic agreement between the EAEU and the PRC will create more favourable conditions for infrastructure construction and investment. At the same time, there is still no reason to talk about a breakthrough in the creation of modern transport and logistics infrastructure of Eurasia.

II. Hurdles and difficulties

There are many circumstances and factors that impede the rapid launch of such large-scale infrastructure projects. Among them is the insufficiency of those options for the development of transport and logistics infrastructure, which reduce the role of most countries and regions along the route of corresponding transport route only to ensuring the transit of goods and passengers. It is necessary to intensify trade production activity along the entire length of the transport corridor, ensuring maximum loading of containers, ships and automobile trucks, and thereby enhancing the economic coherence of the territories and the overall efficiency of infrastructure projects.

Such a statement of the task, in turn, requires from States interested in developing transcontinental infrastructure a new quality of infrastructure policy and traffic management, which can overcome disproportions in the functioning of the transport services market and the system of delivery of foreign trade goods through sea and river ports. However, at present, at the level of inter-State cooperation in the post-Soviet space, there is no operational control authority for the transport of goods in its unified transport system (UTS).[3] Launching giant development projects for the Eurasian transport and logistics infrastructure without breaking down the bottlenecks will initially be doomed to low economic efficiency and, at worst, will lead to the question of their 'autonomisation' regarding the existing UTS management structures and even the transfer of the most important elements infrastructure created under the control of the main investor. Meanwhile, one of the most important tasks that needs to be solved in the process of forming the SREB transport corridors on the territory of the EAEU States is ensuring the economic coherence of the entire macro-region, which requires both the modernisation of the UTS management mechanisms and the regional, industrial, investment and trade policies of individual States of the EAEU integration structures. In

3 V. P. KUPRIYANOVSKIY, P.V. KURENKOV and O.N. MADYAR, "Passenger and cargo transport corridors in the Eurasian digital space", *Transport: science, technology, management. Scientific Information Collection*, 2017(11), p. 8–17.

fact, the point is that the SREB transport corridors must simultaneously become development corridors within the EAEU.

In general, the Agreement will improve the conditions for the access of goods to mutual markets through the rules available in the agreement on trade facilitation, increasing the level of transparency, as well as increasing the level of interaction in all areas of trade cooperation. The document is non-preferential in nature and does not imply automatic reduction of trade barriers. However, it enables targeted reduction of barriers to entry into the Chinese market for interested businesses of the EAEU States and increases regulatory transparency. In addition, business through the Eurasian Economic Commission will be able to solve controversial issues with the Chinese side.

The signed Agreement on Trade and Economic Cooperation between the EAEU and the PRC contains a number of provisions aimed at both stimulating information exchange and developing administrative cooperation between the responsible authorities of the parties (in the format of creating working groups and advisory committees).

It is the next step towards the conjugation of the Eurasian Economic Union and the strategic initiative 'One Belt, One Road', which, of course, is a positive signal to companies to work more actively on joint projects.

III. Solutions taking into account China's priorities

Today, China, according to media reports, ranks second among the foreign trade partners of the EAEU States (13.6% of total trade), significantly lagging behind the collective EU (48.9%). But the share of China is constantly growing. Generally, China is an obvious strategic partner of the EAEU.[4] China continues to increase its economic presence in the EAEU States not only through the development of trade relations, but also through continuous growth in direct investments. The PRC is the leader among Asian countries in terms of accumulated foreign direct investment (FDI) in the region.

According to the Centre for Integration Studies of the Eurasian Development Bank (CIS EADB), since 2008, the total accumulated FDI of Chinese companies in the five EAEU States increased by 138%

[4] China and the EAEU have completed negotiations on a trade and economic agreement: https://ria.ru/economy/20171001/1505949651.html.

and reached 25.7 billion US $ (in 2008 it was about 11 billion US $). Even against the backdrop of the 2015 crisis, the decline in accumulated Chinese FDI in the EAEU was insignificant (by 0.6 billion US $), mainly due to the financial revaluation of assets. The next stage in trade and economic relations with China is the increase in openness regarding the country's trade and customs procedures, which is intended to ensure this agreement.

Taking into account given challenges, the agreement involves the creation of a joint committee at the ministerial level, determines the order of interaction between the customs authorities of the parties, expands the basics of using electronic documents and specifies the areas of cooperation. Main areas of focus:

- trade remedies (anti-dumping, countervailing and protective measures) and subsidies;
- technical regulation (in the future, the development and implementation of international regulations and standards);
- sanitary, phytosanitary and veterinary measures;
- customs regulation;
- protection of intellectual property;
- government procurement, etc.

At the same time, the agreement between the EAEU and the PRC is quite a framework. The absence of more serious agreements and obligations can limit the potential for closer trade and economic cooperation between the parties. The results of cooperation in this case depend on the terms of reference and the effectiveness of the work of the advisory committees and working groups, as well as on the will of Chinese leaders and the EAEU States.

On the other hand, under the conditions of Western sanctions, the unilateral cooperation of the EAEU with China, especially in the area of lending to investment projects, can potentially lead to an imbalance in the form of excessive economic dependence of the EAEU Member-States from Beijing.

Assessing the prospects for the implementation of the agreement, it can be noted that the strengthening and execution of trade and economic cooperation between the EAEU and the PRC can help to attract investment in the production and transport and infrastructure system of the Union. At the same time, the mechanism for selecting priority areas of cooperation existing within the framework of the EAEU does not allow to take into account the multidirectional interests of each of the Union States, which increases the likelihood of the transition of trade and economic relations to a bilateral format. At the same time, it is necessary to take into account the existence of facts of violation of intellectual property rights by Chinese manufacturers. As a result, situations are possible when exporters of the EAEU States are forced to acquire licenses to use their own developments, a patent for which Chinese companies have registered before.

Development by the authorised body in coordination with the EAEU Member-States of a programme for the development of free economic zones associated with China; the use of broad opportunities for expert diplomacy, the organisation of student exchanges, business forums and business exhibitions can create favourable conditions for deepening business and cultural ties.

To improve the business dialogue and to facilitate the appeals of businessmen on various issues of the agreement, the possibility of opening official representative offices of the EAEU in Beijing and other cities of the PRC can be considered; creation of a separate page (or tabs on official websites) for informing entrepreneurs of the EAEU Member-States and China about the opportunities provided by the agreement in Russian, English and Chinese.

At the same time, when implementing the agreement, it is necessary to study the main differences of mentality and cultural characteristics, which will help to find common ground during negotiations. This will be the basis for creating reliable business relationships.

In addition, on 10–13 December 2018 in Moscow, the delegations of the Eurasian Economic Union (EAEU) and the People's Republic of China (PRC) finally agreed on a draft Agreement on the exchange of information on goods and means of international transport moved across the customs borders of the Eurasian Economic Union and the People's Republic of China. The agreement is expected to be signed in 2019.

The document has been developing since 2015. As a result of the negotiation process, the parties agreed to exchange information on goods and means of international transport, exported from China to the EAEU Member-States and from the Union to China, as well as those transit through the territories of the parties to the agreement.

The agreement on the exchange of information has been developed to speed up the procedure for customs clearance of goods imported into the customs territory of the Union and the PRC, as well as goods transported in transit. The parties also plan to use data on goods and vehicles of international transport, obtained during the exchange of information, to improve efficiency in risk management and improve forms of customs control. Such an exchange will simplify international trade procedures and will help to prevent breaches of regulations in the field of customs regulation, will increase mutual trust.

Nevertheless, strategic decisions regarding the development of the Eurasian network of transport corridors in the geographical area of the SREB and the EAEU interface have not yet been made.[5] The Eurasian Economic Union States are in a difficult situation, when hasty and ill-considered decisions can have a high economic price, but excessive delay in their adoption can also lead to not only economic but also serious geopolitical consequences.

Obviously, the EAEU States need not only to develop and maintain unified position regarding cooperation with PRC, but also to ensure the practical implementation of agreements with Beijing at a level that will allow interested external actors to consider the pairing project as successful.

Essentially, the point is that the conjugation of the SREB and the EAEU will give a powerful impetus to the development of the new Eurasian regionalism. At the conceptual level, this was primarily reflected in the development of ideas about Greater Eurasia.[6] The concept of Greater Eurasia, on the one hand, reflects the objective dynamics of growing economic interdependence, and on the other, it contributes to the design of special macro-region based on ideas and identities, harmonisation of

---

5 In September 2017, the design of a high-speed highway Moscow-Kazan was completed, the project was submitted for examination; joint agreements and memorandums on attracting Chinese investments through the Silk Road Fund were prepared. (Russian Railways has completed the design of a high-speed highway Moscow-Kazan): https://lenta.ru/news/2017/09/07/misharin_vsm.

6 T. BORDACHEV, "New Eurasianism", *Russia in Global Politics*, 2015, p. 194–205; D. EFREMENKO, "The birth of Greater Eurasia", *Russia in Global Politics*, 2016(6), p. 28–45; S. KARAGANOV, "From East to West, or Greater Eurasia", *Russia in Global Politics*, 2016: https://eng.globalaffairs.ru/pubcol/From-East-to-West-or-Greater-Eurasia-18440; A. KUZNETSOVA, "Greater Eurasia: Perceptions from Russia, the European Union, and China", in P.W. SCHULZE (Ed.), *Core Europe and Greater Eurasia: A Roadmap for the Future*, Frankfurt am Main, Campus Verlag, 2017, p. 177–191.

which will serve the interests of China, Kazakhstan and other EAEU States, as well as a wider range of Eurasian actors.

*

In conclusion, the hypothesis of an institutionalisation of PRC-EAEU cooperation looms ahead. Following the signing of agreements, the institutionalisation of cooperation mechanisms should be expected. The specific design of joint institutions will allow conclusions to be drawn about the characteristic features of the model of regionalism. Finally, the practical implementation of the agreements reached, ensuring the effective functioning of interfacing institutions and the construction of modern infrastructure of Eurasian transport corridors will allow the EAEU to declare itself in relations with other regions in a new format – in the format of Eurasian regionalism.

With all the problems and risks, the conjugation of the EAEU and the SREB is still an undertaking promising a win to all its participants. It is precisely the conjugation in the coming years that is likely to involve very serious geo-economic and geopolitical transformations on the Eurasian continent. For the same reason, it is not difficult to predict new challenges with which the EAEU States and PRC will have to be in the near future. The success of the conjugation policy is far from being programmed. But the presence of the political will to realise the enormous potential of conjugation may ultimately be successful, which will be enjoyed by the States and people of Greater Eurasia.

Now, scholar lawyers and economists will have to define criteria for identifying specific projects of bilateral and multilateral cooperation to the 'One Belt, One Road' initiative, and for participating States to develop a common action plan based on the stated principles, mechanisms and priorities.

Why, like other African States, does Mali like China?[1]

Éloi DIARRA
Rouen Normandie University, Rouen, France

A Malian site, NIARELA.NET,[2] resuming its archives about the events of 2015, writes: "The Chinese Embassy in Mali, to celebrate the 55th anniversary of the establishment of diplomatic relations between China and Mali, has organised last Tuesday, a reception on its premises. The event recorded, in addition to the presence of the Chinese ambassador to Mali, Lu Huiying and a strong colony of Chinese, several members of the government." The author of the article, Youssouf Coulibaly, could have added that there were more than 300 people, including many Malian officers and other members of the government. For it was on 25 October 1960 that diplomatic relations were established between Mali and China, barely a month after the accession of Sudan, now Mali, to international sovereignty. This shows the speed with which things have been done. And since then, not a Malian President has spent his term without one or more official trips to China, just as very senior Chinese officials are regularly visiting Mali.[3] This is to say the seniority, the depth and the cordiality which preside over relations between the two States. Between them, the terms 'friends' or the expression 'Sino-Malian friendship' are not empty words. Yes, Mali loves China, which does so as well in return.

---

1 Translated from the French and adapted by P. CHABAL.

2 https://niarela.net/politique/diplomatie/mali-chine-plus-dun-demi-siecle-de-relations-diplomatiques, last accessed on 9 June 2019.

3 The author of these lines remembers that, as a young student, he and his comrades were on the verge of tarmac in the Malian capital to greet, with shouts of joy and slogans, the Prime Minister Chou-En-Laï, on an official visit at the beginning of December 1963. It was two months after the signing of the cooperation agreements between the two countries.

Of course, this brief chapter cannot claim to analyse all of these relations nor to examine all their aspects. But if the relations between the two countries are so excellent and defy the time, it is simply because both are in their favour, and Mali, especially in terms of China's participation in its industrialisation and its equipment in various and varied infrastructures (I) and by China's discretion not to be too openly involved in the management of the State in Mali (II). For its part, China benefits from a loyal friend in international forums where votes are regularly issued and also natural agricultural or mining resources. We will focus less on these counterparts in the developments that follow and focus attention on the reasons for Mali's loyalty to its ties with China.

I. China and the economic development of Mali

Here, before going further, it is important to remember that Mali has had three major political periods. The first is from 1960 to 1968. It is the socialist regime of Modibo Kéita, father of the independence of the country. He was overthrown by a military coup on 19 November 1968.[4] While promising to return to civilian political life within six months, the military junta, one way or another, kept power for 23 years, with the same President of the Republic, Mr. Moussa Traore, becoming a general in the meantime. His regime was swept away by a popular revolution backed by a section of the army in March 1991.[5] A new constitution was then elaborated, that of the third republic. Despite these political changes, the political and economic relations between China and Mali have never suffered: they have always been good, but adapting to the new needs of the country, as will be seen in the following developments.

A. The socialist period of Mali

We were then in the midst of the Cold War where two blocs clashed: 'East and West'. The option for socialism automatically removes the new State from its former colonial power, France and all its allies, the US first. Thus, "Mali turns its eyes towards the East as early as 1961,

---

4 A detailed description of the causes and the course of this coup can be found in B. SANANKOUA, *La chute de Modibo Kéita*, Paris, Chaka, 1990.

5 For a presentation of these events, See Cheikh O. DIARRAH, *Vers la 3e République du Mali*, Paris, L'Harmattan, 1992, p. 79–109.

seeing in the USSR the defender of the great ideals of anticolonialist and communist struggle that are dear to him. The Eastern bloc becomes one of the main trading partners of Mali, accounting for 42.8% of trade in the years 1964–1965, far ahead of the US (2.3%)."[6]

But it must be said that the young State of Mali was confronted with another reality: the lack of a class of investors in capital on its territory. If the country wanted to achieve development, hit had no alternative but to appeal to the holders of foreign capital, which would have meant for Mali a formal political independence without a real national economy. Naturally Mali had to build what would later be called 'State capitalism', speaking of China.

In any case, "with its potential as a revolutionary State, Mali attracts the good graces of the two great communists, the Soviet Union and the People's Republic of China… Technical assistance, economic loans, cultural exchanges, these launch in all directions a thrust with the young State".[7] It is in this context that the economic cooperation agreements with China are signed, the first, one year after the independence of Mali, the three others "on November 3, 1964, November 18, 1966 and the last, before the fall of Modibo Keita, May 24, 1968".[8] In particular, these enable Mali to obtain a loan to finance several achievements of the *Office du Niger*. Thus, Chinese aid is primarily sought, at first, because of its expertise in rice, which Mali strongly needs to feed a population that is growing rapidly. Moreover, the agreements will also include imports of Chinese rice.

But cooperation with China also includes a sugar component. Indeed, the irrigation schemes on the Niger River must also enable the production of sugar cane. This is intended for local processing at the Dougabougou plant, a village in the Ségou region. It will be seen later that China will continue to dominate this agro-industrial sector in Mali.

In the competition between the USSR and China in Mali during the Modibo Keita regime, we must recognise the victory of the Soviet Union which dominates in the creation of infrastructure (construction of the omni-sports stadium of Bamako; National School of Administration), supplies of military equipment (weapons, ammunition, military aircraft),

---

6 M. TOURON, "Le Mali, 1960–1968. Exporter la Guerre froide dans le pré-carré français", *Bulletin de l'Institut Pierre Renouvin*, 2017, 45(1), p. 83.

7 *Ibidem*, p. 84.

8 *Ibidem*, p. 85.

and mining research,[9] while China is confined to the agricultural or agro-industrial field.

Beyond these two agricultural domains, many other achievements are to be put to the credit of China in Mali in the agro-industrial field. It is the Society of Canneries of Mali (SOCOMA) for the production of canned tomatoes, mango jam, the National Society of Tobacco and Matches of Mali (SONATAM), the Compagnie Malienne des Textiles (COMATEX), the Oilseed Products Company of Mali (SEPOM), the Tea Factory, the Tannerie-Shoe Complex, the Mali-Milk Factory and many others[10].

The multitude of these companies, all national, of course, since it is a socialist State, enables young people from the school system and major schools of the country to have immediate opportunities. Unemployment is then unknown in Mali, if not for those who are obviously recalcitrant to the Marxist option, reject it or oppose it openly. They are arrested and thrown into prison. But that's another story.

For the moment, suffice it to note that China is very present in the agricultural and agro-industrial field of Mali during this period, in the form of technical assistance and financial assistance, by lending money in Mali and helping with industrial equipment for the creation of national enterprises.

This 'socialist experiment' is therefore interrupted in November 1968 but not cooperation with China.

B. The military period and the UDPM

The military power, *stricto sensu*, runs from 1968 to 1979. At this time, the Military Committee of National Liberation (MCNL) is replaced by a power, a priori civil, single-party, the Democratic Union of the Malian People, having at its head, the same person who ran the MCNL, Mr. Moussa Traoré. Candidate of this party, he is regularly elected, President of the Republic, until the popular revolution of 1991. The ideology of this party is that of a "national economy planned and

---

9 There exists a national mining research company (SONAREM) but its technicians and material means are mainly of Soviet origin.

10 See this list in A.S. TRAORE, *Défense et illustration de l'action de l'Union soudanaise RDA, 1946-1968*, Bamako, La Bouche à Livres, 1995, p. 114–116.

self-centred".[11] Also, in these beginnings, the economic management of the country is difficult to distinguish from that of the previous regime, since the national companies dominate the industrial landscape. However, under pressure from the Bretton Woods institutions and structural adjustment plans, it will be necessary to change their management modalities. It is also driven by increasing openness to the countries of the EU and those of North America. During this long period of 23 years of open or disguised military power, Sino-Malian cooperation will substantially begin to reorient itself. While it is dominated by Chinese agricultural and agro-industrial activity in Mali, it is opening up to new sectors.

It must be recognised: the planned, State-owned economy has posed a major financial risk for Mali. Managers who are not interested and who are often placed in positions of responsibility, not because of their skills but because of their political or family ties, have never put all their capacities in the development of State companies created under the era of Modibo Kéita and maintained artificially in economic survival because of the social weight of the main trade-union that held a majority, the National Union of the workers of Mali. Even though they would like to develop these companies and State enterprises, they often did not have the required training.

Were the soldiers who take power on 19 November 1968 aware of the economic difficulties that awaited them? We can doubt it. In any case, they had to cope with a difficult economic situation, facing an intellectual elite and an administration largely acquiring the socialist theses of Modibo Keita. Also, at first, for more than five years, they will not change anything, or so little, the system set up by the first president of the Republic. At most, without suppressing it, will they reduce the influence of the imposing Malian Import-Export Corporation (SOMIEX), which had the monopoly of importing all agricultural and manufactured products; they will do the same for the Office of Agricultural Products of Mali (OAPM), for the purchase of agricultural products. For the rest, they leave things as they are. The military is content with small diplomatic openings to Europe and the Bretton Woods institutions.

It must be added that their taking the reins of power occurred at odds, because the same year, severe drought hits the country. It will last until 1985. It forces the military regime to seek financing everywhere for essential grain imports to feed a hungry and hostile population, while trying to continue to support the State enterprises and companies. Thus, in the very

---

11 Slogan of the party L'Union démocratique du peuple malien.

near future, the military regime was exposed to over-indebtedness, which soon became unbearable. The debt, which was only 55 billion CFA francs in 1968, reached the record level of 1700 billion in 2001.[12] It reached 100% of GDP in 1990[13] and then declined to 60% in 2003. Or, to put it differently, it is in the order of US $ 700 million in 1980 and about 2,200 million in 1990. This increase is due to foreign borrowing, but it is also combined with the pernicious effects of the deterioration of the terms of trade which prevents Mali from deriving from the export of its cotton the necessary revenue to fill its budget deficit and finance the economy.

In any case,

> "instead of financing development, the many State-owned companies were living in a situation of permanent deficit, which the government had to constantly bail out by swallowing up its meagre resources. Fifty-five of these companies and enterprises and State-owned companies, considered by managers, employees and civil servants as a 'people's asset', employed 24,000 people; their activity accounted for 20% of the output of the secondary sector and 14% of the tertiary sector. But the annual deficit was around 10 billion Malian francs."[14]

Also, in the late 1970s, it is necessary to reorient the management of many companies and State-owned companies. In her way, China is participating in this transformation. This is the era "of co-management where China has become deeply involved. Thus, SUKALA sugar complex, COMATEX, TAMALI, UMPP, PPM[15] were subject to this type of intervention".[16] In this system, the administration and management of the company are entrusted to a foreign country, here China, whose nationals occupy some/most positions of responsibility, assisted by Malians.

However, this form of management can only lead to friction between the managers, because the responsibilities are not sufficiently distinguished and the penalties difficult to distribute. This is why it will be necessary to go further. This will be the work of the 3rd Republic.

---

12 By which date, truly enough, it had been 10 years since the military left power. Still!...

13 The UDPM and its military President lost power the following year.

14 J.R. de BENOIST, *Le Mali*, Paris, L'Harmattan, 1998, p. 137.

15 UMPP: Usine malienne de produits pharmaceutiques; PPM: Pharmacie populaire du Mali.

16 See the Report by Prof. Abdrahamane SANOGO of the Faculty of Economics and Management of the University of Bamako, Mali, 2008, p. 13.

If, during this period, Sino-Malian cooperation has been strengthened in agriculture and agribusiness, it was still open to the health sector, with the creation of the UMPP in 1983 and Chinese support to Mali's Pharmacy, through the regular supply of medicines. Until now, however, China's interest in the infrastructure sector is only moderately seen, with small subsidies for actions such as the construction of the Bamako airport in 1974, the Sélingué dam built between 1976 and 1981. This will come with the Russian disengagement and the collapse of the Soviet world on the one hand, and the inability of the former French public works companies and the new regional companies in the sector to respond to demand. China will go into it. One exception, however, is the investment of the Chinese to improve the exit of the city of Bamako by the creation of the first highway enabling the connection with the airport and the exit of Bamako towards the city of Ségou.

C. The era of the 3rd Republic

Since 1992, Mali has entered the democratic era. It is considered, with regard to the regularity of the elections, and with alternation, as having entered truly a democracy, in spite of the current crisis related to militant Islamic jihadism.[17] Despite this adherence to ideology and liberal democracy, China has not turned its back on Mali. More than ever, cooperation has strengthened and China continues to invest heavily in Mali.

The sign of these good economic relations is that the three presidents of the 3rd Republic[18] all made more than two official trips to the Middle Kingdom Country. The archives of the Presidency of the Republic of Mali contain photos showing the splendour with which the Malian High Commanders are received in China or those of China are received in Mali.[19]

Under the 3rd Republic, more than ever, China is present in the Malian economy. Those of the State-owned companies and corporations

---

17 This is indeed a real danger for democracy, because his victory would mean a religious lead of the slate as Iran experienced.

18 This concerns Mr. Alpha Oumar KONARE, President of the Republic from 1992 to 2002; Mr. Amadou Toumani TOURE, President from 2002 to 2012 and Mr. Ibrahim Boubacar KEITA whose first term began in 2013 and who is presently serving his second term.

19 Among whom the latest two Chinese leaders, Hu Jintao et Xi Jiping.

that have survived outright liquidation owe it, for many, to a change in their legal status. Some were sold entirely to individuals or multinationals, or were converted to semi-public companies, or were privatised; this is the case of COMATEX, with a 20% stake of the Malian State and the rest of the capital being held by the Chinese company COVEC (80%) in 1993. In the case of sugar, is a mixed economy company that took over in 1996 linking the Malian State and the Chinese company SUKALA-SA. Today, in 2019, it manages three flourishing factories. In addition to these areas, the company Huilerie Sino-Malienne (HUSIMA) (SARL) produces oil in Bougouni and Koumantou;[20] the Afro-China Industry Corporation (SACI) is engaged in the manufacture of plastic shoes; DATON, the production of agricultural and agro-industrial equipment; UCEMA[21] in the manufacture of ceramic building materials and the company of enamelling and galvanising of Mali (SEGMA) in the manufacture of household articles.[22]

But it is in the field of construction and public works that China has created and installed many companies in Mali: the National Society of Construction of Hénan or CHECEC-MALI.SA, the General Society of Engineering of China (COVEC), QILU Construction Group (QLCG), QUIGDAO Construction Group (QDCG).

In recent years, these companies have built, especially during the term of Mr. Amadou Toumani Touré, many social housings. To this must be added the construction of ten 'homes for the child and the woman' and the construction of the Administrative City, on Libyan payment, between 2005 and 2007; the construction of the building of the Constitutional Court of Mali, with Chinese financing, in 2008; construction between 2010 and 2012 of the 3rd Bridge over the Niger River in Bamako. To all these constructions, it would be necessary to add the numerous asphalted or paved roads by the same companies, sometimes on Chinese financing, sometimes of Chinese banks such as EXIMBANK China. It should be added the many stadiums built, both in the city of Bamako (Stadium March 26) in the regional capitals.

---

20 Two cities located, respectively, 164 km south of Bamako and 239 km south of Bamako; 75 km separate the two cities.

21 UCEMA: Usine de céramique du Mali.

22 All these data can be found in the 2008 study by Pr. A. SANOGO, *op. cit.*

On the other hand, Mali has not used, to our knowledge, China to revive its railway to Senegal. Perhaps Mali will turn its attention to this, as it is a strategic commercial axis for the country and the various attempts with other partners have all failed.

Indeed, in terms of infrastructure, it is world-known that China has been the preferred investor in Africa for a decade. In 2018, on an African tour, the Chinese President spoke only of infrastructures of all kinds: roads, ports, railways, everywhere in Africa, in Kigali as in Mombassa, Addis Ababa or Naïrobi. For China invests annually in Africa, nearly 50 billion $ in infrastructure, at least half of which in transport. It is as if the grand project of the 'New Silk Road' across Central Asia to Western Europe had been tested first in Africa. Because transport infrastructures are those that have been lacking for African economies for too long: how can they be complementary if products cannot easily move from one State to another? And without doubt, China, a major exporter today, has seen all the interest that these infrastructures could represent for its own manufactured products or for its supply of raw materials that the African continent is only able to provide it with.

II. Chinese political discretion

Yes, Malians love the Chinese presence in their country; for the works of the Chinese are visible; they leave traces which contribute to the improvement of the quality of their life: roads, administrative buildings, hospitals, schools, stadiums and roads. But beyond these material contributions, there is a kind of affective closeness between the Chinese and the Malians. It is not even necessary to recall cultural connections, such as the cult of ancestors. Beyond that, the sensitivity of the Chinese people to nature could also be evoked. But all of this is irrelevant here, since we have to talk about economics and politics.

But it is constantly said: "States have no friends, they only have interests." Really? With regard to Sino-Malian relations. If the adage is true that States are incorporeal beings, ideals, effective legal fiction that enables to organise the social relations between men, it does not prevent that the beings of flesh who administer them, manage them, direct their economic, social and cultural policies may have affinities with such and such counterparts.

And while Malians very much appreciate Chinese investments in their country, they are also very sensitive to Chinese discretion as to the management of their domestic affairs. Certainly, China did not need to blackmail the Malian governments to be recognised.[23]

A. Discretion not to interfere with Malian affairs

If the analysis consisted in presenting the Sino-Malian economic relations by borrowing a historical step, it is not without reason. Indeed, despite the political variations that the country has experienced, economic relations have never been affected and have only been amplified. The military regime has not generated a long-term mistrust of relations between Mali and China. The latter continued to support the companies and public enterprises that had been initiated by the previous regime. Beijing even provided support in improving their management. Better still, new companies have even emerged, giving even more hold to State capitalism over the Malian economy. Similarly, when Mali entered 'democracy as we enter religion', China was not offended by the approach of the Malian people. Beijing took note of it; accepted the opening of the country to other Western countries, as the previous regime had undertaken.

But in the end, it is China that won over again: the renovation of all the streets and roads of the capital and the whole country are China-done. China herself entered the era of the open economy began to create national companies to invest in different areas of the Malian economy. One could even say that China has never had an industrial and financial commitment as important in Mali as today. And Mali has never ceased to use its capital, to the point that some have been moved by the risk of substitution of a financial dependency by another, namely the replacement of dependence on the Bretton Woods institutions and Western States (North America, EU States and the EU itself) by a financial dependence on China. Indeed, the grievance or the fear are not feigned: the danger of a high indebtedness with regard to China does indeed exist. According to the 2017 report of the Malian Ministry of Finance entitled Balance of Payments and International Investment Position, "at the public sector level, interest payments on external debt amounted to

---

23 Indeed, Mali has never given the slightest credit to the Republic of China (Taiwan) that some African states had recognized before the People's Republic of China (China's official political name) put a market in their hands: "either it's me or it's them". Thus, recently, Burkina-Faso, which had diplomatic relations with Taiwan, had to change sides, all shame drunk.

28,200 million after 26,200 million in 2016. These payments are mainly made to the World Bank (22.2%), ADB (11.9%), BOAD (11.5%), IDB (4.6%), China (15.6%), India (6.1%), Saudi Arabia (2.0% and Kuwait (2.8%)"… The burden of repayments to China ($4,4 million) ranks second behind the World Bank ($6.2 million).[24]

But despite this financial dependence, China does not impose any conditions other than financial on its loans: interest rates certainly low, but compensated by shorter grace periods and shorter repayment terms. Thus, in no way did Beijing interfere in domestic political affairs. Nevertheless, only one political condition: support in international bodies. What China had to demand of other African States, she did not even need to ask of Mali, namely the rupture of diplomatic relations with Taiwan. On the other hand, Mali still defends the position of a single China, as the then President of Mali recalled, during an official visit to China in July 2004. Also, the country of the Middle Kingdom does not does not want to teach any lesson in terms of sound financial management, corruption, good administration, or human rights. And Malians appreciate this! Beyond this legendary discretion, Chinese and Malian officials have regularly created real relationships marked by a high reciprocal esteem.

B. An esteem between Chinese/Malian leaders; an old acquaintance between peoples

It can safely be said that there has always been a genuine esteem between Chinese leaders and Malian leaders. This is a historical truth that finds its foundation in the anti-colonialist ideology of which the Malian heads of State, from Modibo Kéita, to Ibrahim Boubacar Kéita, through Moussa Traoré or Alpha Oumar Konaré have always been kneaded. Unlike those of other African heads of State, those of Mali have always shown a strong patriotism, if not a certain nationalism[25] that wants to

---

[24] T. PAIRAULT, "Mali, son endettement et les prêts chinois", 2 février 2019: https://www.pairault.fr/sinaf/index.php/15-references/1551-mali-son-endettement-et-les-prets-chinois, last accessed on 7 June 2019. BAD: Banque africaine de développement (created 1964; headquarter: Abidjan), BOAD: Banque ouest-africaine de développement (created in 1973, headquarter: Lomé, Togo), BID: Banque islamique de développement (created 1975; hq: Djeddah, Arabie Saoudite).

[25] The events from 2012 to the present have struck a serious blow to these virtues, as the country is today managed practically by the international community through

do things for oneself and for oneself. So far, this ideological convergence had facilitated relations between the leaders of the two countries. Does China also explain and justify China's participation in MINUSMA? Undoubtedly, because the country began to engage its own people[26] in such operations only very recently, from only 1990, and choosing well theatres of operation.

In addition to this intellectual and ideological connivance, in the 1960s, Mali sent students to China in the most varied fields. As a result, many Malians know the country well and speak the language. And the sending of 'Chinese cooperants' to Mali in the same period enabled a mutually appreciated acquaintance. This, especially since unlike Western nationals, the Chinese did not hesitate to live in very different and very modest conditions. And since the Chinese expatriate themselves to Mali to create business, they have maintained these old ways, ride a Djakarta motorbike like Malians and live in the usual neighbourhoods, if they are poor, without seeking more comfort. All this creates a proximity that explains the success of Chinese interventions: they do not raise suspicion; they are legible, they are understandable.

This proximity between the two peoples is manifested by many social interventions of China: support at the moment of Ebola epidemy in 2014, various actions in favour of the mother and the child, creation of a hospital in Bamako and trauma centres in regional capitals, etc. In return, Mali wants to be as close to China as we are with a friend. Thus, in 2008, in China, during the earthquake that hit China, Mali made a donation of 50 million CFA francs (about US$85,470) in 2008. The sum is small, very modest even, but a symbol. Symbol of a friendship. At the ceremony mentioned at the beginning of this chapter, the Minister representing the government stated: "Cooperation with China is for us

---

the MINUSMA (United Nations Multidimensional Integrated Mission for the Stabilization of Mali) and by France in the fight that Mali is unable to support in the face of the strike force of the rebels of the National Movement for the liberation of Azawad (MNLA, Tuareg movement) and especially the jihadists of Iyad Ag Ghali and Mamadou Koufa supported by the Movement for Unity and Jihad in West Africa and Boko Haram.

26 As of 31 May 2019, there were 413 Chinese soldiers in MINUSMA: see United Nations website https://peacekeeping.un.org/china, last accessed on 9 June 2019.

a cooperation that has a human face, based on the spirit of solidarity, friendship and solidarity. Fraternity".[27]

*

In conclusion, we can therefore emphasise that Mali likes China, like many other African States, because China it has been anti-colonialist, Malians feel that China really helps Africa in its development, in its equipment in means of production and infrastructures. But above all, China is discreet, does not make a fuss, and, slowly emerging from underdevelopment, remains close to African realities. With these road- or transport-infrastructures, China undoubtedly helps the African States to integrate their economies, but do these realise that they thus enter into a Chinese vision, a Chinese project, that which aims at facilitating the distribution and the expanding trade of Chinese products in their markets? The case is double-edged.

[27] http://french.xinhuanet.com/2015-10/28/c_134758024.htm, last accessed on 9 June 2019.

The implications for South Korea of China's Belt and Road Initiative (BRI) and of the Maritime Economic Cooperation (MEC) in East Asia

Seok-Woo Lee
Law School, Inha University, South Korea

The Background of the 'Belt and Road Initiative' (BRI) – While attending the 21st APEC Summit in Indonesia in October 2013, President Xi Jinping of China outlined the creation of a '21st Century Maritime Silk Road' (MSR) which called for the promotion of maritime cooperation with ASEAN nations and the implementation of measures that would lead to common development and prosperity.[1] He also proposed establishing the Asian Infrastructure Investment Bank (AIIB) to facilitate financing infrastructure construction and to promote regional interconnectivity and economic integration.[2] In the previous month of that same year, President Xi also announced his proposal for a 'Silk Road Economic Belt' (SREB) during his visit to Kazakhstan.[3]

These two initiatives have been described by Chinese academics and officials as the 'One Belt, One Road' and 'Belt and Road Initiative' (BRI) as a strategy that seeks to connect the Chinese economy and other Asian economies to Europe and Africa. Looking back to the Silk Road – the ancient route taken by traders between China and the Mediterranean world – the BRI is certainly an ambitious plan to propel China's economy forward. However, beyond the apparent economic benefits, questions

---

1 W. JIAO and Z. YUNBI, "Xi in call for building of new 'maritime silk road'", *China Daily*, 4 October 2013: http://www.chinadaily.com.cn/china/2013xiapec/2013-10/04/content_17008913.htm.

2 *Ibidem*.

3 "Xi suggests China, Central Asia build Silk Road economic belt", 7 September 2013, Xinhua: http://news.xinhuanet.com/english/china/2013-09/07/c_132700695.htm.

remain as to the political and military strategic implications of this grand Chinese initiative, particularly for South Korea at times when the US, under the Trump Administration, appears to be disengaging from its liberal trade policies that has helped to fuel South Korea's economic growth while China has signalled that it will fill the gap.[4]

Clearly, the BRI intends to incorporate the Asian, African, and European continents and their neighbouring seas. From China's perspective, the purpose of the BRI is to:

> "promote the connectivity of Asian, European and African continents and their adjacent seas, establish and strengthen partnerships among the countries along the Belt and Road, set up all-dimensional, multi-tiered and composite connectivity networks, and realise diversified, independent, balanced and sustainable development in these countries. The connectivity projects of the Initiative will help align and coordinate the development strategies of the countries along the Belt and Road, tap market potential in this region, promote investment and consumption, create demands and job opportunities, enhance people-to-people and cultural exchanges, and mutual learning among the peoples of the relevant countries, and enable them to understand, trust and respect each other and live in harmony, peace and prosperity."[5]

The BRI is an example of a 'pan-Asian initiative' for Asian regional connectivity that has had a number of past iterations from within and without the region: from Asia, India, Japan, and South Korea have helped build or finance greater linkages within the Asian continent, and the US has also pushed for similar efforts; China's efforts have found success by borrowing from and adapting these previous initiatives.[6] Interestingly, South Korea has also advocated for this kind of regional connectivity calling for the building of a 'Silk Road Express' to connect South Korea

---

4 President Xi reiterated this point at the World Economic Forum in Davos, Switzerland in January 2017 where he insisted that "Whether you like it or not, the global economy is the big ocean that you cannot escape from. Any attempt to cut off the flow of capital, technologies, products, industries and people between economies, and channel the waters in the ocean back into isolated lakes and creeks is simply not possible. Indeed, it runs counter to the historical trend. [...] In the face of both opportunities and challenges of economic globalisation, the right thing to do is to seize every opportunity, jointly meet challenges and chart the right course for economic globalisation."

5 Action Plan on the Belt and Road Initiative, Section III, Framework: http://english.gov.cn/archive/publications/2015/03/30/content_281475080249035.htm.

6 E.A. FEIGENBAUM, "China and the World: Dealing with a Reluctant Power", *Foreign Affairs*, January-February 2017, p. 38.

with Europe through Central Asia along with a maritime route linking the Northeast Sea Route with Eurasia.[7]

Over land, the SREB focuses on uniting China, Central Asia, Russia and Europe. The land routes would run along three courses: one route, connecting China to Europe through Central Asia and Russia; the second being a route that would connect China with Middle East through Central Asia; and the last would link China and Southeast Asia, South Asia and the Indian Ocean.[8] The idea would be to build a 'new Eurasian Land Bridge' by developing corridors to and from China by utilising critical industrial areas along these routes as platforms for cooperation between the States in these regions.[9]

In the ocean, the MSR would comprise two pillars: i/ connect China to Europe through the Indian Ocean via the South China Sea and ii/ extend through the South China Sea to the South Pacific. The MSR is designed to strengthen Beijing's relationships with friendly countries, such as Pakistan, Sri Lanka, Cambodia, and Malaysia. This will be accomplished primarily by way of economic incentives, such as infrastructural development and trade agreements.[10]

From China's perspective, the impetus for the BRI brings about regional economic prosperity and cooperation along with bolstering relationships and understanding between the diverse cultures of Asia and promoting world peace and development.[11] To fully realise the BRI,

---

7 President Park Geun-hye speaking at the 2013 International Conference on Global Cooperation in the Era of Eurasia stated: "First, we should unleash a new era by reconnecting Eurasia to make the continent truly one. It is necessary to reconnect the logistics network that has been cut off in Eurasia and overcome physical barriers obstructing exchanges. To this end, we have to build the Silk Road Express, which will run from Busan all the way to Europe via North Korea, Russia, China and Central Asia, by connecting the northeastern part of Eurasia with railways and roads to establish a multi-purpose logistics network, which would eventually be extended to Europe. We also need to redouble our efforts to seek ways to link the eastern end of Eurasia with the sea through connection with the Northern Sea Route, which is newly emerging as a shipping lane."

8 A. BHATTACHARYA, "Conceptualising the Silk Road Initiative in China's Periphery Policy", *East Asia*, 2016, p. 311.

9 Action Plan on the Belt and Road Initiative, Section III, Framework: http://english.gov.cn/archive/publications/2015/03/30/content_281475080249035.htm.

10 W. YALE, "'China' Maritime Silk Road Gamble", *The Diplomat*, 22 April 2015: http://thediplomat.com/2015/04/chinas-maritime-silk-road-gamble/.

11 Action Plan on the Belt and Road Initiative, Preface.

China has identified five areas that need to be developed for its implementation: i/ policy coordination is needed between the national governments; ii/ efforts have to be made to connect the various facilities that will enable transportation and logistics to move along efficiently in a way that is sensitive to the environment; iii/ there must be unimpeded trade such that legal and regulatory barriers to the flow of goods should be removed; iv/ financial integration is needed to support the establishment of the routes that will be created under the BRI as well as the economic activities that will result from economic cooperation; v/ China has identified the need for creating public support between the nations involved in the BRI that would involve increasing exchanges between people to deepen cooperation.[12]

The BRI can be viewed within the context of recent Chinese efforts by China to enhance its image as a global power through 'soft-power' initiatives including institutions which it has proposed such as the New Development Bank, the Asian Infrastructure Investment Bank, and the Free Trade Area of the Asia-Pacific.[13] According to the Chinese government, the objectives and required inputs for the realisation of the BRI are supposed to be mutually beneficial for all who seek to be involved with the initiative.

> "The Initiative seeks mutual benefit. It accommodates the interests and concerns of all parties involved, and seeks a conjunction of interests and the 'biggest common denominator' for cooperation so as to give full play to the wisdom and creativity, strengths and potentials of all parties."[14]

The BRI is marketed as a win-win for the parties who choose to be involved. Rhetorical flourishes aside, the BRI is a 'Chinese-engineered Asian connectivity project'.[15] It is estimated that China is pouring in $40 billion and $25 billion for the SREB and the MSR respectively.[16] By investing such large sums in the BRI, one would expect Chinese expectations of a significant return on investment in regard to its ability

---

12 Action Plan on the Belt and Road Initiative, Section IV, Cooperation Priorities.

13 D. SHAMBAUGH, "China's Soft Power Push", *Foreign Affairs*, July-August 2015, p. 100.

14 Action Plan on the Belt and Road Initiative, Section II, Principles.

15 A. BHATTACHARYA, "Conceptualising the Silk Road Initiative in China's Periphery Policy", *op. cit.*

16 D. SHAMBAUGH, "China's Soft Power Push", *Foreign Affairs*, July-August 2015, p. 100.

to influence and shape the policies of the States which participate:[17] "Actions speak louder than words, and in many parts of the world, China's behaviour on the ground contradicts its benign rhetoric".[18]

For example, while encouraging its neighbouring States to engage in economic cooperation without any political strings attached,[19] China has continued its assertive policy with respect to strengthening its position in the South China Sea, namely, by way of transforming reefs and other submarine maritime features into fully operative islands complete with 3,000-meter runways, air defence installations and so forth.[20] China's MSR and its infrastructure investments and projects also aim to facilitate more frequent People's Liberation Army and Navy (PLAN) deployments in the Indian Ocean and beyond. The plan requires reliable logistics chains across the Sea Lanes of Communication (SLOC) throughout Southeast and South Asia.

The apparent need for the Chinese military to guarantee the security for SLOC and logistical sites and facilities along the MSR and SREB calls into question the extent to which the military and security interests of China are driving the BRI. Naturally, one would not expect China to trumpet the geostrategic implications of the BRI in the advancement of China's national interests, but the BRI has certainly raised the stakes for any State that wishes to consider the implications of engaging China on the BRI.

Thus, the BRI is a double-edged sword: i/ there is a real possibility for States that implement this Chinese initiative in attaining economic rewards and benefits, while ii/ these participating States can become dependent upon and potentially subject to Chinese military intervention along the SREB and MSR.

The seemingly inevitable military component of the BRI warrants the observation that the design of the BRI is to ensure the establishment of

---

17 Despite the significant injection of money and the promise of more to come, China has had a relatively low yield when it comes to actual influence on the policies of the targeted States.

18 *Ibidem.*

19 W. SHANG, "Commentary: Chinese Marshall Plan analogy reveals ignorance, ulterior intentions", *Xinhua*, 11 March 2015: http://news.xinhuanet.com/english/2015-03/11/c_134057346.htm.

20 W. YALE, "'China' Maritime Silk Road Gamble", *The Diplomat*, 22 April 2015: http://thediplomat.com/2015/04/chinas-maritime-silk-road-gamble/.

Chinese hegemony in Asia and extending its reach into other regions of the world.[21] In particular, the extension of Chinese power is more likely in the high seas and other waters along the MSR where the reach of international law is less defined and subject to controversy given the problems of maritime delimitation. Moreover, along with the rapid development of the Chinese navy and its blue-water capacity, China is able to flex its maritime power well beyond its territorial sea and exclusive economic zone.[22]

For a country such as South Korea, that is dependent upon international trade through the carriage of goods by sea, the implications of the BRI on the whole and the MSR in particular are crucial.

I. South Korea and the Implications of the BRI

Though South Korea exists on the Korean peninsula, it is in effect an island since it is surrounded on three sides by water: the West Sea (Yellow Sea); the Korea Strait to the south; the East Sea (Sea of Japan). To the north is North Korea where the movement of goods and people overland is non-existent due to the Demilitarised Zone (DMZ). South Korea depends upon the oceans for its economic livelihood which includes a robust fishing industry and inbound and outbound sea freight traffic which has been vital to South Korea's rapid economic development as an export-oriented economy.

Having from the 1960s followed an export-oriented development strategy, South Korea has emphasised foreign trade as a mechanism for economic development. The country has become a legitimate maritime power as the world's 13th largest economy, 10th in maritime trade volume, a global leader in shipbuilding, ranked 5th in handling containers. These achievements would not have been possible but for the stability of sea lanes connecting South Korea to the world. 73% of South Korea's

---

21 A. BHATTACHARYA, "Conceptualising the Silk Road Initiative in China's Periphery Policy", *op. cit.*, p. 312.

22 At the beginning of the 21st century, China's naval capacity was largely limited to China's coastal areas. Since then, China has embarked upon an ambitious modernisation programme. According to China's Defense White Paper released in 2013, it noted that the Chinese navy "endeavors to accelerate the modernisation of its forces for comprehensive offshore operations… [and] develop blue water capabilities". R. O'ROURKE, *China Naval Modernisation: Implications for U.S. Navy Capabilities – Background and Issues for Congress*, Congressional Research Service, 17 June 2016, 80: https://fas.org/sgp/crs/row/RL33153.pdf.

GDP is dependent upon foreign trade while 99.7% of the country's entire trade volume is transported over the sea.[23] Furthermore, as the country does not have any domestic production of oil, South Korea is wholly dependent upon oil imports, 80% of which is transported from the Middle East through two of the world's major oil transit chokepoints, the Strait of Hormuz and the Strait of Singapore/Malacca.[24] Any disruption of vessels carrying oil to South Korea through these sea-lanes of communication would have a potentially devastating effect on the South Korean economy.[25] Consequently, sea-lane safety and the securing of passageways has been necessary for South Korea to sustain its economic growth through foreign trade and maintaining sea power for national security. The waters surrounding South Korea and beyond are important from an economic, military, and strategic perspective. In short, the South Korean economy is wholly dependent on secure global SLOC.[26]

Similarly, the majority of China's seaborne energy imports come through the regions mentioned above; and much like Seoul, Beijing places a high level of importance to the security of the SLOCs and has growing strategic interests in ensuring unimpeded access in the Indian Ocean and South China Sea.[27] China is already involved in a number of ongoing port projects in Gwadar (Pakistan), and in Colombo and Hambantota (Sri Lanka).[28] In other parts of South Asia such as Bangladesh, Beijing is engaged in Chittagong and has been pushing for the development of a deep-sea port at Sonadia Island.[29] Beijing has also established its first overseas military outpost in Djibouti that would give it a significant foothold in the Gulf of Aden and thus influence Suez Canal traffic. China's

---

23 H. JEONG, "Korea's Sea Lane Security Strategy [Hankuke Haeroanbojeollyak]", in *Sea Lane Security of East Asia*, KIMS, 2007, p. 197.

24 Korea Energy Economics Institute, *Energy Statistics 2008*: http://www.kesis.net/flex/eng_main.jsp.

25 L.V. MING and L. CHENG, "Maritime Insurance against Piracy: A Shield or a Sword?", in J. HO (Ed.), *Realising Safe and Secure Seas for All: International Maritime Security Conference*, 2009, p. 151–152.

26 Republic of Korea Ministry of Land, Transport and Maritime Affairs, *Statistical Yearbook of MLTM*, 2008.

27 Peter Roell, "China's Maritime Silk Road – An Ambitious Undertaking: A View from Europe", *ISPSW Strategy Series: Focus on Defense and International Security*, No. 423, May 2016: https://www.files.ethz.ch/isn/196395/411_Roell.pdf.

28 *Ibidem*.

29 *Ibidem*.

design and implementation of the MSR has been the cause for concern from some of its Asian neighbours.[30]

The greatest challenge to the MSR is a deep level of mistrust among some Asian countries towards Beijing with the disputes in the East and South China Seas as representative examples. There is evidence that a number of countries in Southeast Asia are sceptical of China's intentions.[31] India is concerned that China may use these ports for strategic purposes, thus undermining India's position in the Indian Ocean and its neighbouring States.[32] Little wonder, then, that in its endeavour to counter-balance China's influence, India is currently seeking to strengthen its relations with the U.S., Japan, several ASEAN countries, Australia as well as with the EU.

As to South Korea, the BRI brings both risks and rewards that are complicated given its relations with both China and the US States.

II. South Korean Perspectives on the BRI

China's rise has put South Korea in a strategic bind. Seoul's traditional (?) ally is the US. Since 1953, the US has stationed troops in the country which contributed to relative stability on the peninsula. In addition to military cooperation, the US was South Korea's largest trading partner for many years, a major factor in South Korea's rapid economic

---

30 Japan has long been involved in providing overseas development assistance (ODA) and investing in Asian countries providing massive amounts of money and direction for the development of roads, rail lines, metro systems, and ports across Asia through financing vehicles such as Asian Development Bank (ADB) and the Japan International Cooperation Agency (JICA). Japan has responded to China's BRI by creating a new financing effort called the Japan Infrastructure Initiative and Prime Minister Abe's promise of $200 billion for infrastructure projects in Asia and Africa. W. SHEPARD, "Japan Ups Its Game Against China's Belt and Road", *Forbes*, 1 December 2016: https://www.forbes.com/sites/wadeshepard/2016/12/01/japan-ups-its-infrastructure-game-against-chinas-belt-and-road/#10f8e2e3223c.

31 Vietnam and the Philippines have confronted China over China's maritime claims in the South China Sea while Indonesia was angered with China's claim that Indonesia's Natuna Island exclusive economic zone fell within China's Nine-Dash Lines. A. BHATTACHARYA, "Conceptualising the Silk Road Initiative in China's Periphery Policy", 323.

32 India is also concerned about the construction of the China-Pakistan Economic Corridor which passes through Pakistan Occupied Kashmir which India considers an infringement of territorial sovereignty. A. BHATTACHARYA, "Conceptualising the Silk Road Initiative in China's Periphery Policy", 324.

development. However, due to China's massive economic growth and its geographic proximity to South Korea, Seoul has become increasingly dependent upon the Chinese economy. According to WTO data, China has become South Korea's main trading partner. The Chinese market accounts for 26.1% of South Korea's total exports with China accounting for 16.1% of what South Korea imports.[33] Given these realities, "South Korea has to dually manage its security, which is grounded in the ROK-U.S. alliance, and its economic well-being, which is dependent on the ROK-China strategic cooperative partnership".[34]

Not surprisingly, opinion on the BRI is polarised. Economic and industrial interests, including the Korea Railroad Corporation (KORAIL), support South Korean involvement in the BRI and closer economic interactions with China. They see how the BRI fits nicely with ex-President Park Geun-hye's 'Eurasia Initiative', and anticipate significant commercial benefits for South Korea from better connections to energy-rich Russia and the consumer markets of Europe and Central Asia. They welcome the prospect of reduced trade-barriers between China and South Korea, and of improved transport infrastructure, and perceive the political risks as manageable.

In September 2013, ex-President Park announced her controversial 'Look North' policy, of which the most salient aspect is the 'Eurasia Initiative'. This comprises various proposals designed to overcome existing constraints by developing new markets and creating new economic partners in continental areas from which South Korea has been alienated since the end of WWII, and this dovetails nicely with China's BRI. The concepts of the 'Silk Road Rail Express' (SRX) and the 'East Sea Rim Maritime Community' (ESRMC) have also been discussed. SRX is at present a purely symbolic railroad project intended to encourage individual, cultural, trade and diplomatic exchanges. ESRMC is a model for establishing an *ad hoc* community to promote regional economic cooperation around the East Sea. Ex-President Park's 'Eurasia Initiative' sought South Korean investment for Northeast Asia to complement Russian plans such as the 'Northern Energy Road' built by Gazprom,

---

33 S. DENNEY, "South Korea's Economic Dependence on China", *The Diplomat*, 4 September 2015: http://thediplomat.com/2015/09/south-koreas-economic-dependence-on-china/.

34 H. SUK-HEE, "South Korea Seeks to Balance Relations with China and the US", *Council on Foreign Relations*, November 2012.

and Chinese plans such as the Chang-Ji-Tu Development Plan for the North Korean port of Rajin.

However, some ardent pro-US groups worry that the political risks of the BRI are too high. They cast doubt on the feasibility of implementing the BRI, and warn that although it has been portrayed primarily in economic terms, it actually reveals a crucial Chinese geopolitical strategy. They are fearful of China's growing regional dominance and that the BRI is ultimately a means to supplant the prevailing US-led regional security structure and restore the Middle Kingdom order, with China as the only power that matters in the region. According to this view, once China has complete control of the regional logistics hubs and sea ports, this will severely limit the autonomy of China's neighbours, including South Korea, both economically and politically, nay risk their own peace and prosperity. Moreover, the US and South Korea have already renegotiated the Korea-US Free Trade Agreement, signing a revised pact in 2018 leaving South Korea with fewer options economically when it comes to trade.

Despite the fact that the Chinese government portrays the BRI as a win-win opportunity which will harm no one's interests, some South Korean commentators[35] have interpreted it as much more than just a trade and development deal: they focus on the geopolitical implications and the possibility that the balance of power in Asia will be disturbed. South Korea depends upon its military-security alliance with the US to deter North Korean threats, and yet cannot afford to be left out of a project which could transform the economic and logistical linkage between Asia and Europe. Given its negative reception by the US, however, South Korea has so far expressed only lukewarm support for the BRI.

Opponents of the BRI also doubt that its putative benefits can be realised, at least in the short term, arguing that creating the necessary rail interconnections may be too costly.

*

In conclusion, what is the way forward for South Korea? The current strategic cooperative partnership between South Korea and China will not suffice to deal with the potential risks and problems which will arise from South Korea's involvement in the BRI: the terms of interaction must change. Some may consider this as an impediment to closer

[35] "South Korea should walk diplomatic tightrope," *Korea Times*, 19 November 2018: https://www.koreatimes.co.kr/www/opinion/2018/11/202_258954.html.

cooperation, but it would be better to interpret it as an opportunity, and there is every reason to hope that new arrangements can be established.

i/ South Korea has demonstrated an ability to separate economic decisions from political ones, and this approach needs to become more robust. An example comes from a recent issue that has given encouragement that this might be possible. The planned deployment of the Terminal High Altitude Area Defense (THAAD) anti-ballistic missile system from the US on South Korean soil has yet to cause a serious breach in relations with China though not completely without its strains.[36] Indeed, South Korea shares a deep historical and cultural background with China, and moreover the two countries have no maritime territorial disputes, and also conduct active military exchanges and cooperation, despite the problem of North Korea.

ii/ China is economically an indispensable partner for South Korea, but China also derives immense benefit from the relationship. China is South Korea's most important market, and with economic growth in South Korea expected to remain sluggish, the recent surge in Chinese direct investment in South Korea, which more than doubled in 2015, is welcome. And the economic interdependence between China and South Korea can increase after the free trade agreement between them came into effect in 2015. In this light, the BRI is simply another aspect of a natural trend for South Korea to cooperate with China.

iii/ North Korea, although its obstructionism is a critical problem, since it is blocking the creation of a land corridor between China and South Korea, this difficulty can surely be resolved by coordinated action. Both China and South Korea should show flexibility toward North Korea to provide it with obvious and definite economic benefits from joining the BRI and the AIIB.

South Korea's former Foreign Minister recently expressed the view that the country's unique strategic position enables it to make an important contribution to regional peace and prosperity.[37] If it is possible to

---

36 It appears that China is retaliating against Korean firms doing business in China as there have been calls for boycotting popular Korean products and tour travels to Korea. Adam JOURDAN, "China hints at trade war strategy in South Korea standoff", Reuters, 3 March 2017.

37 H. SUNG-JOO, "Grand Strategy for South Korea? An Overview," *The Asian Forum*, 13 August 2015: http://www.theasanforum.org/grand-strategy-for-south-korea-an-overview/.

continue the recent diplomatic *finesse* in balancing the influence of the two great powers, China and the US, then South Korea should be able to share its outcome.

China insists that its investment in the BRI is economically motivated, and highlights the economic benefits for the other countries involved. A 'Community of Common Destiny' is being built, if the Chinese slogans are to be believed; and the expansion and integration of regional trade and logistics networks really do offer a win-win outcome, both for China and the world.

Even if the BRI is an exclusively economic strategy, however, it still would have clear strategic implications, since China has proven its willingness to use economic coercion to pursue its geopolitical interests, making any economic investment a potential weapon; so China need not send its navy to the newly constructed ports to exert increased control over regional shipping lanes. Of course, from a Chinese perspective, the economic and geopolitical ramifications of the BRI run in parallel: both recall China's historical dominance, fitting in nicely with Xi Jinping's favourite theme of the Chinese Dream.

In recent years, China and South Korea have become very close. The connections between individuals, companies and institutions of the two nations constitute a shared modality that integrates tradition and history with complementary governance and the international legal regime. For this reason, South Korea's involvement in the BRI offers opportunities which China cannot obtain from any other country. It therefore makes sense for both countries that South Korea should cooperate closely with the BRI, despite the possibility that the US will take *ombrage*. Indeed, the BRI seems likely to play a central role in South Korea's progress from being a weak and divided nation to become a genuine and acknowledged middle power.

South Korea has recently shown its capacity to rise to the challenge of sustaining an autonomous position equidistant from the two great powers and demonstrated its ability to engage in a delicate balancing act. It has upset China, by moving forward with THAAD deployment, but it has also upset the US by joining the AIIB as a founding member and by cooperating with the BRI; and yet South Korea has remained on good terms with both countries. Doubtless, South Korean involvement in the BRI will bring its own challenges, but South Korea will need to address them skilfully and steadfastly – the potential economic benefits are too great to ignore.

Part IV

The challenges of change in civil law and human aspects

Introduction

Amandine Cayol
Caen Normandie University, Demolombe Institute, Caen, France

Part IV of the book addresses legal issues concerning changes that affect individuals, whether it be their rights in armed conflicts, their *rapport* to privacy or modern forms of communication, their own physical body or their medical situations.

The function of law is to regulate social life. Subjects of law are bearers of rights and duties. They have to respect rules necessary for life in society: rules of civil law, commercial law, labour law, criminal law, and so on. If the majority of these rules are determined by the internal law of each State, many of them now come from regional Law, for instance European law, or from international law. Human rights are thus protected by international humanitarian law, in particular in arm conflicts. Serious violations of humanitarian law entail international criminal responsibility. However, the number of armed conflicts involving such violations but without an international character increased noticeably in recent years. The changing nature of armed conflicts has created an impetus for change to reassess which actors can contribute to prosecute those responsible for violations of international humanitarian law. It becomes now necessary to grant the extended jurisdiction of national courts (cf. Danila Tatarinov and Karimzhan Shakirov, "The jurisdiction of national courts in the implementation of prosecution of violations of international humanitarian law").

Law must indeed adapt to the changes in our society. Digitalization is one of the greatest challenges of modern society that legal systems have to face. We enter in the 'digital age', which leads to profound social and economic changes, and raises the question of how fundamental rights can be protected. If freedom of expression is undoubtedly strengthened, the right to privacy, for its part, is weakened. The Internet giants (the GAFA) collect information about consumer's browsing habits or behaviours, without them knowing it. In order to prevent from such invasions of privacy, the European Union recently modified its legislation concerning personal data protection: the European institutions adopted a European Data Protection Regulation (GDPR) on 27 April 2016, which entered into force on 25 May 2018 and reinforced the rights of individuals as regards the processing of personal data concerning them (cf. Fanny Rogue, "The legal challenges of personal data protection").

If dematerialization is thus a risk, it also has important logistical advantages, as it makes access to the content of databases easier and with a greater level of security. Hence, dematerialization can be a vector of the fight against fraud, especially in international relations. The example of the '*apostille*' can illustrate this idea (cf. Catherine Golhen, "The challenges of dematerialisation in law: the example of the '*apostille*' ").

Medical progress also represents a major challenge for legal systems. Due to scientific progress, change is going on in man's perception about the human body and this leads to a deep reflection about the appropriate legal status of the human body. It is no longer possible to ignore the question of the legal status of human body before birth or after death, nor the question of the legal status of elements or products detached from human body (cf. Amandine Cayol, "The challenges of change for the legal status of the human body").

Advances in medical knowledge also cast doubt on euthanasia, which poses ethical, moral and juridical problems. The increase in the number of life-sustaining treatments raises the question of the rights of patients in end-of-life situation. It is necessary to clarify the standard for determining whether to discontinue life-sustaining treatment and to permit removal of life-prolonging treatment (cf. Hyun-Jin Kim, "Proposal of an 'healthcare agent' as 'end-of-life' options in Korea").

This last part of the book provides a useful complement to the rest of the analyses of the first three parts that address more macro-level issues.

The jurisdiction of national courts in the implementation of prosecution of violations of international humanitarian law

Karimzhan SHAKIROV, Danila TATARINOV
al-Farabi Kazakh National University, Almaty, Kazakhstan

In accordance with the basic principles of international humanitarian law applicable in armed conflict, the Geneva Conventions[1] and Additional Protocol[2] contains a list of specific actions defined as 'grave breaches', which entail international criminal responsibility in the case of non-compliance with standards and international humanitarian law requirements. This list of 'serious violations' of international humanitarian law is rather extensive and exhaustive, but taking into account the development of the military industry, new technologies used in warfare should not be limited by the existing list and rely solely on international jurisdiction to prosecute the perpetrators of such violations. Now it becomes necessary to grant the extended jurisdiction of national courts to prosecute those responsible for violations of international humanitarian law.

In this regard, it should be noted that the rules of international humanitarian law set for such crimes individual responsibility of individuals who have committed or have ordered the commission of these crimes. Speaking about violations of international humanitarian law, it is necessary to focus on the fact that until now it was thought that such rules apply only in respect of international armed conflict and shall not apply to the internal (non-international) armed conflicts. This is due to

---

1 Geneva Conventions of 12 August 1949 and Additional Protocol to them. – M.: MKKK, 2005.

2 Additional Protocol I to Geneva Conventions of 12 August 1949 concerning to the protecting of victims of international armed conflicts // Geneva Conventions of 12 August 1949 and Additional Protocol to them. – M.: MKKK, 2005.

the fact that at the time of the adoption of 'Additional Protocol I' a view occurred that the application of the system to prevent 'serious breaches' to internal conflicts is unacceptable interference in the internal affairs of the State.

But the reality of recent years shows that the majority of armed conflicts have non-international character, in the course of the commission of numerous violations of international humanitarian law. Acts committed during such conflicts, in its cruelty and mass violation of human rights, are not inferior to acts characterised as 'serious violations' of international humanitarian law that are considered, in turn, as war crimes. That is why the international legal doctrine and international jurisdiction formed an opinion on the recognition of the need to extend the mechanism of suppression of 'serious violations' of international humanitarian law in internal armed conflicts and the importance of extending the repression of such crimes to the national courts.

In this regard, efforts that States should take to implement the criminal prosecution of those responsible for 'serious violations' of international humanitarian law forms an emerging theory. In the absence of a recognised permanent international criminal court, the preventive function of war crimes falls on a fraction of States. Although the Rome Statute of the International Criminal Court[3] (hereinafter – the Statute of the ICC) entered into force in 2002, many States such as China, the US and Russia have not ratified it. As a result, it cannot be considered that the Rome Statute of the ICC is universal. What is more, it can be assumed that the main burden to stop the violations of international humanitarian law lies upon the States.

Thus, in the case of many other international offences, the obligation to prevent war crimes is an alternative form of *aut dedere aut judicare* or *aut prosequi*. In accordance with this obligation, a State must search executors of war crimes or crimes against humanity and bring them to justice for these acts, regardless of the nationality of the executors or of their victims, as well as the place where the acts committed or extradite executors under the law of the State to which the request is made.[4] From this it follows that the State has the right to carry out a so-called 'universal

3 Rome Statute of the International Criminal Court: adopted 17 July 1998, with amendments and additions from 25 September 1998 and 18 May 1999 // Preparation Commission for International Criminal Court. UN. – New York, 1999.

4 E. DAVID, "Principy prava vooruzhennyh konflictov", M.: MKKK, 2011, p. 647.

criminal jurisdiction' in respect of the person (persons) who have committed violations of international humanitarian law, or, if not, to give it to any interested State under the conditions provided by its national legislation.

I. The imperfection of existing positive law

This alternative obligation is formulated in general terms in various UN General Assembly`s resolutions, which are always accepted without objection and processed like normative documents. Therefore, these documents are binding for any State recognised them. Regarding to executors of military crimes, the obligation to prosecute and extradite them is formulated in the Geneva Conventions of 1949: I, 49; II, 50; III of, 129, and IV, 146 (as well as in paragraph 1 of article 85 of Additional Protocol I of 1977, because it contains a reference to these provisions). Such a rule is set in the Conventions on genocide (articles III and IV) and apartheid (articles 4 and 11) with regard to executors of the relevant actions.

The obligation *aut dedere aut judicare* is not explicitly present in the conventions that do not establish a universal criminal jurisdiction. They are spoken in general terms only about the obligation of signatory States to cooperate with each other in solving problems that may arise in relation to the aim or in connection with the implementation of the provisions of such Convention:

1. The UN Convention on the Prohibition of the Development, Production and Stockpiling of Bacteriological (Biological) and Toxin Weapons and on their Destruction 1972 (Art. 5);[5]
2. Convention on the Prohibition of Military or Any Other Hostile Use of Environmental Modification Techniques 1976 (p. 1, Art. 5);[6]

---

5 The Convention on the Prohibition of the Development, Production and Stockpiling of Bacteriological (Biological) and Toxin Weapons and on their Destruction, 10 April 1972, Official page of International Committee of the Red Cross: http://www.icrc.org/rus/resources/documents/misc/convention-biological-weapons-100472.htm.

6 Convention on the Prohibition of Military or Any Other Hostile Use of Environmental Modification Techniques. Recommended for consideration, signing and ratification by all States by resolution 31/72 of General Assembly from 10 December 1976, Official page of UN Organisation: http://www.un.org/ru/documents/decl_conv/conventions/hostenv.shtml.

3. Convention on the Prohibition of the Development, Production, Stockpiling and Use of Chemical Weapons and on their Destruction, which says: "Each State Party shall cooperate with other States Parties and afford the appropriate form of legal assistance to facilitate the implementation of the obligations under paragraph 1" (including to recognise in domestic law the criminal actions considering by Convention) (p. 2, Art. VII).[7]

In these general terms it is very difficult to discern the source of the obligation to extradite military criminals. However, since, for example, the use of chemical weapons would be qualified as a crime against humanity, obligation provided by customary law to prosecute and extradite those guilty persons is able to make up the bad drafting of these conventions.

In the case of accepting direct normative-legal act in a particular State, granting the national judge with the universal jurisdiction for analysis cases of the facts, recognised by a violation of norms of the international humanitarian law, there are a number of important questions:

- is the law of a particular State applicable to acts committed abroad by foreigner in respect of other foreigners in the framework of conflict under the Additional Protocols I and II, considering that international law military do not recognise crimes committed in conflicts of this kind?
- is this law applicable to military crimes committed in an armed conflict which is not regulated by the Additional Protocols I and II under the fact that: i/ one of the parties in the conflict is not bound by these agreements, while the conflict itself is one of those, which are discussed in the documents; ii/even if the parties in the conflict are bound by the Protocol, the conflict itself is not considered in them?

For a full solution of problems of expanding the jurisdiction of national courts in the implementation of prosecution of violations of international humanitarian law, it is necessary to consider these situations separately.

---

7 Convention on the Prohibition of the Development, Production, Stockpiling and Use of Chemical Weapons and on their Destruction. Open for signing in 1993, Official page of organisation on prohibiting chemical weapon: http://www.opcw.org/ru/konvencija-o-khimicheskom-oruzhii.

For the beginning, let us consider cases where the application of the law does not depend on the fact that violations of international humanitarian law committed in non-international armed conflicts are not recognised as criminal.

The ability of the State to exercise jurisdiction over the extraterritorial nature of the investigation of criminal cases has already been recognised in international law. The problem that still occurs in this connection is: could a State give itself universal jurisdiction which is not provided by international law? Is not this an abuse of sovereignty from the part of this State and will it not break the principle of legality and proportionality of penalties?

Of course, when the State reacts to an act prohibited by international law, there is no abuse of sovereignty. Even if a breach of 'Additional Protocol II' is not recognised as criminal under international law, the fact remains that these actions are beyond the scope of the exclusive jurisdiction of the State and apply to all countries, united by this provision, not only States that have signed the Protocol, but also those bound by obligations before the international community in the field of human rights if the relevant acts may amount to a violation of these rights, as is the case of prisoner`s torture or executions of non-combatant.

If these violations fall under the Article 3, which is common to the four Geneva Conventions of 1949, States can and should respond in accordance with article 1, also common to the four Geneva Conventions of 1949, which obliges States to 'ensure respect' all provisions of these documents. Thus, the fact that the government takes actions to stop violations is not either an abuse of sovereignty or interference in the internal affairs of the State in the territory which gone civil war.

II. The dialectics of national/international jurisdictions over territoriality

There is an open question about the prosecution by national courts of persons who have violated international humanitarian law during armed conflict (international or non-international) in the country, which is not bound by the obligations arising from the Geneva Conventions and their Additional Protocols I and II. This problem could only arise in respect of the Additional Protocols, since it is known that almost all States that are members of the international community are parties of the Geneva

Conventions 1949, but Additional Protocols is not binding for a third of them.

Does that mean that, because of this lack of ratification of the Additional Protocols I and II, their rules are not applicable to the unlawful acts committed during the war, and that therefore, the national provisions will also not apply to actions under the Protocol? This is not entirely true, since the prosecution for actions recognised by national law as offences will be possible, but in condition that these actions are prohibited by a customary rule similar to the norm of the corresponding Protocol. Each party in the conflict, even if not bound by the Additional Protocols I and II, remains bound by customary norms. Thus, the action discussed here is not necessarily taken place in a legal vacuum. Being under the action of customary norm, similar to the contractual norm, these actions are prohibited and the law can be applied to them, although it refers to the Protocols, not to the custom. Not to apply it to a particular action on the pretext that the identical material norm has another formal source (custom, not the Protocol), would be contrary to the spirit of the law.[8]

The Geneva Conventions and their Additional Protocols apply only in certain situations of armed conflict: the Geneva Conventions and Additional Protocol I – international armed conflicts; Additional Protocol II – non-international armed conflicts, in which i/ the government and ii/ organised armed forces are involved, controlling part of the territory.

Nevertheless, there is a question about non-international armed conflicts falling solely under article 3, common to the four Geneva Conventions of 1949, the scope of which is broader than the Additional Protocol II and whether the norms adopted under the national level will apply in respect of such cases. Most likely, the State will take the path of least resistance and such laws will only apply to serious violations taking place in the internal conflict in the territory of that State, provided by the Additional Protocol II.

But in any case, for the prosecution of executors of violations of international humanitarian law, an effective mechanism is required, as that should serve the national law of a particular State. This law should be referred to the violations, i.e., "wrongful act or omission in respect of persons and (or) property protected under international conventions".

---

[8] E. DAVID, "Principy prava vooruzhennyh konflictov", M., 2000, p. 189–190.

Moreover, persons affected by common article 3 of the Geneva Conventions of 1949, belong to the category of persons enjoying the patronage of these conventions. Thus, a national law aimed to prosecute those persons, who are responsible for violations of international humanitarian law, should not make much difference between the victims considered as violations. Victims of violation, committed in the conflict under common article 3, are 'protected person' within the meaning of the Geneva Conventions and, therefore, are victims of violations recognised as criminal in this law. Moreover, the law by means of which the jurisdiction of national courts will expand for prosecuting persons responsible for violations of international humanitarian law, must refer to the Additional Protocols I and II, because it relates to common article 3. It follows from this that these violations of norms of international law will correspond to the offences contained in the enactment of national laws and under the jurisdiction of national courts.

At the same time, if a national legislator has not possibility to make reference to the common article 3 of the Geneva Conventions of 1949 and their Additional Protocols I and II, this does not entail the impossibility of adopting and applying such national law to the violations of international humanitarian law. The legislator in view of the sovereignty of the State is able to give a normative-legal act to determine the acts constituting the offence.

Consequently, the scope of the crime stipulated in such law is not related to the scope of the definition of crimes contained in the Geneva Conventions and their Additional Protocols I and II, i.e. the scope of the law will be limited only by the notion of 'persons and property… under the auspices of the Conventions and Protocols I and II…', and persons, using the patronage of common article 3, necessarily fall into the category of persons using the patronage of the Conventions that contain this article.

Implementation of jurisdiction by national courts over criminal offences are based on such basic principles as the principle of territoriality and nationality. It should be noted that the principle of territoriality according with jurisdiction is vested to the courts of the State in the territory of which the crime was committed. It is an expression of a territorial nature in its essence of State sovereignty and the presumption that the crime affects the interests of the State where it was committed.[9] International practice and legal doctrine have long been considered the

---

[9] J. M. VAN BEMMELEN, "Reflections and Observations on International Criminal Law", *A Treaties on International Criminal Law*, vol. 1, p. 80.

principle of a place of fulfilment and citizenship as generally accepted principles. However, the latter is considered to some extent subordinate to the first.[10] At the same time, it does not prevent States to take the initiative and acknowledge the criminal act in their domestic legislation as violations of international law, which are not recognised as such from the point of view of international law.

In addition, for extending the jurisdiction of national courts in the prosecution of those who violate international humanitarian law, States may adopt internal legal act, from which it follows that any violation of the Geneva Conventions and their Additional Protocols I and II, not being included in the category of 'serious violation', will still be considered as the basis for prosecution under the national criminal law of a State. In this case, we disagree with the view that:

> "Possessing a distinctive feature of the principle of universality, allowing jurisdiction over non-citizens will be extended to the national courts of States. Because now this principle is regarded as the basis of international criminal jurisdiction over individuals who commit international crimes".[11]

III. Preventing violations of international humanitarian law by national courts: right or duty?

Preventing war crimes and crimes against humanity is an important task of all mankind, which one way or another, turns into an obligation. This is due to the fact that some of the classic obstacles to the extradition and prosecution in the legislation of a number of States were eliminated in respect of crimes against the peace and security of mankind. In this case, we are talking about the principle of the 'universality', the 'inevitability' of punishment, the political nature of the crimes, the period of limitations, amnesty, even non-retroactivity – as 'obstacles' to criminal prosecution.

Acting for preventing of violations of international humanitarian law by national courts is more an obligation than a right. A 1935 study on the issues of criminal jurisdiction of States conducted by the Harvard Law Institute suggested the universality principle to be applied in addition to

---

10 Y. BROUNLI, "Mezhdunarodnoe pravo:Kniga pervaya", M., 1977, p. 428–433.

11 U. A. RESHETOV, "Bor`ba s mezhdunarodnimi prestuplenyami protiv mira i bezopasnosti", M., 1983, p. 173.

principles such as: place of the act, citizenship, principle of passive personal conduct of the State having arrested the criminal, in the case that the committed crime is punishable according to the law of the State to which the offender is legally relevant but that State refuses to carry out the procedure. In this case, it refers to the already mentioned principle of *aut dedere aut punier.*

The principle of universality has received the greatest development in relation to international crimes against the peace and security of mankind, when suspected persons may be punished by any State. In this regard,

> "the existence of 'international crimes' as concept, i.e. delicts encroaching on the fundamental values of the international community, led to the emergence of the principle of universality, according to which any State as a member of this community has the right to oppose these offenses, no matter where they were committed".[12]

In this regard, J. Dotrikura suggests that international criminal jurisdiction is the answer to the main problem of our time – the fight for universal peace.[13] Consequently, executors of international crimes should be punished regardless of where the crime was committed and at the same time all States shall take the necessary measures for the arrest and deportation of those persons, responsible for international crimes to those countries where they have committed them for trial and punishment according to the laws of those countries. Consequently, every State is obliged to take all measures for such combating and punishing, possibly through the adoption of a special normative-legal act, extending the jurisdiction of the national courts on this issue.

In particular, this is confirmed in the Principles of international cooperation in the detection, arrest, extradition and punishment of persons, responsible in military crimes and crimes against humanity adopted by the UN General Assembly on 3 December 1973. For example, principle 5 states: "Persons against whom there is evidence that they have committed war crimes and crimes against humanity shall be subject to trial and, if found guilty, to punishment, as a general rule, in the countries where

---

12 S. Z. FELLER, "Jurisdiction over Offenses with a Foreign Element", in M. C. BASSIOUNI and V. P. NANDA (Eds.), *A Treatise on International Criminal Law*, vol. V, Springfield, Ill., Thomas, 1973, p. 41, 43.

13 J. DAUTRICOURT, "The International Criminal Court", *A Treaties on International Criminal Law*, vol. 1, p. 653–654.

they committed these crimes. In line with this States shall cooperate on questions of extraditing such persons".[14]

At the same time, there are circumstances excluding responsibility. Accused to stop the persecution to which they are exposed, often refer to two classic circumstances precluding responsibility. These justifications are i/ the requirements of the law or authority, and ii/ a state of emergency. Thus, the prescription of law or government – is the classic method of protection, but it was declared irrelevant for military crimes and crimes against humanity in the Charter of the International Military Tribunals at Nuremberg (art. 8.) and Tokyo (art. 6), as well as in their indictments.

*

In conclusion, the jurisdiction of national courts in the implementation of prosecution of executors of violations of international humanitarian law is determined by the national legal acts. States, being full participants in international relations, are required to bring their *national* legislation in accordance with international regulations, which naturally leads to the fact that States do not just have the right, but an obligation, to prosecute those persons responsible for violations of international humanitarian law.

---

[14] Principles of international cooperation in the detection, arrest, extradition and punishment of persons, responsible in military crimes and crimes against humanity. Adopted by resolution 3074 (XXVIII UN General Assembly from 3 December 1973, UN Organisation`s official page: http://www.un.org/ru/documents/decl_conv/conventions/warcrimes_principles.shtml.

The legal challenges of personal data protection

Fanny Rogue
Caen Normandie University, Demolombe Institute, Caen, France

The need to protect personal data arose from the development of IT tools. Over forty years ago, France was a pioneer in this field, with the *Loi Informatique et Libertés* (LIL) adopted on 6 January 1978,[1] following the *SAFARI* case, named after the file that the French State intended to create for the interconnection of all computerised files managed by public authorities, based on the social security number. The French legislation was one of the bases for the EU Directive of 24 October 1995, ensuring the protection of personal data within the Union. Since the objective of harmonisation of the relevant regulations could not be fully achieved on the sole basis of this text, the European institutions adopted a European Data Protection Regulation (GDPR) on 27 April 2016, which entered into force on 25 May 2018.[2]

This new regulatory framework incorporates the fundamental rules on the protection of personal data and seeks to strengthen the framework for data processing by imposing new obligations on controllers and processors and the rights of individuals with regard to their personal data. However, the application of the GDPR can be experienced as a real challenge, as an obstacle or even a provocation, for companies and organisations that must comply with it. From a legal point of view, however, the GDPR does not represent a revolution in itself since it is in line with

[1] Law n° 78-17 of 6 January 1978 relating to data processing, files and freedoms, *J.O.R.F.*, 7 January 1978, p. 227.

[2] Regulation (EU) 2016/679 of the European parliament and of the Council of 27 April 2016 on the protection of individuals with regard to the processing of personal data and on the free movement of such data and repealing Directive 95/46/EC (General Data Protection Regulation), *O.J.E.U.*, 4 May 2016, L119/1.

the European and French texts that preceded it. However, it will not be so easy to reach the general targets which it is intended to achieve in the field of personal data protection.

This chapter raises certain questions, the outcome of which will determine the effectiveness of personal data protection. While some questions may arise from the very notion of personal data (I), the real issue is linked to the fundamental principles of data protection (II).

I. Legal challenges raised by the very notion of 'personal' data

The notion of personal data covers "any information relating to an identified or identifiable natural person [...] by reference to an identifier, such as a name, registration number, location data, online identifier, or to one or more elements specific to his physical, physiological, genetic, psychological, economic, cultural or social identity".[3] Any information that enables a direct or indirect identification of a natural person is therefore qualified as such. *Conversely*, data that may not be qualified as personal will not receive the same degree of protection, and more particularly, will not be subject to the rules and principles set out in the GDPR.

The European legislator recently adopted a new regulation,[4] establishing a framework for the free flow of non-personal data in the EU. This Regulation should apply to any processing of electronic data that is not personal.[5] It aims to facilitate the free flow of such non-personal data, "by establishing rules on data location requirements, data availability for competent authorities and data porting for professional users".[6] As these data are not linked to a private person, they are subject to a less strict regulatory framework. The issue may therefore be seeking to qualify the data processed as non-personal in order to avoid applying the GDPR.

In this respect, it should be noted that the GDPR is intended to be applied broadly. Indeed, many data can be qualified as personal, if they enable the identification, even indirectly, of a natural person. As such,

---

3 GDPR, art. 4.

4 EU Regulation of 14 November 2018.

5 Regulation of 14 November 2018, art. 2.

6 Regulation of 14 November 2018, art. 1.

the GDPR distinguishes between anonymised data and data that would simply be pseudonymised. Pseudonymisation can be defined as

> "processing of personal data in such a way that it can no longer be attributed to a specific data subject without recourse to additional information, provided that this additional information is kept separately and subject to technical and organisational measures to ensure that the personal data are not attributed to an identified or identifiable natural person".[7]

This is the case for data linked to a person not through their civil identity but by a randomly generated code. In the file, each individual is identified by a different code, that does not directly identify them. Nevertheless, for reasons of security or public health, for example, there is a reading key, available within the responsible organisation that enables each code to be linked to the civil identity of each data subject. Before the GDPR came into force, such a technique was considered as a modality for anonymising data. However, this is no longer the case as long as a data subject can be indirectly identified. This is what justifies the use of the word pseudonymisation.

The definition of the word 'anonymisation' has a much more restrictive meaning since any data that does not concern an identified or identifiable person or any data that is anonymised in such a way that the person concerned is not or no longer identifiable is considered anonymous – or anonymised. Anonymisation is irreversible by nature; it consists in removing any character identifying a data set. In practice, this means that all directly or indirectly identifying information is deleted or modified, thus making it impossible to re-identify individuals (for example: a case of measles in Caen; a sale made on a particular date on a particular website; a consultation of a particular page of the website on a particular day). While the provisions of the GDPR do not apply to anonymous or anonymised data, the same does not apply to data that is simply pseudonymised.[8]

In view of the increasing evolution of new technologies, less and less data can be qualified as anonymous or anonymised. One may even question the possibility of such a qualification in the future. We have indeed entered the era of *Big Data*.[9] It is now possible to collect, process, analyse, modify, etc., a very large amount of data, of personal nature or not, and which are more and more diversified. As individuals, we all

---

[7] GDPR, art. 4.

[8] GDPR, recital 26.

[9] Megadata or massive data.

generate a multitude of data about us every day. These data feed giant databases, characterised by the 3V rule: *Volume* (large number of data), *Variety* (great diversity of data) and *Velocity* (great speed of data collection and sharing).[10] These files collecting personal information about individuals can be used for marketing and advertising purposes – facilitating for example targeted online advertising – but also to set up population monitoring tools – such as the NSA's PRISM software – or feed algorithms related to artificial intelligence.

However, while *Big Data* develops in all disciplinary fields, the technological solutions are refined to maximise the potential of this mass data, thus making it possible to interconnect these different data. Such an interconnection of data, even if anonymised, is intended to enable the natural individuals concerned to be re-identified. It has been shown that it is possible to re-identify nearly 90% of American citizens via postal codes, genders and dates of birth.

The advent of *Big Data* also raises questions about the legal nature of the right that is granted to each individual over his or her personal data. Is this right personal or proprietary? Traditionally, at least in France and Europe, the protection of personal data is linked to the protection of privacy. Thus, the right granted to a person over his or her own data is a right of personality, i.e. inherent to his or her person. Personality rights are among the extra-patrimonial rights, which are therefore unavailable, inalienable and unseizable. They also have a 'life annuities' character, since they cannot be exercised by the heirs after the death of their holders. The rights granted by the GDPR and the French data protection act to a natural person over their personal data have such characteristics. In particular, the heirs of the deceased may not exercise these rights subsequent to death, unless there are exceptions under specific provisions in the French law only[11] and in particular the possibility of drafting advance directives in this regard[12]. Nevertheless, many actors in the sector – lawyers, entrepreneurs, technicians or politicians – advocate recognition of the proprietary nature of natural persons' rights to their personal data.

---

10 Or even 5V; to the previous 3 mentioned above, can be added Veracity (reliability of data) and Value (profit that can be derived from these megadata).

11 LIL, art. 84 and seq. The GDPR remains surprisingly silent on the issue of the exercise of the rights of the people concerned after their death.

12 LIL, art. 85.

This debate has been given a new impetus since the entry into force of the GDPR. For the proponents of this concept, the recognition of the patrimonial nature of personal data would promote better control by individuals over their own data and a more effective protection. This approach does not seem convincing. From an economic point of view, the asset value of the raw data is minimal. It varies, according to recent estimations, between 0.5 cents and $15, depending on the nature of the data (e-mail address, name…). Even if individuals generate a lot of data, it is difficult to see it as a real source of remuneration. What can be valued is not so much the raw data, but the approval of these data, their interconnection, their selection according to specific criteria. We therefore believe that all collection and processing work can be valued on the market. From a legal point of view, such an approach is possible, but does not shed light on the current regulation of personal data protection stated in the GDPR.[13] It is difficult to accept that the data subject actually holds the *usus*, *fructus* or *abusus* rights on his or her personal data. Indeed, what would happen if one's data were sold to a third party? Would this enable the buyer to use his identifying data, such as his name, first name,[14] e-mail address?

At present, it is not so much the data itself that is the subject of a patrimoniality, but the processing of these personal data. In the *Big Data context*, volume and diversity give heritage value to a set of personal data.

II. Legal challenges raised by the fundamental principles of personal data protection

The entry into force of the GDPR leads to a paradigm shift in the protection of personal data in Europe. From a protection based essentially on the formalism of declaration and authorisation given by the supervisory authority (the CNIL in France) or the State itself, we have moved on to a protection that requires the controller to play a proactive part. The

13 *Contra*, in application of modern property theory: A. CAYOL, "L'homme 'disséminé' par le développement de la e-santé : vers la reconnaissance d'un droit de propriété sur les données personnelles", Interdisciplinary Symposium n° 1 of the workshop "L'humain en transformation", organised by GDR NoST, December 2018, proceedings to be published.

14 There would also be a difficulty in reconciling this patrimoniality of personal data with the unavailability of the status of individuals, including surname, first name, sex and adress.

controller has to ensure the good compliance of his organisation to the provisions stated in the GDPR and this by virtue of a principle of *accountability.*[15] It is his responsibility to implement technical and organisational measures to ensure compliance with the GDPR. This obligation to *comply with the* regulations in force requires practical adaptation (a challenge?) and a good knowledge of the obligations imposed on him.[16]

What we will focus on here is not so much a descriptive study of the obligations imposed on the controller, but rather on the light shed upon certain legal questions that will have to be raised to guarantee the effectiveness of the protection of personal data. Thus, according to Article 5 of the GDPR, data-processing must be lawful; it must be consistent with one of the 6 legal bases set out in Article 6. The main legal basis of the processing operation is the *consent* of the data subject to the processing operation. If it already existed under the 1995 Directive, the objective of the GDPR was undoubtedly to give it a more important role. It is the first legal basis set out in the text. The other 5 alternative grounds are all justified by a criterion of *necessity* of the processing. Therefore, unless it can be demonstrated that the processing is necessary in the light of these legal bases, a processing operation can only be lawfully if it is carried out with the consent of the data subject.

Consent to processing may at first sight appear to be the preferred legal basis for the controller. Based on the will of the data subject, it is the one that best complies with rights and freedoms, in particular because the processing of personal data cannot be done without his or her knowledge. Nevertheless, there is a risk for the controller to base his process on consent. Indeed, the conditions for consent to validly provide an acceptable justification for processing data are very strict. It is defined by the GDPR as the "free, specific, enlightened and unambiguous expression of will by which the data subject accepts, by a clear declaration or positive act, that personal data relating to him or her may be processed". Consent cannot be inferred from silence or a pre-checked box. It must be formulated in an oral or written statement or, tacitly, it must be inferred from explicit and unambiguous consent. In addition, it is the controller's responsibility

---

15 GDPR, art. 5, 2: "The controller is responsible for compliance with paragraph 1 and is able to demonstrate it".

16 In particular, the obligation to store compliance documents, the obligation to keep a register, the obligation to carry out an impact assessment when the processing presents a high risk to the rights and freedoms of the data subject, the obligation to appoint a Data Protection Officer…

to ensure that he or she has proof that the data subject has given his or her consent. This will lead to technical and organisational arrangements that can be costly (e.g. documents storage).

Consent may also be precarious, which may lead to legal uncertainty. Indeed, Article 7 of the GDPR explicitly authorises the data subject to withdraw his or her consent to the processing operation at any time. If this withdrawal does not affect the previous lawfulness of the processing, it will be unlawful if the controller continues to process the data of the person after his/her withdrawal. However, from a technical point of view, it cannot be affirmed that the overall processing operation is not affected by the withdrawal of someone's consent to the processing of his data. It will therefore be up to the controller to put in place the necessary technical measures to ensure that, despite the withdrawal of consent by a single person, he or she can continue to process the data of all others, which, once again, could be costly.

The difficulties will increase if the controller intends to process data from vulnerable individuals. Mechanisms for the legal protection of minors or incapacitated adults will have to be used to assess the validity of the required consent. It should be noted in this respect that young people under 18 can validly consent alone from the age of 16[17] as soon as the processing is carried out as part of the direct offer of information society services (social networks, website, mobile applications).[18] Below this age-threshold, the consent of the parents, as holders of parental authority, is required. The controller will thus have to check the age of the individual and the consent given by their parents (parents' e-mail address, copy of a parents' identity document, which are also personal data specifically concerning them).

The GDPR has extended the rights granted to natural persons whose personal data are processed. The rights of access, rectification and opposition are reaffirmed and new rights are enshrined, in particular the right to portability and the right to erasure. The right to portability enables a person to receive personal data concerning him or her that he or she has provided to the controller, in a structured, commonly used and machine-readable format. This right to portability thus makes it possible to transmit one's data to another controller, if necessary, directly by

---

17 Unless national derogations provide for another threshold, within the age limit of 13 years. In France, the threshold has been set at 15 years.

18 GDPR, art. 8.

the former to the latter, where this is technically possible. Such a right enables individuals to better control the use made of their data. However, its effectiveness will depend on the technical means put in place by the controllers. This right to portability is interesting because it makes it possible to transmit personal data, but this will only be possible if the support and structuring of the data enables it to be used by the second controller. This right is likely to remain 'dead letter' and will only consist of a method of returning the data to the data subject. Moreover, this right to portability does not in itself imply a cessation of data processing by the first controller. If the data subject wishes to stop the processing of his or her data, he or she must request their erasure. However, this right is subject to strict[19] conditions. Deletion is necessary in particular in the event of withdrawal of consent to the processing operation, where there is no other legal basis, or where the processing operation is unlawful.

This right to erasure, which is exercised with the controller, is coupled with a right to de-referencing, which has been imposed on the operator of a search engine, since the *Google Spain* decision of the CJEU.[20] The data subject may, under certain conditions, obtain the expungement of certain content appearing when a search is made on a search engine, by using his or her surname and first name, in the name of the right to privacy. This right is more of a 'right to be forgotten' than a right to erasure because the 'source' content is not deleted. To do so, the person must contact the referenced site to request the deletion of his or her data, if the conditions for exercising this right are met. The *Google Spain* case law is therefore intended to continue, even after the entry into force of the GDPR. For the time being, uncertainty has not yet been removed with regard of the application of this case law. If the CNIL considers that the request is valid for all extensions of the search engine, Google opposes a limitation of this right to the European territory. The real effectiveness of this modality of personal data protection will depend on the decision of the CJEU.

More globally speaking, while the GDPR strongly enshrines the rights of the data subject, so that some authors may speak of *empowerment* in the sense of rebalancing the forces between the natural persons whose personal data are processed and the data controllers, the fact remains that

---

[19] GDPR, art. 17.

[20] CJEU, 13 May 2014, *Google Spain*, Case C-131/12.

this rebalancing will only be effective if citizens effectively exercise these new rights, both individually and collectively.

*

Other important issues could also have been considered here, such as those raised by connected objects, decision-making based on automated algorithmic processing and compliance with the principles of equality and non-discrimination. In this respect, the effectiveness of strong personal data protection in the EU in the context of a globalised economy, or the interactions of the Blockchain technology with personal data protection must be questioned. All these questions testify to the topicality and necessity of the protection of personal data.

The challenges of dematerialisation in law: the example of the '*apostille*'

Catherine GOLHEN
Caen Normandie University, Demolombe Institute, Caen, France

When we take a closer look at the stakes of change in law and political sciences, we think of dematerialisation, a global environment transformation factor. The use of new technologies, such as digital ones, improves the data-movement process and makes it easier to access information. Some authors do not hesitate to qualify the digital technology progression as a 'third industrial revolution'.[1] The second industrial revolution was born from the simultaneous apparition of new communication technologies and of new energy systems: printing/coal. As for the third industrial revolution, it comes from the combined apparition of the computer, the internet and renewable energies. Nowadays, human activity is being digitalised.

The apparition of the digital technology is symmetrical to the apparition of data dematerialisation. Dematerialisation can be defined as the process that replaces material data supports, i.e. paper, with digital files. It became a major stake for all activity sectors: firms, public administrations but also individuals. This dematerialisation is primarily a social fact due to its numerous advantages. It makes it possible to open up remote areas thanks to the internet, enabling them to access online services.

However, one of the main advantages of data dematerialisation is logistical. That is what is referred to as *paperless*. An archive room can contain 23 000 pages per square meter. Digital storage brings in great change because a single 1-terra-octet hard drive is the equivalent of an archive room of more than 43 000 square meters if word processing documents

---

1 J. RIFKIN, *The third industrial revolution: how lateral power is transforming energy, the economy, and the world*, New York, Palgrave Macmillan, 2013.

were stored in it. Saving place is an opportunity for all actors of the legal and economic world. It obviously has a non-negligible impact on the environment. One of the main advantages of the dematerialisation is that it makes access to the content of databases easier. It is not only possible to access data remotely, but also to quickly and efficiently interrogate the database. Dematerialisation also eases data sharing.

The potential of dematerialisation is also considerable for the public services of the justice system. The whole jurisdictional process can be dematerialised, "whether it be the initial pleadings, the exchange of legal documents, presenting evidence or pronouncing the judgement".[2] It is now possible for all parties to access their digitised files. Dematerialisation has a considerable impact on the economics of the proceedings. It affects the person answerable to the law as well as the Officers of the Court or the legal institution itself. The aim here is to increase the productivity and efficiency of the justice system.

Naturally, these advantages must not make us lose sight of the fact that dematerialisation is also a risk source. Dematerialisation of public services causes the dematerialisation of human relations. The digitised data breaching risk cannot be eclipsed, whether the data is personal or professional. Fraud risks facilitated by the use of digital tools cannot be kept silenced either. As such, stakes and regulations of digital security must be understood.

The law must adapt to this dematerialisation factual movement – and in every State. In each matter, the law must draw the consequences of the modifications induced by the dematerialisation and adapt its regulations. The new on-line sale modes require adjustments to consumer-protection and seller-liability. Using social networks also implies data protection. There are many examples that pertain to all legal fields: civil, criminal, public, commercial law… As is clear, the entirety of the law in its various components must adapt to the dematerialisation movement and must go along with it in order to supervise it. One of the stakes of dematerialisation is the adaptation of our rights to the phenomenon.

The EU became aware of the need to supervise the dematerialisation movement. Two recent instances of this are illustrative:

---

2 G. CANIVET, "Les facteurs de transformation du droit", *Enjeux numériques*, September 2018, p. 38.

i/ the adoption of a Regulation of the European parliament and of the Council of 27 April 2016. This text, called GDPR – General data protection regulation – regards the protection of natural persons about the processing of personal data and the free movement of such data. It will constitute the new European framework concerning personal data processing and movement. Its objective is to supervise data processing in an egalitarian manner on the EU territory.

ii/ a regulation called eIDAS (Electronic IDentification and Trust Services) adopted on 23 July 2014. This regulation concerns the electronic identification and trust services for electronic transactions inside the Internal Market. Its objective is to institute a legal homogenous framework for the recognition of electronic signatures. The aim is to develop a European Single Market by removing what hinders the functioning of electronic signatures. With the setting of this new regulation, the European Commission wishes to reinforce the legal security of dematerialised documents by creating the status of trust service provider offering recognised services on the European territory. The idea is to secure and guarantee a trust-based relationship between signatories. To achieve this, the Regulation organises the issuing, the validation and the preservation of certificates qualified as electronic signatures, electronic seals and certificates of authentication of internet sites.

Of note is also the 2016 recent French reform on the law of contract and of proof of obligation. With this reform, the French legislator wished to "clarify, simplify all regulations applicable to the law on the proof of obligation". He took into consideration the evolutions of society and especially dematerialisation. He integrated a specific corpus of regulations to the contract signed by electronic means[3] or even to the electronic proof[4] to which he gives the same convincing strength as the written paper support. In the context of this reform, the legislator kept another important aspect of dematerialisation in mind: the notions of original and copy. The new texts postulate that a reliable copy has the same convincing strength as the original one, whether there exists an original or not. In other words, the fact that an original remains or not has no incidence on the convincing value of the copy. This text is quite

3 French Civil Code, art. 1125 to 1127-4.

4 French Civil Code, art. 1366 and 1367.

certainly one of the most important ones of the reform since it will enable to make the electronic archiving, and dematerialisation, easier.

The purpose of all these texts is to give a legal framework to the dematerialising process in order to avoid, for instance, the fraud risks or personal data breach mentioned before. Paradoxically enough, dematerialisation can be a vector of the fight against fraud, especially in international relations. This lesser known aspect of dematerialisation is what this chapter wishes to bring up. To illustrate this idea, it dwells on the example of the *apostille*.

An *apostille* is a formality that enables to certify the authenticity of a public document written in another State. To begin with, why choose example of the *apostille*? Other examples could have been used but it seems more coherent to choose the *apostille* in the context of this book. The *apostille* originates from an international convention: The Hague Convention of 5 October 1961. This convention was ratified by France on 24 January 1965 as well as Korea on 14 July 2007 and Kazakhstan on 30 January 2001.

Providing a document in a State other than the one it originates from is quite frequently needed. In order to get a certain social security benefit or even to adopt a child abroad, a marriage certificate, a diploma, a criminal record certificate, etc., may need to be presented. To that end, different public documents have to be certified. The certification proves the authenticity of foreign public acts. It can be defined as "the formality by which is confirmed the authenticity of the signature, the capacity in which the signatory acts and, where appropriate, the identity of the seal or stamp borne by the record".[5]

And if the certification seems imperative in the international order, it is because in a given legal order, if an internal act validates its own origin, that is because it is presented in a form and with expressions that are known and easily verifiable. But these external signs of authenticity are obviously different from one State to another. A French birth certificate does not look like a Korean birth certificate which itself does not look like a Kazakh birth certificate. Each of these three States has its own forms. So, a French act cannot, with its mere appearance, convince a Kazakh

---

[5] It is the most often used definition in international conventions, for instance in the Convention of the International Commission of Civil Status, signed in Athens on 15 September 1977, on the exemption from legalisation of certain records and documents.

public officer of its authenticity and conversely, since it is unknown to the country's authority. The moment one has to verify that a foreign public authority authentically received an act or recorded a fact, the least to be done is to ensure the capacity of the foreign authority who signed the act. This is why most States still demand the formality of certification.

Despite being imperative, certification is a complex and long procedure that has often been denounced. In its classical form, certification does consist in a chain of individual authentications of the document that involves embassies or consulates of the States or Ministries of foreign affairs. The complexity of certification is the source of The Hague Convention of 5 October 1961 that suppresses the requirement for certification of foreign public acts. In order to make the movements of public documents easier, this convention replaced the certification with a much simpler formality: the *apostille*. The Convention foresees that the only formality that can be demanded to authenticate a public act written in a State signatory of the Convention, and that must be presented in another signatory State, is the affixing of an *apostille* delivered by the competent authority of the State from which the document originates.[6] Such an *apostille* can be a simple square of about 9 cm with standardised notes.

Before delivering the *apostille*, the competent authority in the State from which the document originates must verify the authenticity of the act. In Korea, for instance, that is the Ministry of Justice and the Ministry of Foreign Affairs. In France, competence belongs normally to *procureurs généraux* (general public prosecutors) in the courts of appeal. To verify the act's origin, each State keeps a database of signatures and seals. After verifying the act's authenticity, the *apostille* is affixed to the act.

The *apostille* then presents a two-fold advantage: its simplicity and its security. Simplicity, because the only requirement is the affixing of an *apostille*. Security, because *apostilles* are submitted to a public numbering and recording. Each State keeps a register of *apostilles* delivered. As such, if it is extremely easy to make a fake *apostille*, the fake document will be easily detectable since it will not have been recorded on the register. The register or the file that makes the inventory of *apostilles* is an essential tool of the fight against fraud, since it enables one to confirm an *apostille*'s origin. If the recipient of an *apostille* intends to verify its origin, they must contact the authority that produced the *apostille* and will check whether

6 Article 3 of the Convention.

the inscriptions on the *apostille* correspond to those of the register or the file.[7]

The 1961 Hague Convention was a success in terms of ratification. Suffice it to look at the number of contracting States to see this: 117 States by 12 November 2018 out of 197 States recognised by the UN. Among Member-States of the convention, the missing ones are China, Canada and most African States.

Turning now to the link between the *apostille* and dematerialisation. This convention is not perfect; or rather, its practice is not. It does not specify the affixing conditions of the *apostille*. The latter can be directly affixed on the public act or on a separate piece of paper, on an annex. The convention does not tell how the annex should be attached. Some *apostilles* are attached with mere staples, which makes them easily detachable from the document with which it must, though, remain. Authentic *apostilles* can thus circulate on fake documents. Also, in practice, registers are not verified, mostly for linguistic reasons. To check the register, the authority that produced the *apostille* must be contacted, which implies being able to speak the same language. This difficulty entails that in most States, documents that were affixed an *apostille* in another State are received without checking the *apostille* register. Yet, this is the very step that guarantees security as a fake *apostille* is quite easily made.

It is here that dematerialisation can offer a higher legal security and limit frauds. And the The Hague Conference thus aims to develop an e-*apostille*/e-register programme in order to facilitate the checking of produced *apostilles*. Given the exponential increase of the number of electronic documents produced around the world, the e-*apostille* component is the only way to affix *apostilles* onto electronic public acts while keeping the advantages that these documents offer in terms of security, efficiency and ease of transmission. Some States only produce e-*apostilles* for public acts electronically generated, and still produce paper *apostilles* for paper public acts, while others produce e-*apostilles* for electronic public acts as well as public acts made on paper and then digitised.

An e-register is an electronic register to which the recipient of an *apostille* can access online. It makes it easier to check the origin of the *apostille*. Currently, e-registers are divided into three main categories depending

7 Article 7 of the Convention.

on the information displayed in response to a recipient demanding to check the origin of an *apostille*:

- Category 1 (basic information): The e-register only displays basic information confirming that an *apostille* bearing the corresponding number and date was produced (it is generally a "yes" or "no" answer type).
- Category 2 (additional information): The e-register does not only confirm that an *apostille* bearing the corresponding number and date was produced. It also gives information about the *apostille* and / or the public act it is affixed to.
- Category 3 (advanced information): The e-register does not only give information about the *apostille* and/or the public act it is affixed to. It also enables to check digitally the *apostille* and/or the public act it is affixed to.

Here are three examples, referring to, respectively, Andorra, New Zealand and Bulgaria as countries of Eurasia and the Asia-Pacific.

Andorra adopted the simplest system. The number of the *apostille* and the date of the act are entered and the website immediately responds that the *apostille* does exist in the register. Here, the dematerialisation of the verification corresponds to the phone-call that could be made to the register, but without the comprehension problems linked to language differences between speakers. But legal security is not complete, if this verification dematerialisation process does guarantee the existence of the *apostille*, nothing guarantees that it circulates with the right document. Other States have thus pushed dematerialisation farther for a higher legal security.

New Zealand, for instance. On the interface, just like for Andorra, the user enters the number of the *apostille* and the date of the act. And just like for Andorra, dematerialisation guarantees the existence of the *apostille* in the register, but on top of that the user has a short description of the act: its author, etc.

But if pushing dematerialisation even further, one can then guarantee an increased legal security. That is Bulgaria's system. The interface is similar, and the number of the *apostille* and the date of the act are entered in it. But the website's answer is much more detailed. The existence of the *apostille* in the register is of course guaranteed, but there is also a digitised picture of the *apostille* and of the document with which it circulates. Dematerialisation enables here to fight efficiently against fraud. Only a dematerialised system can give a quick, immediate answer, without the language barrier.

The contracting States are free to decide if they want to use one or the other component of the e-APP or both (e-*apostilles* and e-registers). Each component can be used independently, meaning that the e-*apostille* component does not need to be used at the same time as the e-register component. So far, 35 States have already started using the e-*apostille* programme, or 30% of the signatory States to the The Hague Convention. The list of countries that chose the e-*apostille* is easily accessible on the website of the The Hague conference. Amon the States that that already use the e-*apostille*, South Korea adopted the system for all the acts produced after November 2016. France as well as Kazakhstan have not done it yet, but we can hope that they will do it soon.

*

The purpose of this chapter is to address one the lesser-known aspects of dematerialisation: offering a guarantee of the security of legal acts. If one often brings up its negative aspects – fraud risks, personal data breach, etc. – one should not forget that dematerialisation can also be a useful tool. As was just seen, with the example of the *apostille*, dematerialisation does not only save time or reduce costs. It can also overcome the language barrier between the administrations of different States and enable a better cooperation between States. Above all, it offers a higher legal security since it enables verifications that were before inexistent for practical reasons.

The challenges of change for the legal status of the human body

Amandine Cayol
Caen Normandie University, Demolombe Institute, Caen, France

The French Civil Code is based on the legal distinction between persons and things. *Persons* are subjects of law whereas *things* are objects of law. Persons enjoy the capacity in their own name to have rights and obligations of all kinds, to make contracts or accomplish other legal acts and to sue and be sued; and they can become the owner of things. French Law recognise two types of persons: i/ legal entities and ii/ natural persons. Companies, associations, public bodies are legal entities; they do not have a body in the biological sense. Natural persons are all human beings.

When first written-up in 1804, the French Civil Code did not contain any rule about the human body. It was solely focused on the concept of person in the legal sense. Considering that human beings need a body to live, and that they are all natural persons under French Law (since slavery has been abolished), it seemed like human body was a part of natural persons; their "substratum".[1] Human body was assimilated to the person given that it was considered as inseparable of her.[2] It was consequently protected by the rules governing persons.

Due to scientific progress, change is going on in man's perception about human body and leads to a deep reflection about its appropriate legal status. It is no more possible to ignore the question of the legal

---

1 J. CARBONNIER, *Droit civil*, t. 1, Paris, Presses universitaires de France, 2004, n° 196.

2 *Dictionnaire de la culture juridique*, V° Corps humain, par X. LABBÉE, Paris, Lamy-Presses universitaires de France, 2003; CE, *Sciences de la vie. De l'éthique au droit*, 1988, p. 16 (the whole human body is not a thing); S. PRIEUR, *La disposition par l'individu de son corps*, Bordeaux, Les Études hospitalières, 1999, p. 12 (the body is "the person itself").

status of human body before birth or after death, nor the question of the legal status of elements or products detached from human body.

The 1975 authorisation of abortion in France raised the question of the legal status of embryos. Then, medically-assisted procreation led to the creation of 'surplus embryos', whose legal status was provided for in the 1994 law. These 'excess embryos' are cryogenically frozen. They can be donated for the treatment of others or for research or stored for some time and then destroyed if they are no longer the subject of a 'parental project'. Their existence is thus submitted to the will of their parents. Does it not lead to the objectification of human life? At the same time, organ-donation also raised the question of the legal status of human dead body. Should it be considered as a common property resource in order to ensure the health of living human beings?

Scientific advances also led to the possibility to extract elements and products from the living human body, as blood, gametes and organs (kidney for example). Parts of human body can be replaced by those of other human bodies, or even by artificial ones. According to the transhumanist ideology, it will even soon be possible to change the whole body, which is treated as a machine. This raised the question of the legal status of the living human body. Is it still possible to consider that human body is inseparable of the natural person? Should we not consider that the living human body is a thing in the legal sense? Should each natural person be considered as the owner of their own body? Such a proposition seems dangerous, paving the way for the human body's commercialisation.

Identifying an appropriate legal status for the human body is indeed a major challenge because it raises several ethical questions. To ensure an appropriate response, it seems necessary to distinguish between human body before birth and after death on one hand (I), and human body between birth and death on the other hand (II). A legal framework has already been clearly defined for the first situation. The second one is still being discussed.

I. The legal status of the human body before birth and after death

French Law recognises that legal existence is acquired at birth by a live-born child able to sustain life, and is extinguished with death. Consequently, even if a human body still exists after death, this corpse has no legal personality.[3] Dead persons do not have personality-rights any more. It is impossible to punish invasion of privacy concerning them after their death. Since 1999, the French Court of Cassation has ruled that "the right of action to defend the right to privacy ends with the death of the person concerned".[4] A dead human body is undoubtedly a thing in the legal sense.[5] Only living human beings are subjects of law. French trial judges have already stated that a corpse was a familial co-ownership.[6] Furthermore, since 1976, it is necessary to specify that the French law enables organ-donation to occur unless otherwise specified.[7] The consent is thus presumed.[8] Such a solution led some authors to consider that it is a kind of 'corpse nationalisation'.[9]

The matter is more complicated concerning the human body before birth. There is considerable debate over the ethical, moral and legal status of human embryos. Should human life not be protected from the moment of conception? Is it not yet a "potential person"?[10] Many authors proposed recognising the legal personality of embryos.[11] Other suggested creating intermediary categories between things and persons.[12] However, in the French legal system, persons do not gain legal status and rights until after a live-birth. A foetus has to be born alive before any legal rights of person-hood can accrue. Consequently, embryos are unquestionably

---

3 It is thus possible to says that they are "bodies without persons": F. BELLIVIER, *Droit des personnes*, Paris, LGDJ, 2015, p. 185.

4 French Court of Cassation, First Civil Room, on 14 December 1999, n° 97-15.756.

5 *Contra*, supporting the existence of a "half-personality" concerning dead people: G. TIMBAL, *La condition juridique des morts*, Toulouse, Privat, 1903, p. 132; M. MARTIN, "Vers un genre juridique commun à l'animal, l'embryon et le cadavre", *Revue générale du droit*, 2015(4).

6 Lille Court of first instance, on 5 December 1996.

7 Law of 22 December 1976.

8 Article L.1232-1 of the Code of the public health.

9 X. LABBÉE, *La condition juridique du corps humain avant la naissance et après la mort*, Villeneuve-d'Ascq, Presses du Septentrion, 2012, p. 325.

10 CCNE, Avis n° 1 du 22 mai 1984.

11 N. MASSAGER, *Les droits de l'enfant à naître*, Bruxelles, Bruylant, 1997, p. 389; R. ANDORNO, *La distinction juridique entre les personnes et les choses à l'épreuve des procréations artificielles*, Paris, LGDJ, 1996, p. 289; M.-A. HERMITTE, "L'embryon aléatoire", *Le Magasin des enfants*, 1990, p. 263, who suggests a "limited subject of law", a "new category of incapable persons".

12 C. SUREAU, "L'être prénatal. Illusion biologique, réalité humaine ou enjeu politique", in N. LE DOUARIN et C. PUIGELIER (dir.), *Science, éthique et droit*, Paris, Odile Jacob, 2007, p. 217.

things in the legal sense. The French Court of Cassation concludes that it cannot be a victim of homicide[13]. For example, if an embryo is killed in a car accident, the person responsible for the accident cannot be convicted for homicide but only be convicted for assault and battery of the pregnant woman.

Thus, scientific progress revealed the challenges raised by the very notion of *person*. It led to the distinction between *human person* and *legal person*. Before birth and after death the notions of *human person* (human being) and *legal person* (natural person) do not coincide. Law considers the human body before birth or after death as a thing. Nevertheless, this thing belongs to the human species. It is consequently protected by the principle of human dignity.[14] The origins of this principle are the ideas of the philosopher Emmanuel Kant. It means that all human beings are equally important and must be respected: they must *be treated as an end and never simply as means.* This principle expressly applies to *human* persons ("human dignity"), not to *legal* persons.

Consequently, violations of the physical integrity of dead people are punishable under the French Criminal Code.[15] Article 16-1-1 of the French Civil Code also stipulates that the requirement to treat a person with respect does not cease to apply after death. In order to preserve the physical integrity of corpses, the French law since 2004 has banned genetic identification after death.[16] The memory of deceased persons is also protected. The principle of human dignity is a limit on the freedom of expression of journalists. For example, the French Court of Cassation stated in the *Erignac* case that the publication of a photography that represented a murdered Prefect was contrary to the principle of human dignity.[17]

Embryos are also protected by the principle of human dignity. The first article of the Simone Veil Law legalising abortion clearly presents it as an exception to the principle of respect of all human beings from

---

13 French Court of Cassation, Criminal Room, on 30 June 1999.

14 X. BIOY, *Droits fondamentaux et libertés publiques*, 4e éd., Paris, LGDJ, 2016, n° 405; C. LABRUSSE-RIOU, *Écrits de bioéthique*, Paris, Presses universitaires de France, 2007, p. 404.

15 Article 225-17 of the French Criminal Code.

16 Article 16-11 of the French Civil Code.

17 French Court of Cassation, First civil room, on 20 December 2000.

their very beginning.[18] The French Constitutional Council affirmed in 1975 that this principle applies to embryos.[19] They are already human persons whose destruction is therefore regulated. However, these rules do not apply to *in vitro* embryos.[20] There is no human person before the implantation of the embryo in the mother's uterus.[21] Thus, the 'morning-after' pill is not covered by the legislation on abortion. It is regarded as a method of contraception.[22]

In conclusion of part I, we can say that lawyers had to adapt theirs concepts to the changing realities of our society arising from medical advances. As the human body before birth and after death has been taken into account, the notions of *human person* and *legal person* had to be distinguished: embryos and corpses are things in the legal sense even if they belong to the human species and are, for this reason, protected by the principle of human dignity. Searching an appropriate legal status for the human body between birth and death is even more difficult.

II. The legal status of the human body between birth and death

All human beings are natural persons from their birth till their death. Their body is traditionally considered as inseparable of their person. Hence the traditional principle is the non-commercialisation of the human body. According to article 16-1 of the French Civil Code "The human body, its elements and products cannot be the object of any rights of patrimony". Article 16-5 provides that "conventions with a view to confer rights of patrimony to the human body, its elements, or its products, are null and void". The human body cannot be marketed, and hence cannot be a source of financial gain.

Even if it is not expressly written in the French Civil Code, the French Court of Cassation stated in 1992 that the human body is inalienable (in French: *indisponible*) concerning a case about a surrogacy agreement. The prohibition of this type of contract was then in 1994 enshrined in

---

18 Article 16 of the French Civil Code.

19 French Constitutional Council, on 15 January 1975.

20 French Constitutional Council, on 27 July 1994.

21 X. BIOY, *op. cit.*, n° 393.

22 French Council of State, on 30 June 2000.

the Civil Code:[23] it is impossible to enter into such a contract in France. However, the inalienability (*indisponibilité*) of the human body is still not expressly stated in the French Civil Code, which leads to question this principle. The latter means that human body is not a thing which could be the subject of a contract. However, it is irrefutable that many contracts concern the human body, such as medical contracts between doctors and their patients. Consequently, it seems more relevant to retain the principle of non patrimoniality instead of the principle of inalienability concerning the human body. In this way, it is possible to donate blood but not to sell it.[24]

Indeed, scientific progress now makes it possible to separate 'components' or 'products' from the human body. These elements detached from the body are regarded in law as things and not as persons any more. It does not matter if they come from a corpse or a living human body. Such a solution led to question the legal status of the whole body: if components and products of the human body are things in the legal sense, should it not be the same about the whole body? It is incorrect to say that human body is inseparable of the natural person, who is only an abstract concept, a legal notion. The legal person "only designate a bundle of rights and obligations"[25] and does not need a body: legal entities do not have one! The concepts of *person* in a biological sense (*human person*) and in a legal sense (*legal person*) must be clearly distinguished. Although the human body unquestionably belongs to the human species, it should be treated as a thing under the law.[26]

Such a materialist vision of the human body raises concerns about its patrimonialisation.[27] Considered as a thing in the legal sense, the body

---

[23] Article 16-7 of the French Civil Code.

[24] Article 16-6 of the French Civil Code: "No payment can be made for allowing [...] the taking of elements or products from the human body".

[25] H. KELSEN, *Théorie pure du droit : introduction à la science du droit* (trad. H. THÉVENAZ), Neuchâtel, La Baconnière, 1953, p. 113.

[26] F. ZENATI-CASTAING et T. REVET, *Manuel de droit des personnes*, Paris, Presses universitaires de France, 2006, n° 270; A. CAYOL, *Droit des biens*, Paris, Ellipses, 2019.

[27] M.-A. HERMITTE, "L'affaire Moore ou la diabolique notion de propriété", *Le Monde diplomatique*, mai 1992. Defending such a libertarian conception, see B. LEMENNICIER, "Le corps humain, propriété de l'État ou propriété de soi ?", *Droits*, 1991, n° 13, p. 111.

might then be an object of property.[28] Property right is usually presented in France as a patrimonial right. However, a new type of approach has been proposed by Frédérick Zenati in his doctoral thesis: property right would mean "the right to prevent others from using an appropriate thing".[29] Its characteristic would thus be "exclusivism". Objects of property right could be patrimonials or extra-patrimonials. The human body could thus be appropriated despite its non-patrimoniality.

According to article 16-1 of the French Civil Code, "everyone has the right to respect for their own bodies" and "human body is inviolable". This prevents harm to the physical integrity of a person without her consent.[30] Would it not be possible to consider such an exclusive right as a property right? Recognising a property right to the human body seems to be the best way to protect it.[31] Because of the impossibility to separate the body from the natural person of which it is the support, the owner could only be this natural person. It would be a kind of 'inborn property'.[32]

Such a proposition is not as dangerous as it may seem, because abusive use of human body by its owner would be prohibited in application of the principle of human dignity. If it can be designed, in an individualistic way, as a freedom, it can also be designed as duties with regards to the Humanity. As the philosopher Kant said: "Act so that humanity, in whatever shape, is for you an end, and not merely the means to an end".[33] Every human being has the duty to respect his own dignity. Any act contrary to the principle of human dignity would be sanctioned.[34]

*

---

[28] T. REVET, "Le corps humain est-il une chose appropriée?", *RTD civ.*, 2017, p. 587; R. LIBCHABER, "La recodification du droit des biens", in *Le Code civil, 1804-2004, Livre du bicentenaire*, Paris, Dalloz-Litec, 2004, n° 40; Amandine CAYOL, *op. cit.*

[29] F. ZENATI, *Essai sur la nature juridique de la propriété*, Thèse Lyon III, 1981.

[30] Even if some exceptions exist, like medical necessity: article 16-3 of the French Civil Code.

[31] J.-P. BAUD, *L'affaire de la main volée : une histoire juridique du corps*, Paris, Seuil, 1993, p. 77.

[32] F. ZENATI-CASTAING et T. REVET, *Les biens*, *op. cit.*, n° 8c, p. 30; F. ZENATI, *op. cit.*, n° 571, p. 786–787. Previously, about this notion: Aubry et Rau, 5e éd., II, § 162.

[33] E. KANT, *Les fondements de la métaphysique des mœurs*, II (trad. V. DELBOS), Paris, Delagrave, 1988, p. 150.

[34] Cf. The famous French case about "dwarf launch": CE, 27 octobre 1995, "Commune de Morsang-sur-Orge".

In conclusion, scientific progress has revealed the need to change the traditional view concerning the human body. It is not possible any more to claim that the human body is inseparable from the person and must consequently be treated as a part of legal person. Before birth and after death, the human body is already considered as a thing in the legal sense. It is the same when products are detached from the whole body. Is it not time yet to recognise that the whole living human body is also a thing in a legal sense? The distinction between the notions of *human person* and *legal person* makes it possible.

However, such a materialist vision of the human body could be worrying because it seems to leave the way open to the transhumanist ideology, whose goal is to develop technologies in order to enhance human intellectual, physical, and psychological capacities. If the human body is a vulgar thing, it should be repaired or even upgraded as a machine. Man-machines interfaces could even be envisaged, leading to the prophesied "Singularity". The robotisation of human beings, as the humanisation of machines (with the advent of "strong artificial intelligence") will again raise the question of the distinction between *persons* and *things*. It is certainly one of the most important challenge for the Humanity in the coming years.[35]

[35] A. CAYOL and É. GAILLARD, "*Transhumanisme(s) et droit(s)*", Research program financed by the French Ministry of Justice between March 2019 and March 2021.

Proposal of an 'healthcare agent' as 'end-of-life' options in Korea

Hyun-Jin Kim
Law School, Inha University, South Korea

In August 2017, Korea officially became an 'aged society', meaning that persons over 65years number over 14% of the total population. Ageing has triggered several legal issues, such as the problem of adult guardianship and testamentary capacity. On the other hand, the development of a dependence on medicine is producing a social problem called 'life-sustaining-treatment', for the maintenance of life rather than for the recovery of a biological function. Average life-expectancy of Koreans extended to 82.36 years in 2016 – that is 85.40 years for ladies and 79.30 years for gentlemen. Surveys show that more than half of all medical costs over one's lifespan are consumed during the last years, just before death only for sustaining life – not for curing disease.

However, news often stirs our sympathy informing us that celebrities died naturally with dignity without any meaningless sustaining treatment: a Korean Cardinal Kim Su-Hwan in February 2009, a Singaporean politician Lee Kuan-Yew in March 2015, and recently an American patriot John McCain in August 2018. In eighty countries, there exists a measurement of the quality of palliative care: The Economist Intelligence Unit's Quality of Death Index (EIUQDI). As to this index, Korea managed to move fourteen steps forward from 32th in 2010 to 18th in 2015. What happened in Korea between those years?

After two well-known decisions by Korean Courts, based in fact on the same patient, were released in 2009, legislation creating new rights in favour of patients in end-of-life situations was adopted in 2016 after a long debate in parliament. It entered into force on 4 February 2018 and the revised one on 20 March 2019. This chapter follows the trajectory for establishing this Act and introduces the contents of the Act, However, we will see that there is still a way to go.

I. The 'Grandma Kim' case

A. Background Facts

One cannot mention 'end-of-life' situations without commenting on a milestone, the so-called 'Grandmother Kim (Kim Halmeoni) case', which has rehashed the debate on euthanasia in Korea. Ok-kyung Kim is a patient in her late 70s who has been in a permanent vegetative state since suffering brain damage caused by hypoxia and has received medical treatment such as the administration of antibiotics, artificial feeding and hydration solution, etc.

Kim's son and daughters requested the medical staff to halt any medical treatment for her, refusing to receive what they termed 'treatment of life extension', but the demand was refused by the hospital. Upon this, the complainants (including the special representative on behalf of Kim) filed two lawsuits against the Hospital and the State: i/ a lawsuit against the Yonsei hospital seeking the removal of the medical devices, ii/ they sought the Constitutional Court to confirm the unconstitutionality of the legislative omission on 11 May 2008, arguing that

> "In case where a dying patient's intent to refuse to receive life sustaining treatment that would not restore functions, could be confirmed, such as Kim in this case, a fundamental right to die should be acknowledged, and the complainants' human value, right to pursue happiness, property rights, etc. are infringed by the legislature's omission to enact a related law to protect this right."

Before looking into the holding of the two decisions, it is a prerequisite to review briefly one decision, the so-called *Boramae Hospital Case*[1]. The facts are as follows: The day after brain surgery (removal of the hematoma & mounting of artificial respirator), a patient's wife requested discharge from Hospital due to burden of medical expenses. The doctor refused several times warning of his death but finally the doctor could not help giving up medical treatment and allowing a discharge after the patient's wife messed up the hospital. The patient died right after stopping ambu

---

1 Supreme Court, 2002Do995, 24 June 2004 (S. Kor.).

bagging and deleting spile. The patient's sister accused the hospital and the doctor. Surprisingly, the Supreme Court sentenced the doctor guilty of murder in *en banc* decision! This ruling brought about a tremendous impact on the medical profession: the medical practices of discharging a patient even according to the request of the patient's family could be a crime of murder. It is noticeable that in this case the patient had medical possibility of recovering consciousness. Nevertheless, it made doctors and hospitals shrink in discontinue of life-sustaining treatment.

B. En banc decision on 21 May 2009

The Supreme Court seemed to show a proactive stance. In her *en banc* decision on 21 May 2009, the Supreme Court set aside the appellate court's decision that had refused to allow the hospital to remove life-sustaining devices, by ruling that the patient entered an irrecoverable stage of death and the patient's intent to seek discontinuance of life-sustaining treatment could be shown[2]. This is the first ruling to clarify the standard for determining whether to discontinue life-sustaining treatment and to permit removal of life-prolonging treatment. There were three dissents, i/ inquiring whether she had entered the irrecoverable stage of death, ii/ focusing on whether an intention to discontinue life-sustaining treatment can be inferred, and iii/ involving the criteria of permitting discontinuance of life-sustaining treatment. We will review them one by one in reverse order.

i/ First and foremost, whether to allow discontinuation of such treatment should be determined on a different set of criteria according to whether the patient's intent could be confirmed. When a patient expressed in advance his/her wish to reject life-sustaining treatment to a medical practitioner, although the patient could not exercise the right to self-determination at the time of discontinuing treatment, the original intent could be respected. When a patient enters an irrecoverable stage of death without providing prior medical instruction, the patient cannot be expected to express his/her intention since he/she has no possibility of regaining consciousness. However, in cases where it can be presumed that the patient would have chosen to discontinue life-sustaining treatment even when given the opportunity to exercise the right to

---

2 Supreme Court [S Ct], 2009Da17417, 21 May 2009 (S. Kor.).

self-determination, based on the recognition that discontinuation would be objectively consistent with the patient's best interests in light of the patient's usual values or beliefs, it is reasonable and compatible with social norms to presume the patient's intent for the discontinuance. Such presumption of the patient's intention should be made objectively. The dissenting opinion was stricter in admitting a patient's right to self-determination, however.[3] In cases of treatment directly connected to life, a patient's right to self-determination can be exercised in a passive way by rejecting treatment, but not in an active way by discontinuing treatment through the removal of a life-sustaining device, such as an artificial respirator inserted into a patient's body. It is because discontinuation or removal of life-sustaining device would likely lead to or advance the patient's death, that it is treated as a suicide, unless there exist special circumstances.

ii/ Secondly, as to whether an intention to discontinue life-sustaining treatment can be inferred, the dissenting opinion claimed that there was insufficient basis to presume the patient's intention.[4] If discontinuing life-sustaining treatment is justified based on the patient's right to self-determination, the 'presumed intention' can be recognised only when the patient's intention can be presumed from objective circumstances and it not by 'assumptive intention' as described in the majority opinion.

iii/ Last but not the least, whether the patient has entered the irrecoverable stage of death (the impossibility of recovering consciousness, loss of critical biological function, and having only a short time to live) should be determined by considering the attending physician's medical opinion and other expert opinions through factual inquiry, treatment record review, etc. In the *Grandmother Kim* case, the patient's brain-MRI showed severe contraction in the brain and the cerebral cortex was damaged to the point of looking like a mere thin band, and the brain stem and cerebellum were contracted owing to severe damage. The medical practitioner who reviewed the treatment records had an opinion that Kim was nearly brain-dead (much more serious than being in a vegetative state) due to not being able to breathe on her own. Doctors in charge of physical examination opined that she had virtually no possibility of recovery owing to being in a vegetative state and relying on an

---

3 By Lee Hong-hoon J. and Kim Nung-hwan J.

4 By Ahn Dai-hee J. and Yang Chang-Soo J.

> artificial respirator. Considering these facts, the majority opinion came to the conclusion that Kim had entered an irrecoverable stage of death. However, the dissenting opinion did not agree that she has entered the irrecoverable stage of death, based on the attending physician's opinion that the patient was just in a vegetative state, not brain-dead, and had a life expectancy of four months, with less than 5% possibility of recovering consciousness.[5]

Undeniably, this monumental ruling brought about serious debates on whether and how to permit end-of-life or euthanasia in Korean society. This case has put a limitation that the lengthening treatment must be futile with the patient's opinion presumed, but it has the significance as the first case to admit euthanasia de facto. Surprisingly, Grandmother Kim survived more than 100 days after the removal of life-sustaining devices according to this decision, dying on 10 January 2010.

C. Decision of 26 November 2009

The Constitutional Court seemed to be passive, when it had a chance to review the constitutionality of legislative omission regarding the withdrawal of life-sustaining treatment, filed by a patient herself as well as her son and daughters. On 26 November 2009, the Constitutional Court ruled that it was difficult to conclude that the State was obligated to legislate an "Act on withdrawal of life sustaining treatment" to protect Law, even though the right of self-determination on withdrawal of life-sustaining treatment is one of the basic rights guaranteed by the Constitution.[6] It added that disputes over withdrawal of life-sustaining treatment can be resolved by a trial court and the right of self-determination on withdrawal of life-sustaining treatment can be effectively protected by the requirements and procedures for allowing the withdrawal set by the trial court, even though this is not perfect. Because the issue of choosing to cease life-sustaining treatment and to die a natural death through exercising the right to self-determination is related to the constitutional value system of protecting the right to life and is a matter of grave importance in connection with not only law and medical science but also religion, ethics and further, philosophical discussion of human existence, it requires a sufficient social consensus. Therefore, the enactment of legislation related to

---

5 By Lee Hong-hoon J. and Kim Nung-hwan J.

6 Constitutional Court, 2008 Hun-ma385, 26 November 2009 (S. Kor).

this issue should be possible only after social discussion on this becomes mature, yields a public consensus and then the legislature accepted such necessity as a result.

Further, the National Assembly has discretion to decide which of the options would be desirable as means to guarantee the "right of self-determination on withdrawal of life sustaining treatment". Although the Constitutional Court rendered a decision of dismissal on the ground that the constitutional complaint is not justiciable because the legislative omission does not fall under the "non-exercise of governmental power" stipulated in Article 68(1) of the Constitutional Court Code (*Heonbeop Jaepansobeop*), in the filing by the patient herself, it is widely considered that this judgment has great significance: it clarifies that the right of self-determination on withdrawal of life-sustaining treatment is authorised as one of the basic rights guaranteed by the Constitution.

II. Legislation of Korean 'Well-Dying Law'

A. Establishment of the Act

Since these 2009 milestone-decisions of Korean Court, there has been long and assiduous debates in the public as well as in the Korean parliament. Finally, legislation creating new rights in favour of patients in end-of-life situations, the "Act on Decisions on Life-Sustaining Treatment for Patients in the Hospice and Palliative Care or at the End of Life",[7] came into full effect in 4 February 2018.[8] Surprisingly, a draft amendment was already submitted to the National Assembly, a few days after it was completely implemented.[9] And it was revised on 27 March 2018.

---

7 Act No. 14013 (3 February 2016).

8 Before then, a pilot programme for the above law was implemented from 23 October 2017 to 15 January 2018 to raise public awareness of the impending law. The programme also serves to uncover any potential problems so that they can be fixed before the law is implemented. A total of 13 hospitals and foundations nationwide are taking part in the trial implementation.

9 The National Health and Welfare Commission of Korea (NHRI) convened a preliminary review of the bill on 21 February 2018 and decided to revise the reform bill.

B. Main content of the Act

The nickname 'Well-Dying Law' referred to the fact that the Act was made to protect the dignity and value of human beings by assuring the best interests of the patients and by respecting their self-determination. It allows the doctor in charge to reject life-extending treatment only if his/her patient at the end of life falls under any of the following cases: i/ patient should be at the end of life, ii/ verification of patient's intent by Advance Directive, iii/ deliberation by the Institutional Ethics Committee on matters requested regarding a determination to terminate life-sustaining treatment and implementation thereof.

The Act enables patients to refuse four devices 1. cardiopulmonary resuscitation, 2. hemodialysis, 3. anti-cancer treatment, 4. mechanical ventilation (Article 2(4) and Articles 15 and 16). However, there are more diverse health-care practices used in actual medical practice. As medical technology develops, new procedures are also emerging. Therefore, as confronted to the criticism from the medical practices, the revised Act adds that medical procedures prescribed by the Presidential Decree refer to the extension of the term of the termination without treatment. The revised Act reflects this point and allows a presidential decree to add medical treatments.

Advance Directives in this Act could be previously made by the patient, only if the patient at the end of life falls under any of the following cases; 1) where there is a "Life-Sustaining Treatment Plan" prepared at a medical institute, 2) where there is an "Advance Medical Directive (AMD)" prepared by the patient and the doctor confirm it, or 3) where there is an AMD, but the patient currently does not have full capacity to confirm it, but the doctor in charge and one medical specialist confirm that the AMD was properly drawn up.

In cases not falling under the above conditions and when the patient is not in a condition to express his/her will, there are two possible options to permit discontinuation:

i/ a patient's intention could be presumed through a family member (art. 17): the doctor in charge and one medical specialist should verify the patient' intention through two or more identical

---

If there is no big difference between the 2 parties, the amendment plan passed the plenary session on 28 February 2018.

statements of the family members that the patient had consistently expressed his/her will to reject life-extending treatment. a) the spouse, b) a lineal descendant, c) a lineal ascendant, d) a sibling, where no person falls under any of item (a) through (c) and there is no contradictory evidence.

ii/ all the family members determined unanimously for the patients (art. 18): where all members of the patient's family have unanimously expressed an intention to decide discontinuance of life-sustaining treatment. Whereas, a legal representative with parental authority of a patient who is a minor has expressed an intention to terminate those treatment & the doctor in charge and one medical specialist have verified such intention.

C. Problems arising from the Act

However, there are big hindrances. It is first of all difficult to prove the patient's continuous intention by two family members for presumption of the patient, notably if the patient expressed the view without any written document. Furthermore, it is unrealistic to derive a unanimous agreement among all the family members including grandchildren, family members living abroad or being disconnected: usually it requires that certificates of Family Relations and signatures of all family members. There was a real tragic case: in this family there was a 'skeleton in the closet' who broke a relationship with his family after continuous juvenile frequencies, and for the unanimous agreement to discontinue his grandmother (in her late eighties)'s treatment, his consent was needed. But nobody knew where he lived, and after desperate seeking of families, he was found to be in prison. It then took a long time and a burdensome process to get his signature after visits in the prison. We can easily confirm the inefficiency of unanimous accord of family members. Fortunately, the height of this hindrance was a lowered due to the reform of the Act. Now the act requires only his/her spouse, parents and children.

Another crucial weak point rests in the risk of presuming the patient's intent through family members. People vaguely think their loved ones know what they want, but this is oftentimes untrue. Studies show that when questioned, friends or families often incorrectly assume others' wishes about end-of-life options. Therefore, their 'unanimous' opinion, even though their opinions reached to an accord, could be totally different from that of the principal patient.

D. Proposal of healthcare agent

I propose that the system of the Medical Power of Attorney (MPA) should be introduced in the Korean Act. The MPA is a person appointed as one's healthcare agent in order to make medical decisions on determination to terminate life-sustaining treatment and hospice care on one's behalf when the person one trusts and to whom one explain one's wishes regarding end-of-life options: one's personal values and what makes living meaningful for one; one's current medical condition and decisions one may foresee in the future; specific concerns one may have regarding life support or aggressive interventions, hospice or long-term care; what concerns one most about death and dying; and how one would want to spend the last month of one's life. If a person authorises an agent to make medical decisions for his/her behalf, then the agent can do it but only if that person is unable to do it.

Of course, the Korean Civil Act knows of the Adult Guardianship & Healthcare agent in the two situations: i/ where an adult ward is unable to give consent to the medical treatment that harms his/her body, the adult guardian may give consent thereto on behalf of the ward (Korean Civil Act art. 947-2 (2)) and ii/ where an adult guardian intends to isolate the adult ward in a psychiatric hospital or any other place to undergo medical treatment, etc., he/she shall obtain permission from the Family Court (same art. 3). However, these articles cannot be applied because the decision to discontinue life-sustaining treatment, is not the decision for medical treatment that harms his/her body nor that for isolation in any hospital. Therefore, we need to reform the Act in order to establish the power of medical attorney.

The patient could appoint a person as his/her healthcare agent in order to make decisions to terminate life-sustaining treatment or hospice care for him/herself by written statement. This document (Advance Health Care Directive) should be registered on the database of National Agency for Management of Life-sustaining Treatment. Where there is Advance Health Care Directive prepared by the patient, the healthcare agent's intention shall be construed as patient's intention

*

In conclusion, the rapid ageing of Korean society makes many older patients and their families suffer from pain and disability for a long time towards the end of life. Regrettably, however, there is still a long way to go. One cannot deny the necessity of admitting a medical power of attorney or health care proxy, which allows one to appoint a trusted person as one's health care agent (surrogate decision-maker). The health care proxy is authorised to make medical decisions on the patient's behalf, but only if one is unable to make one's own medical decisions. It is essential that one explains one's wishes to this person because, as studies have shown, people often wrongly assume that their loved ones know what they want.

However, the current 'Well-Dying Law' does not have any provision about this. Rather, it prescribes that when the patient enters an irrecoverable stage of death and the patient's intent to seek discontinuance of life-sustaining treatment could be confirmed, all family members of the patient should agree to reject life-extending treatment and the doctor in charge and a medical specialist in the relevant field should verify such intentions. This toxic provision seems to be a barrier to the implementation and settlement of the new system. Better solutions ought to be found through collaboration between academia and practice.

Conclusion

Remus Titiriga
Law School, InHa University, South Korea

This conclusion shall let the constituent chapters of the book speak for themselves. These are simply gathered around main ideas, interrogations and intrinsic relations. In this way, it follows the counsel by P. Chabal who considers in this volume that in order to understand 'the New Asia' it is necessary to leave aside to a large extent European 'categories of the mind'.

The analysis of chapters in the volume reveals two parallel narratives in relation to Eurasia. On the one hand, there is a narrative of general changes imposed to Eurasian actors by challenges such as modernisation-secularism, institutional developments and the new technological evolutions (I), and on the other there is a narrative focusing on the challenge and changes induced by the Belt-and-Road or parallel initiatives by China and the positive or negative responses to it (II).

I- A first group of chapters examines the **challenges created by 'pure' change** – the passing of time – to Eurasian actors. These challenges impose a new relation to tradition, a push for modernisation or even the hyper-modernisation (adapting legal systems to realities of two technological revolutions). One can thus distinguish challenges to the forces of tradition (a) and challenges created by the hyper-modernisation (b).

a) Challenges to the **forces of tradition** and the needed change in mentalities, in legal-political systems, or institutional/constitutional arrangements within Eurasian actors.

Eccentric to the Eurasian space but overlapping, are the Arab countries, covered in a chapter by Nasreddine El Hage, assessing the limited compatibility between European legal influences and the legal solutions embraced by countries which adopted at various degrees the *Shari'*.

The message of the chapter is a pledge for a push in the legal modernisation of Arab countries.

In the same vein, the chapter by Philippe Gast focuses on secularism and Islam and qualify the Central Asian states as secular and as a model for other Muslim countries. However, these states are under religious, cultural and economic pressures created by poles of influence such as a Russian-Orthodox, Sino-Confucian, Islamist (Turkey, Iran, Saudi Arabia) or even American (universities with a Protestant influence). Paradoxically, for the author, the greatest challenge to secularism is represented by the Sino-Confucian pole of influence, linked to the growing economic power of China within the region.

On the side of institutional modernisation, one can mention the somewhat provocative chapter by Élise Frêlon which underlines the institutional evolution of the Parliament in France, from the *Ancien Régime* to the present day. The French Parliament changes its nature from a jurisdictional body to a representative legal assembly. That evolution might continue in unexpected ways, maybe similar to those followed historically by Roman institutions.

While the chapter by Bing Chen analyses the development and transformation of the Rule of Law since 'Reform and Opening' in the P.R. China, the chapter by Professor Tai-Uk Chung introduces a new taxonomy of communist systems, able to cover the nature of the North Korean regime and its eventual reform. Overcoming a formalist approach, the author discovers that North Korea has established a one-person rule (similar to the Emperor – *Princeps* of Ancient Rome), where the power of the Communist Party is not as strong as the ruling parties of the other two communist countries (China or Vietnam). Therefore, the first step in a constitutional reform of the North Korean regime would be to shift from a 'Principate' to a 'Party-State' regime.

Two chapters focus on the institutional challenges for two Eurasian integrative initiatives: the EAEU and the EU. According to Ilya Lifshits, the treaty on the Eurasian Economic Union (EAEU) established a Customs union and a Single economic space for five post-soviet States and has equipped it with several attributes of an integration grouping. Since the Union's legal order was not complete, it had to be complemented with legal concepts developed by the Court of the EAEU in the three years since its establishment in 2015.The EAEU seems to follow on the steps of the EU.

Analysing the more advanced integrative initiative of the EU, Michel Bruno, considers that EU Europe has failed in its harmonising taxation and social rights, in the migration policy and in respect for the fundamental rights of the human person. The daring suggestion of the author is the signing of a new treaty including such dispositions but only after the original states of the Community of Six would quit the EU, based on article 50 of the actual Treaty.

In the same vein, of challenges and change, this time in relation to *Lex mercatoria*, one should mention the chapter by Chan-Mo Chung. The author is assessing the jurisdictional practice of investor-State dispute settlement (ISDS) in Eurasia, where investment treaties usually include a clause for a most-favoured-nation treatment (MFN) guaranteeing no-less favourable treatment to investors from a contracting party than that which the other party provides to investors and investments from a third country. The author criticises the still restrictive jurisdictional practice for the streamlining of the procedure – the reluctance of arbitral courts to allow, for example, to bring a case directly to arbitration without recourse to the preliminary negotiation or local procedure.

b) Challenges created by the **hyper-modernisation** (the emergent the new technologies) to the legal- political systems within Eurasia.

In their chapter, Karimzhan Shakirov and Danila Tatarinov notice the evolving nature of modern military conflicts, with the development of the military industry, the new technologies used in warfare and the mainly internal nature of the majority of armed conflict impose an extensive reading of the international humanitarian law of responsibility applicable in armed conflict. Hence the States must update their internal legislation and have the right, or even the obligation to carry out a so-called 'universal criminal jurisdiction' in respect of the person (persons) who have committed violations of international humanitarian law.

The chapter by Fanny Rogue focuses on the challenges created by IT instruments to the privacy of individuals and the answer provided at the Europe Union level by the new GDP Regulation. The author raises certain questions, in relation to the effectiveness of personal data protection, in relation to the very notion of personal data or to the fundamental principles of data protection within the Regulation.

The chapter by Catherine Golhen examines the *apostille*, a formality that can certify the authenticity of a public document written-up in another State. Given the exponential increase of the number of electronic documents produced around the world, and the dematerialisation of documents, The Hague Conference added to its old regulation, new dispositions aiming to develop an *e-apostille/e-register* programme in order to facilitate the checking of produced *apostilles*.

The evolution of biotechnology has created new challenges for the legal apprehension of the person and their body. This is the substance of the chapter by Amandine Cayol. The 'body' was traditionally considered as inseparable from the 'person' and was protected by rules governing persons. Scientific progress made possible to separate 'components' from 'products' of the human body, components regarded by law as 'things' and not as 'persons'. The author wishes to extend this qualification of 'thing' to the whole human body, and as such the body would become, in a legal sense, an object of property. Such a very interesting hypothesis is considered by the author as not being dangerous since the abusive use of human body by its owner would be prohibited by application of the principle of human dignity.

The chapter by Hyun-Jin Kim, deals with the highly controversial subject of euthanasia. The rapidly ageing population of Korea forced many older patients and their families to experience the pain and disability related to the end of life Medicaid treatment. The current Korean 'Well-Dying Law' prescribes that when the patient enters an irrecoverable terminal stage and the explicit patient's intent to end the life-sustaining treatment can be confirmed, all family members must agree to stop life-extending treatment and the doctor in charge and a medical specialist should certify these intentions. The author considers this provision as 'toxic' and defends the necessity of admitting the medical power of an attorney or 'health care proxy', which enables to appoint a trusted person as a 'patient's health care agent' (a surrogate decision-maker). Such health care proxy would be authorised to make medical decisions on the patient's behalf, but only if one is unable to make one's own medical decisions.

II- Another group of chapters deal with the **challenges and changes, created specifically** by the 'Belt and Road Initiative' (BRI) of China and the positive or negative reactions to it. One group examines the BRI initiative in itself (a), another the explicit or implicit challenge to the BRI (b)

a) A first group of chapters examines the 'Belt and Road Initiative' in itself and in **relation to other** parallel regional, synchronic approaches or projects.

In his chapter, Éloi Diarra praises the relations between Mali and China, the role of China's participation in Mali's industrialisation and in the building of infrastructures and China's discretion in regard to the internal affairs of Mali.

The chapter by Sagyngalyi Aidarbayev provide an overview of the 'Belt and Road' Project in Kazakhstan and its consonant interaction with Kazakhstan's 'Nurly Zhol' Project. The chapter by Duman Zhekenov, Askhat Darkenbaev and Zhassulan Zhunisov analyses further the interrelations between the two projects.

The chapter by Zhuldyz Sairambaeva and Gulmira Mashymbaeva is a legal assessment of the 'Silk Road Economic Belt' initiative, which was implemented, initially, by separate agreements, memorandums or programmes between China and each Central Asian country. The chapter further assesses the prospect of the institutionalisation of cooperation between China and the regional integration initiative of EAEU.

b) Another group of chapters examines the 'Belt and Road Initiative' and the **explicit or implicit challenge** to it, either within the countries party to the project, or from external actors, such as the USA.

The chapter by Kuralay Baizakova and Fatima Kukeeva examines, from the point of view of Kazakhstan, the interrelations between 'Nurly Zhol', the BRI (as part of OBOR initiative), and the EAEU. The authors consider that the EAEU and BRI might lay the foundation for a Greater United Eurasian Economic Community (GUEAEC). However, they equally notice certain problems, since the anti-Chinese sentiments are a serious roadblock to the implementation of the BRI. One of the most widespread fears is that Chinese economic, demographic, and military expansion will lead to a loss of sovereignty.

The legal migration, a contentious subject between Kazakhstan and China, is analysed in a chapter by Zulfiya Baimagambetova and Leila Delovarova from the perspective of coordination between the two countries, and Kazakhstan's legal provisions. That analysis probes deeper in the chapter by Yesbol Omizhanov and Almagul Tusupova, who acknowledge that the attitude of local populations to the Chinese has changed in the recent years in a negative way. A subject of contention is the fact that since 2017, ethnic Kazakhs are being persecuted on religious belief in China, where authorities wage a campaign against 'separatists' in the western Xinjiang Autonomous Uyghur Region, and apply to Kazakhs the same restrictions as those imposed on Uyghurs. In order to assuage such tension, the authors consider that Kazakhstan would have to reform its policy in the regulation and control of external labour migration. Since Chinese companies prefer to employ workers with knowledge of the Chinese language, the Kazakh side has the right to require Chinese companies to hire ethnic Kazakhs from China who speak Chinese. This, in turn, would solve the problem of shortage of workers with knowledge of the Chinese language and would also contribute to the decline of an anti-Chinese sentiment in society.

c) Another group of chapters focuses on the **external influences** to the region and their conflictual impact in relation, among others, with the Belt and Road initiative.

Foreign to the Eurasian space, the USA, as the main super-power, initiated a new foreign trade policy under the leadership of President Trump. The US is acting as a global challenger of the regional Eurasian challenger – China. This is the subject of the article by Remus Titiriga which deconstructs the declarations of President Trump and the actions of his Administration in order to understand the US trade actions in relation to China, the EU, Japan and, eventually, the WTO. The author considers that the US trade war with China would undoubtedly disrupt the Belt and Road Initiative with far-reaching consequences for Eurasia.

In the same direction is the chapter by Seok-Woo Lee. The US is the main defence and security partner of South Korea while China has become, in the last years, its main economic partner. This situation imposes a delicate balancing act for South Korea, especially now, when the US, under the Trump Administration is disengaging from its liberal trade policies. However South Korea has shown its capacity to rise up to the demand and to sustain an autonomous position equidistant from the two super powers and competitors.

In all, this book, the fourth in a series that has already looked at *The limits of regionalism* and at *The responses of regional law* as well as at *The origins of Eurasian legal and political systems*, enables the reader to grasp the essentials of present evolution in two regions, and to do so in a comparative manner.

Postface

Integration as a tool

Ilya Lifshits
Russian Foreign Trade Academy, Moscow, Russia

Integration is one of the most popular words in modern economic relations. This term and phenomenon which defined by it could be perceived as setting up closer economic ties between different States, it could be realised via establishment of international organisations and groupings, and it could be promoted through creation of communities of States where the degree of economic and social cohesion is much higher than it two other forms.

We observe all these examples in Eurasia: the Belt and Road initiative supposes that China and its partners coordinate their economic activities for the purpose of constructing transport and logistics corridors from Asia to Europe. All these projects, no doubt, facilitate integration, as a rule they are realised via bilateral agreements,[1] they may create a beneficial investment treatment of Chinese persons and companies. The good research of B&R projects in Kazakhstan has been performed by participants of the Fourth international conference in Almaty. The outcome of this conference we are presenting in this book.

The activities of international groupings and organisations such as ASEAN, Shanghai cooperation organisation, BRICS, Asian Infrastructure Investment Bank contribute much to economic development and underpin international peace and stability. As a rule, the legal arrangements such institutions contain multilateral instruments.[2]

---

1 See for example the list of deliverables of the Second Belt and Road Forum in April 2019: http://www.beltandroadforum.org/english/n100/2019/0427/c36-1312.html, last accessed on 22 May 2019.

2 See, for a example, last documents of SCO at http://eng.sectsco.org/documents/; Articles of Agreement of the AIIB at https://www.aiib.org/en/about-aiib/basic-documents/articles-of-agreement/index.html, last accessed on 22 May 2019.

Communities of the States always function on the basis of the treaties, such unions have its own bodies including courts of justice, competence in different matter, international capacity and legal system. The notable example of such a community is the Eurasian Economic Union which was established in 2015 and comprises five States at the moment.[3] Bodies of the EAEU include representatives of the Member-States on the parity basis, the resolutions of such bodies together with treaties tend to form the 'Union law". Member-States conferred the competence to conclude international trade agreements to the Union's bodies, to date there are several such agreements.[4] It means that the new era of economic relations could be defined as integration of integrations. This phenomenon represents an interesting topic for scientific research and our future conferences might be devoted to it.

---

3 The article on the legal order if the EAEU is included in this book.

4 Free Trade Agreement between the Eurasian Economic Union and its Member States, of the one part, and the Socialist Republic of Viet Nam, of the other part of 29 May 2015; Agreement on economic and trade cooperation between the Eurasian Economic Union and its Member-States, of the one part, and the People's Republic of China, of the other part of 17 May 2018; Interim Agreement leading to formation of a free trade area between the Eurasian Economic Union and its Member States, of the one part, and the Islamic Republic of Iran, of the other part of 17 May 2018. Available at https://docs.eaeunion.org/en-us, last accessed on 22 May 2019.

List of contributors

Sagyngaliy AIDARBAYEV, Doctor of Law, Professor, Dean of International relations Faculty, *al-Farabi* Kazakh National University, Almaty, Kazakhstan, is a leading expert in the field of public and private international law. He has a number of fundamental studies in the field of integration law, WTO law, the status of the CIS, EAEU and other areas.

Zulfiya BAIMAGAMBETOVA, Doctor PhD, associate Professor of International Law Department, *al-Farabi* Kazakh National University, Almaty, Kazakhstan, is Director of the WTO Center and International Trade Law. Author of the monograph "International-legal issues of the unification of the rules are governing international trade" and about fifty scientific articles and publication

Kuralay BAIZAKOVA, Doctor of History of International Relations, Professor of International Relations Department, *al-Farabi* Kazakh National University, is Director of the Institute for Security and Cooperation studies, Almaty, Kazakhstan. Since 2014, she has written over 18 international publications and was granted more than 10 international grants

Zhulduz BAIZAKOVA, Candidate of History of International Relations, Senior Lecturer of International Relations Department, *al-Farabi* Kazakh National University, Almaty, Kazakhstan.

Michel BRUNO, specialises in EU policies and material law and is Director of the LexFEIM research centre. He was Dean of the Faculty of International Affairs of the University of Le Havre (2006–2011) and Director of the Law Department (2012–2014, 1996–2001). He coordinated a Tempus project 1994–1997 – Valencia, Antwerp, Le Havre – and another one with the University of Vladikavkaz (Russia). His publications deal with EU law EU policies and on human rights.

Amandine CAYOL, Senior Lecturer in Private Law at the Faculty of Law, Caen Normandie University. Member of the Demolombe Institute (EA967). Co-director of the master's in Insurance Law. Her fields are

Tort Law, Contract Law and Property Law. She defended her thesis entitled *Le contrat d'ouvrage* in 2009 (published at Bibliothèque de l'Institut de recherche juridique de la Sorbonne, 2013), which led to a renewed analysis of work contracts under the angle of Tort Law: as owner of workforce, the contractor is also the original owner of the work produced by his workforce. She is now particularly interested in the legal status of the human body. She organized a 2016 symposium in Caen on this and heads a two-year collective research project on the topic "Transhumanism(s) & Law(s)", Research Mission Law and Justice, French Ministry of Justice.

Pierre CHABAL, Dr in Political Science (IEPG, *alumnus* of EUI in Florence), Dr Habil. in Political Science (IEP, Paris), teaches at Le Havre University and on the IEP *Europe-Asia* campus. He is invited professor in Mongolia (NUM), Kazakhstan (KazNU, EKSU), Kyrgyzstan (AUCA), Uzbekistan (UMED). He authored *La coopération de Shanghai: conceptualiser 'la nouvelle Asie'* (2019) and directed *L'OCS et la construction de 'la nouvelle Asie'* (2016) and *Concurrences interrégionales Europe-Asie au XXIe siècle* (2015). He is the founder of two research networks: i/ Comparative regional dynamics in Europe-Asia; ii/ legal approaches to regions (France, Kazakhstan, Korea, China, Russia), which have yielded since 2012 a dozen conferences and fifteen international publications. In 2016, the Republic of Mongolia's Presidency awarded him the *Altan Gadas* State distinction, in recognition of his efforts to promote Eurasian academic links.

Bing CHEN, is 'Young Talent Professor' of Law, Ph.D. Tutor, Nankai University, Director of Research Centre of Competition Law and Policy, Ph.D. in Law.

Chan-Mo CHUNG, Professor at the Inha University School of Law since 2007, specializes in International Economic Law and Information Technology Law. Prior to 2007, he was a senior research fellow at the Korea Information Society Development Institute (KISDI) as a director of the Centers for *Law and Information Society* and *for IT Trade* Policy. A graduate of Oxford Univ. (D. Phil, 1995), Korea Univ. (LL.M, 1989) and SNU (BA, 1987), he was visiting scholar to NYU (2005), Le Havre (2012), Yale (2012), NTHU (2016). A panelist in domain-name dispute-resolution (KIDRC, ADNDRC), he presided in 2015 the Korean Society of International Economic Law.

Tai-Uk CHUNG, is Professor at School of Law, Inha University, South Korea. He received Ph.D. from School of Law, Seoul National University 1995. He is teaching philosophy of law, history of political and constitutional thought, peace and humanity on Korean Peninsula. He has been serving as a vice-president of Korean Association of Legal Philosophy since 2010. He was a co-editor of The Collected Papers of the 8th East Asian Conference on Philosophy of Law held in Taipei 2012. He was an invited speaker in the 10th and 11th East Asian Conference on Philosophy of Law held in Beijing 2016 and in Hong Kong 2018.

Askhat DARKENBAEV, Doctor PhD, associate Professor of International Law Department, *al-Farabi* Kazakh National University, Almaty, Kazakhstan. He is a specialist in the field of constitutional law, has more than 30 publications in recent years in this field.

Leila DELOVAROVA, PhD in International Relations, Associated Professor of International Relations Department, Head of the UNAI Hub, Al-Farabi Kazakh National University, Almaty, Kazakhstan. Her key research interests cover International Migration, Regional Cooperation, Sustainable Development, Refugees and Statelessness Studies.

Éloi DIARRA, professor of Public Law, University Rouen Normandie. Member of Constitutional Commission of Mali.

Nasreddine EL HAGE, Dr Hab. in Private law – Docteur d'État en droit –, teaches private law, criminology and penology at Le Havre Normandie University. His doctoral thesis dealt with the respective roles of the 'innate' and that of the 'acquired' in human violence. He has published numerous articles in legal journals. He is also a co-author of several collective works on the principles of law, criminology, religious diversity, human rights and European law.

Élise FRÊLON, is associate Dr Habil professor in Roman and French Law History at the Faculty of Law, University of Poitiers, France. She is a specialist in French parliamentary history (XVI-XVIII Century). Her PhD thesis, published by De Boccard, Paris, 2011 dealt with "The Parliament of Bordeaux and the law (1451–1547)", received various scientific awards and honorific distinctions. Its approach is of law compared in time, putting in perspective the past and present institutions, in order to improve their functioning in the future.

Philippe GAST, received his PhD in Law from the university of Paris 2 Panthéon-Assas. He specialises in the philosophy of law, researching mostly relations between religion and law as his doctoral thesis published under the title *The spiritual experience consciousness and law*. He teaches intellectual property and criminal prosecution. He was a practicing lawyer/barrister for 15 years at the Paris Appeals Court.

Catherine GOLHEN, Assistant Professor in Private Law at the Faculty of Law of the University of Caen-Normandie. Member of the **Demolombe** Institute (EA 967). Co-director of the University Diploma VIB (Valorization of biological innovations) of the University of Caen-Normandie.

Hyun-Jin KIM, is Professor and Vice-Dean at the Inha University School of Law, Korea. She specializes in Civil Law, including contract law, family law and succession law. Prior to joining Inha in 2012, she practiced as a lawyer. She is a graduate of Seoul National University (Ph.D. 2011, LL.M. 2004, BA 1998) and Northwestern Law School (LL.M 2014) and published *Economic Consequences of Divorce in Korea* (Brill, 2016).

Fatima KUKEYEVA, Doctor of History of International Relations, Professor of International Relations Department, al-Farabi Kazakh National University, Director of Resource Centre for American and Democratic studies, Almaty, Kazakhstan. Since 2014: wrote over 20 international publications and was granted more than 10 international grants.

Seok-Woo LEE, Professor of Law, InHa University, Korea.

Ilya LIFSHITS, PhD in Law, Associate professor of international law department of Russian Foreign Trade Academy, Moscow. Professional interests: international financial law, legal regulation of financial services, securities market, WTO law, financial integration in the EAEU.

Gulmira MASHIMBAYEVA, Doctor PhD, associate Professor of International Law Department, *al-Farabi* Kazakh National University, Almaty, Kazakhstan. He is a specialist in the field of international consular law, the author of a large number of publications in various areas of international law.

Yesbol OMIRZHANOV, Doctor PhD, associate Professor of International Relations Department, *al-Farabi* Kazakh National University, Almaty, Kazakhstan. He studies problems of the modern state and law, deals with the problems of human rights and the development of civil society in Kazakhstan.

Fanny ROGUE, Senior Lecturer in Private Law at the Faculty of Law of the University of Caen Normandie. Member of the Demolombe Institute (EA967). Co-director of the University Diploma DPO (*Data Protection Officer*) of the University of Caen Normandie (fanny.rogue@unicaen.fr).

Zhuldyz SAIRAMBAEVA, Doctor PhD, Associate Professor, Head of International Law Department. *al-Farabi* Kazakh National University, Almaty, Kazakhstan. She has a number of scientific publications on various aspects of international economic law, manages a fundamental research project funded by the Ministry of education of the Republic of Kazakhstan.

Karimzhan SHAKIROV, Doctor of Law, Professor of International Law Department, *al-Farabi* Kazakh National University, Almaty, Kazakhstan. Director of the Center for Assistance to G-global. Author of more than 160 scientific publications on topical issues of international politics, law, criminal procedure, criminology, forensic examination and educational activities.

Danila TATARINOV, Doctor PhD, associate Professor of International Law Department, *al-Farabi* Kazakh National University, Almaty, Kazakhstan. Director of European Law Center. Author of more than 40 publications on international humanitarian law, human rights, cybercrime.

Remus TITIRIGA, is a law professor at INHA Law School, in Incheon, South Korea. He has received (in 2000) an LLM in EU Law and (in 2008) a Ph.D. in EU Law from University Nancy 2 of France. He has published a book (*La comparaison, technique essentielle du juge européen*, Paris, L'Harmattan, 2011) and some articles on IT law (such as "Cyber attacks and International Law of Armed Conflicts: a 'jus ad bellum' perspective", *Journal of International Commercial Law and Technology*, July 2013, 8(3), p. 179–189.

Almagul TUSUPOVA, Doctor PhD, associate Professor of International Law Department, *al-Farabi* Kazakh National University, Almaty, Kazakhstan. He is a specialist in the field of constitutional law, has a big number of publications in this field.

Yong-Ho YANG, Head of Eurasia Business Association, Korea.

Duman ZHEKENOV, Doctor PhD, associate Professor of International Relations Department, *al-Farabi* Kazakh National University, Almaty, Kazakhstan.

Zhassulan ZHUNISOV, Senior lecturer of International Law Department, *al-Farabi* Kazakh National University, Almaty, Kazakhstan.

Cultures juridiques et politiques

Vol. 1 Stephanie Rohlfing-Dijoux (éd)
La Transmission de Terminologie et de Concepts Juridiques dans l'espace Européen. Allemagne / France / Russie
2012, ISBN 978-3-0343-1094-9

Vol. 2 Otmar Seul & Tomas Davulis (éds./Hrsg.)
La Solidarité dans l'union Européenne / Solidarität in der Europäischen Union. Actes de la 5ème Université d'été franco-germano-lituanienne et européenne en sciences juridiques Vilnius, 3-10 juillet 2008 / Tagungsband der 5. Deutsch-Französisch-Litauischen und Europäischen Sommeruniversität in den Rechtswissenschaften,Vilnius 3.-10. Juli 2008
2012, ISBN 978-3-0343-1122-9

Vol. 3 Ralf Alleweldt, Raphaël Callsen, Jeanne Dupendant (eds.)
Human rights abuses in the contemporary world.
Tri-National Workshop,Tbilisi, September 2011
2012, ISBN 978-3-0343-1147-2

Vol. 4 Stefanie Bouquet
La réglementation européenne relative à la discrimination fondée sur l'âge: conséquences sur le droit du travail français.
Préface du Professeur Joachim Gruber, Université Paris Ouest - Nanterre La Défense
2012, ISBN 978-3-0343-1174-8

Vol. 5 Izabela Krasnicka & Magdalena Perkowska (éds.)
How to Become a Lawyer?
2013, ISBN 978-3-0343-1290-5

Vol. 6 Kerstin Peglow et Géraldine Demme (dir.)
La protection des intérêts privés sur le marché intérieur. La situation des consommateurs et entrepreneurs.
2015, ISBN 978-3-0343-1615-6

Vol. 7 Sam Lyes
Crimes internationaux et immunité de l'acte de fonction des anciens dirigeants étatiques.
2015, ISBN 978-3-0343-1690-3

Vol. 8 Fabien Bottini, Harold Gaba et Pierre Chabal (dir.)
Le régionalisme et ses limites. Regards croisés franco-kazakhs.
2016, ISBN 978-2-87574-335-0

Vol. 9 Otmar Seul, Kaïs Slama, Kerstin Peglow (Hrsg.)
Kulturvermittlung und Interkulturalität, ein deutschfranzösisch-tunesischer Dialog. Politische, rechtliche und sozio-linguistische Aspekte
2017, ISBN 978-2-8076-0133-8

Vol. 10 Stephanie Rohlfing-Dijoux (ed./dir.)
Developing Intraregional Exchanges through the Abolition of Commercial and Tariff Barriers. Myth or Reality?
L'abolition des barrières commerciales et tarifaires dans la région de l'océan Indien. Mythe ou réalité?
2017, ISBN 978-2-8076-0126-0

Vol. 11 Sagyngaliy Aidarbayev, Pierre Chabal, Zhuldyz Sairambaeva (dir.) Mutations de société et réponses du droit.
Perspectives franco-asiatiques comparées.
2017, ISBN 978-2-8076-0187-1

Vol. 12 Tomas Davulis (ed.)
Labour Law Reforms in Eastern and Western Europe.
2017, ISBN 978-2-8076-0416-2

Vol. 13 Tai-Uk Chung, Zhuldyz Sairambaeva, Pierre Chabal (eds.)
On the Asian and European Origins of Legal and Political Systems. Views from Korea, Kazakhstan and France
2018, ISBN 978-2-8076-0732-3

Vol. 14 Manuel Goehrs
Coopération transfrontalière et intégration européenne. Contribution à l'étude du principe fédéraliste
2018, ISBN 978-2-8076-0409-4

Vol. 15 Amandine Cayol, Zhuldyz Sairambaeva, Pierre Chabal (eds.)
The challenge of change for the legal and political systems of Eurasia. The impact of the New Silk Road
2020, ISBN 978-2-8076-1382-9

www.ingramcontent.com/pod-product-compliance
Ingram Content Group UK Ltd.
Pitfield, Milton Keynes, MK11 3LW, UK
UKHW020153290926
15471UKWH00005B/853

9 782807 613829